MELVYN BRAGG

Melvyn Bragg was born in Wigton, Cumbria, in 1939 and is the author of twelve highly acclaimed novels, including THE MAID OF BUTTERMERE. He has also written several works of non-fiction such as SPEAK FOR ENGLAND and, most recently, the authorised biography of Richard Burton.

Melvyn Bragg combines his writing career with positions as Head of the Arts Department at London Weekend Television, editor/presenter of the South Bank Show and President of the National Campaign for the Arts.

sceptre

Melvyn Bragg

LAURENCE OLIVIER

For Ian McKellen

CONTENTS

Foreword   9
Introduction   13
Prologue   23
Early Days   29
Fame and Hollywood   49
Shakespeare and England   69
'The Entertainer' and the National   95
Soldiering On   115
Epilogue   125

LAURENCE OLIVIER
22nd May 1907 – 11th July 1989

After his 'death' as Lord Marchmain in *Brideshead Revisited,* Olivier told his friends, 'it was a good rehearsal.' It was in fact one of the most affecting scenes in that famous television adaptation. Suddenly Olivier turned on his power and theatricality and the vague Lord Marchmain seized our emotions. Olivier's own death, it seems, was no less affecting. It is the death that all of us could wish for. Surrounded by his family, after fifteen years of mighty struggle against massed forces of affliction – including cancer – he passed away peacefully in his sleep. His Master called and he could not say no.

The British rediscovered their love for him and their pride in him. Never has an actor had such a press. The reaction was on a par with that which would greet a monarch or a prime minister. Not only here but in Europe, in America, in Australasia, he was headlines around the world. There is no doubt that we had lost one of our great men of the century.

His achievement is so grand as to beg a hyperbole. For many people he was the greatest actor they had ever seen, the greatest actor in the world. It was he whose force of character and integrity created the National Theatre. He who put Shakespeare onto film. He who set the standard and a marker for British actors for almost three generations. He who united the classical and contemporary strains in British theatre when he did John Osborne's *The Entertainer*. He dominated the stage of his age.

When I finished working with him on the films which were the inspiration for this essay, he was striving towards King Lear. This he did triumphantly for television and won yet another clutch of awards. It was his last great role and if you have to have a curtain, what better? As usual, as always, his choice and sense of occasion were impeccable.

After Lear, he did some cameo performances when his ailing health would allow. He was Admiral Hood in *The Bounty*; Henry Breasley in John Fowles' elegant *The Ebony Tower*; in *Wagner* he appeared in a memorable sequence with his old sparring partners, John Gielgud and Ralph Richardson; he was Rudolf Hess, he was King William III, he was 'keeping working' at the job he never wanted to give up. He then became ethereal as a hologram in the musical, *Time*, when he was beamed down from the other world of his transcendental reputation to visit the teenage earthlings.

The last extended time I spent with him was on his most recent Christmas party. These were dashing affairs. It was open house in Mulberry Walk with the grandees of the British theatre, the family, old pals who had not hit the top notes, all drifting in and out of the illuminated house with the holly wreath on the door. It was in fact like a party after a long, taxing but hugely successful tour.

About midnight, Joan Plowright, his wife, came up and asked if I would like to go and talk to him, 'the old boy'. We all knew he was ill again, but, typically, the party went on. I went upstairs in some trepidation. Was he failing? What would there be to say? Difficult to imagine him other than his powerful self.

I need not have worried. It was Sir Laurence in full command. He lolled on a gracious sofa like a monarch of the ancien régime. He had turned his tiredness into a welcoming attitude. Champagne was to hand, sipped without restraint. There was not the faintest reference to illness and sympathy was nowhere near the agenda.

Although he loved tittle-tattle, he wanted to talk about Shakespeare. What, I asked him, was the hardest role of all? Lear? 'No: he's easy. You have to have strong arms.' Hamlet? 'Anybody can do Hamlet: nobody can do him properly; but we can all do him.' As usual, as I had come to expect, he adored to use his incisive, intuitive intelligence to undercut any philosophical or pretentious talk about the Art of Acting. To him – so he gave out (although this too was an act and one of the characteristics of this multi-layered man) – it was only a matter of learning the lines and of not bumping into the furniture, as his old pal Noel Coward had taught him. So what was the hardest part?

'Othello', he said. Why? 'Because of the big speeches, the big scenes come so fast after one another that there is no time to take breath, no time to work up to the new climax, no room to prepare yourself.' Then he spoke wittily and jokingly but it was like someone chatting to Shakespeare across the centuries and, despite the outrageousness of what he said, perhaps getting it right.

'I've always thought that William was a bit jealous of Burbage', he said. Burbage was the great actor in

Shakespeare's company, the toast of London, the delight of the aristocracy, the fat purse, the superstar. 'He was quite simply jealous,' Olivier giggled – he was capable of that sort of disarming giggle which charmed you completely. 'So dear old William thought – I'll get that sod, I'll write *Othello*. And he did, and he handed it to Burbage and he said: "Right, Burbage, here is a play with un-actable scenes about a man who makes no sense and the lines now and then are sublime but almost unspeakable and he's black. Get out of that!"'

I've never seen anyone 'get out of that' better than Olivier himself. That was his genius.

July 1989

INTRODUCTION

When you first meet Laurence Olivier you feel that you are encountering a pageant. You have seen him rearing high on his white horse, sword unsheathed, urging on England as Henry V. You have been drawn to his icy, at-odds quality amid the athletic antics in the *Spartacus* epic. In a school party you saw *Hamlet*, and were chastened. In *Rebecca* he assumed the restless, upper-class poise which seemed to personify elegance, and in *Wuthering Heights* he somehow made that fantastical male monster, hero of the Moors, into a credible Heathcliff. He has been Restoration man, Marathon man, Suburban man, the Ambassador, the Fop, the Evil Kingly Genius, the Drunk, the Smutty Comic. Your imagination is infested with a Dickensian population of characters, faces, expressions, gestures, roles, moments of piercing awareness. The man you meet, always courteous in a pleasant, old-fashioned way, has a face very like the thousand faces you see every day in a city street. He is a clean slate, almost a blank.

The contrast between this ordinariness, this anonymous private face, and the powerful variety of public masks never ceases to impress and bewilder you. It is as if, having seen the pageant in all its gold and plumage, it disappears when you come upon it, dissolving itself into the mundane figure of an average-sized man in an average-looking suit giving you the perfectly normal time of day, softly shaking hands and shattering all illusions. Which, of course, he intends to do: this private mask is also deliberate. That is to say, the 'private' mask he assumes at first for someone like myself – a stranger, with a request. I wanted to make a portrait of Olivier for television. I knew he had been very ill and was still not well (this was 1981). I knew he was hauling himself back into circulation by the lifeline of an autobiography. I knew that he was very wary of publicity especially in the country of his birth (he had, after all, appeared in advertisements on American television, advertisements which were never to be shown in England). I arranged to see him in my office.

The reason for this was simple. The only way in which I could persuade him to come in with us and spend the time necessary to make a decent portrait was to show him what we intended to do. We had made up a reel of clips from some of his most memorable roles on film and television; we had copied up some newsreel material; we had sorted out some photographs; we had already prepared a list of the people, places, locations which would feature in the film. He came along, tired-looking, even sad in his stooped bearing, whispering that yes, he would appreciate a cup of tea and no, he preferred a hard chair thank you. We ran the reel. It lasted about two hours.

At first he commented a little – always to exclaim about another actor – 'Oh, that's old . . .', 'Dear me, it's . . .', 'And look at . . . isn't she marvellous'. Never emphatic, these comments; perhaps wistful. Then there was silence. His roles fled by on the screen before him in ten-minute segments. He was sitting a yard or so in front of me and so I could not see his face. The screen images looked out at the old and ill man sitting in the hard chair. He had told me – and I believed him – that he had seen scarcely any of these films since the day they were finished. Here he was, fifty years ago, forty, thirty, twenty years ago – wonderfully handsome, now full of power, now astonishingly bold, now bitten into a furious inner passion. As the silence thickened, I felt that I could not have done anything more tactless. Here was someone who had exhausted himself in a massive fight against cancer, who had said he would never have the 'guts' to go onto the stage – his indisputable great love – ever again in his life, who must have known – he who knew his own face and look so profoundly well – that he appeared no more than a wisp of the man he had been: and what had I done but thrown in that face the clearest possible proofs of his former, past, irretrievable greatness. I wanted to apologise, to pull the plug on the relentless reel which pushed out image after extraordinary image at this man – grey-haired, in a dandruffed striped suit, intent and immobile before the glorious passage of his many lives.

Finally, thank God, it was over. I was almost choking with embarrassment. Olivier did not turn round and I said nothing.

When he did turn round his eyes were red from weeping. He had not made a sound. He reached out and took my hand. 'OK, old boy,' he said. 'Let's give it a go.'

I kept notes over the next eighteen months. I saw films, television plays, stage adaptations, newsreels, archive footage, publicity material from the studios, out-takes. There were interviews with Sir Ralph Richardson, Sir John Gielgud, Dame Peggy Ashcroft, John Osborne and dozens of others who had known and worked with him, most especially, of course, Joan Plowright (Lady Olivier). The early draft of his autobiography was read, as were some of the many books, reviews, appreciations and reports of a man who seemed to have enjoyed at least five major careers. Finally there were the photographs, hundreds of them.

There is, I believe, a profound sense in which the look of Olivier describes the man: or rather, in which the many looks, faces, masks reveal the many men he is.

This is not a biography. The best and fullest biography I have read is John Cottrell's *Laurence Olivier*: it is amply detailed and set beside Olivier's own equally full *Confessions of an Actor* gives a substantial helping of information about how he can be recorded from the outside and how he feels he wants to present himself from within. Nor can I carry the authority of those who worked long and closely with him – Sybil Thorndike, for example, Noel Coward, Tyrone Guthrie, Terence Rattigan, John Osborne, Kenneth Tynan. They knew him intimately and have often spoken and written acutely, in Tynan's case dazzlingly, about him. And there has been a long line of critics. Ivor Brown, James Agate, Richard Findlater, Bernard Levin, W. A. Darlington, Harold Hobson, Irving Wardle, Michael Billington et al. are observers whose descriptions of his many particular performances often read as well as anything they have written. Olivier's genius seems to have spurred them on. There is no sense in which I can attempt to match that compendium of regular, industrious criticism. This is an essay. It comes out of a fascination with the man and an attempt to understand him.

Whenever I met Olivier – after that initiation in my office – I met him armed to ask questions. Together with the production team – Bob Bee, Nick Evans, Jill Freeman, Jenny King, Gabriel Clare-Hunt and Chris Haydon, – I prepared myself as thoroughly as possible. Not just because that is normal practice. An extra concentration and anxiety came into it because we were filming over a long period during which Olivier was prone to sudden relapses and intent, with much of his greedily harboured energy, on writing his autobiography. The result was that both parties were directing their attention to the same object – Olivier's life-work; consequently he may have been readier to answer since his own preoccupation evidently dovetailed with our ambition. He wanted to organise his life for print: we wanted to portray it in film.

One of the advantages of doing a public interview with any artist about his work – the source and routes of which are often resolutely private – is that, once the invitation to take part in the interview has been accepted, there are the obligations of courtesy and 'public face' which promote honest responses. Curious though it may seem, I have often been able to hold more intimate, more detailed and more fruitful conversations with an artist – about his or her work – in public than in private. Privacy allows the elisions of shorthand and the loopholes of ambiguity. Put an artist in a public spot such as television and a sense of occasion, of decency, of playing straight, of not being caught out by the inevitable claque of friends and enemies severally gathered around their screens, generally prevails. Television is a good lie detector and sensitive people know it.

Olivier, of course, is ten thousand times accomplished as a man on the public podium, in the eye of a storm of publicity, at the centre of a furore, followed and haloed, as most of his professional life has been, by lights. That was a problem. Would he be merely on parade for us as well? We took our cameras to him time and again over those eighteen months. Even when we met for a meal or a resumé there would be notes taken. He came to trust us, I think. He said so, and was most generous in his appreciation of the final product. But perhaps he tricked all of us all of the time. Certainly some of the television critics were swift to point out that Olivier was 'acting the interviewee'. To which one could only reply, 'But of course.' Of course. The interesting questions are: why was he acting, who was he acting and how much of the Olivier we were concerned with was more truthfully revealed by this acting?

We were all in the game within the first ten minutes of the first morning's shooting. He had just been finishing his autobiography and was full of the pains of authorship. He reclined on a sofa, needing to keep his left leg up because of the danger of clotting; nevertheless it was a grand, authorial pose with a shelf of books just peeping into the right of frame. He wore a fawn, leather-buttoned cardigan of a type I vaguely remembered being sported by Simenon, and one or two of the better-regarded English writers of the forties. His spectacles were firmly fastened to his nose although all he had to look at was me, four or five feet away, and all he had to avoid was the camera,

six or seven feet away. Avoid! But it was the pipe
that did it. The pipe was a little too heavy for the teeth,
that was the trouble, and a touch temperamental, or
was it that its smoker was no great pipeman? 'A good
prop, you see,' he acknowledged, a couple of seconds
before the thought articulated itself in our minds. 'All
authors smoke pipes, don't they?' And the tease was
on.

In one sense it never stopped. I never expected it
to. This was the game he played to tell this sort of
truth: the truth about himself as he was prepared to
admit it. Meanwhile, though, there were the off-
camera times, the observation of the process whereby
Olivier could 'touch' so accurately and often so deli-
cately on people he had been – the boy, the youth,
the matinée idol, the film star, the bureaucrat – and
the parts he had played. Because we filmed on several
occasions we found him mellow, we found him merry,
we found him tetchy, brusque, even angry; we found
him morose, sentimental, abstracted. So was he
always cunning?

I think not. I think that he might well have taken
for his motto this couplet from Congreve's *The Double
Dealer*:

No mask like open truth to cover lies
As to go naked is the best disguise.

The more I thought about it, the more I saw the
thousands of feet of rushes and yards and yards of
celluloid of others talking about him, of him in role
after role, flickering from youth to age, from gorgeous
princeliness to plain weariness across those small
screens in the film cutting rooms, the more I came to
believe that couplet from *The Double Dealer* very
useful; it is when he is in disguise that he is naked.

He is telling the truth about himself all the time, whatever role he plays.

He himself has insisted on this, bluntly, with an unostentatious shrug of words, on many occasions. 'The only time I ever feel really alive is when I am acting,' he has said, in many variations. And as to the purpose of acting, he has been equally firm. 'There are many dimensions in the art of acting,' he said when speaking to some drama students, 'but none of them are good or interesting unless they are invested with the appearance or complete illusion of the truth.' When not acting he has consistently described himself as 'bored' or 'boring', with 'no point oi view': he once said 'without acting I would die, I suppose'. 'People would never believe how very *ordinary* he is at home,' Joan Plowright has said. Acting himself as the writer/ interviewee, then, was his only method of telling us all he could bear to tell us about the work and life on which we questioned him. For at the time of being interviewed he was indeed a writer and a distinguished elder statesman of the theatre looking back on a life of achievement: we got some truth in that.

This truth presumes that we believe what he says and take it for granted that he believes it too. I have found that many highly complex artists are prepared to describe themselves in simple terms and abide by the description. I believe Olivier when he says that the only time he ever feels really alive is when he is acting: I believe that when he is not acting one part or another he is bored, very 'ordinary', even a cipher. I think the extraordinary thing about Olivier is that, in whatever role, he is always telling the 'open truth', always 'going naked', and also always 'in disguise'. That *is* the real self.

I have declared the modesty of my credentials compared with a considerable number of others who have written about Olivier – and indeed, as the man said, there is a great deal to be modest about. Let me now balance this with a conceit. The essay is divided into five parts, preceded by a prologue, followed by an epilogue. In nothing else but that can I imitate and pay tribute to the writer whose creatures have most certainly hoisted Olivier to greatness. Each part – or shall we let loose all restraint and release a coven of hostages to fortune? – each Act includes a description of a place in which I met and interviewed Olivier over the period I spent with him. The hope is to let first-hand reporting rub words with the reflections of Olivier himself, the observations of others and my own attempt at understanding.

When he became a peer – the first actor to be raised to the peerage – Olivier, who still prefers 'Sir' to 'Lord', dug up his family motto. *Sicut Oliva Virent Laetor in Aede Dei*: 'I rejoice in the House of the Lord, even as the olive tree flourishes.' Faith and Nature were kin.

It is a remarkably accurate comment on his life and work.

PROLOGUE

It is a truism that we are different people to different people. A woman can assume the roles of wife, mother, daughter, lover, careerist, friend, intimate, acquaintance, enemy, zealot, nag, refuge, and she will be the same basic person but each time reveal a different aspect of herself. It is a truism also that many of us want to be different people. A man might want to be a famous writer, or a spy, a political hero, a hermit, a scholar, a soldier, a scoundrel, an Olympic athlete, a decent family man, a Beat. However impossible the ambition, the wish can be nonetheless keen.

When we are children, both these truisms seem true. When children play games, they do not bother to pretend to be the characters they are assuming, they adopt them wholesale, they swallow them in a gulp. 'I'm Robin Hood – you be Will Scarlet.' 'I'm Luke Skywalker – you're Darth Vader.' 'I'm a nurse.' 'I'm a mother – he's the baby.' 'I'm Spiderman – she's Wonderwoman.' I am. You are. We are. No qualifications. The impression of any strong character makes a complete imprint on a child and out comes the small self-declared clone. Children seem to have no trouble at all in 'being' other people: it is entirely a pleasure and apparently both effortless and natural.

Aging brings limitations. Childhood's easy access

to a multiplicity of possible lives narrows to a track or two – the routes or ruts we have to follow. Most of us realise, too late, that we have but one life, that much of it has already been determined and that most of it is now spoken for. The full realisation of that terrible restriction is like the clamping on of an iron mask. All those sensual dreams of potential, of possibility, of variety, of alternatives – all are expelled from the riveted face of reality. The game is up.

Yet it will not lie down. And it is those who create characters – writers, film makers, comedians, newspapers sometimes, and actors perhaps most of all – who keep it active. They provide the inspiration for the expiring body of our imaginative needs. We are sucked into their novels, their movies, their media-invented lives and, most surely of all, we are most willingly seduced out of ourselves by actors. They play the parts we once could so easily have reached. They live out the many lives we know we could and should have enjoyed. They tell us what we are not, which is so often what we want to be. They are all the futures we will never have. And when one man – such as Olivier – portrays in himself alone so royal a flush of possibilities then we are moved not only to admiration but also to curiosity. Not – how does he do it, so much as – how does he dare do it?

For in some low throb of memory, we can dimly call up the times when we too could 'be' multitudes: we turned our backs on those multitudes, thinking that less was more, that to specialise was not only inevitable it was mature, not only sensible but profitable. Yet in Olivier we are faced with a man who retained his multitudinous existence and is also mature, has profited, has proved that more is more. How has he held onto that easy childish boldness? Where did he get the nerve to sweat out the imperatives of 'growing up', 'settling down', 'setting your sights', 'specialising', 'stop dreaming', 'stick at one thing'?

Look at the photographs of Olivier. He wants to be everybody. He uses every bit of skill and private sorcery to convince himself and us that he is anybody he wants to be. And he is. A blood-blinded Greek; a spinsterish, old, country justice; a crippled, malicious, envenomed King; a modest young naval officer; a swarthy, vain, wild, jealous Moor; a gallant; a tinselled prince; an oh-so-very-English-county squire; a fashionable husband; a wild, romantic lover; a London clubman; a drunken failure; a conservative with nothing but the preservation of kippers on the Brighton Belle to occupy his mind; an old, wild, tragic and mad-demented King; an administrator. He has brought so many lives into him and discharged them as his own. We press our faces against that in admiration and envy like Victorian street urchins pressing their noses against the panes of richly furnished shop windows.

And this allows him to be the heroes we want to be but never, quite, manage: he is the villains we dread being and sometimes, almost, succeed at. He can let his courage storm the stage and his cowardice palpitate in the spotlight. He can be the most ecstatic lover and the impotent. He can use all the reaches of his many selves and summon up those embryos of other lives we have crushed on our way to the security of singleness.

Not that this singleness does not bring its own rewards and compensations: and it is undoubtedly true that some of the best and most valuable work done is accomplished by people of fierce, limited

dedication. But there are all the other glories of those
unused, unknown lives, all inside us, forever unable
to get out. As if we were a hive of bees and only one,
or at the most two, were allowed to pass into the outer
world, the rest condemned to a perpetual buzzing in
the frustrated dark. Those who create characters –
on the page, on celluloid or on the stage – and most
strikingly those who inhabit other characters, tell us
what we want, perhaps what we need, to know: that
we are various, that we are not one but many.

That Olivier has done this over a vast range of
characters and decades is undeniable. His many roles,
even in close-up camera shots, record what? A master
of disguise? Of make-up? Of camera-spooking trick-
ery? He is the same man, yet he can appear so
different. As we all can. But his differences and his
different appearances are on such a scale, cover such
a range as to leave our commonplace manoeuvrings
from role to role as no more than the fumblings of a
beginner. The different people in him are loosed on
the world in full war paint. And the disguise, the
make-up, all the artifice, are little more than gestures.
The real change is deep within Olivier himself: for it
is different parts of himself he reaches for as the
demands of the many characters rise up to meet him.
It is himself he lays on the line. His own heroism; his
own cynicism; his own villainy; his own fury; his own
tenderness. 'There must have been something of
Archie in me all along,' he said of Archie Rice – 'The
Entertainer'. 'It's what I might so easily have become.'
So with all the others. Olivier, like all supreme actors
– and authors in many forms – is driven by the
relentless compulsion to let out this whole Pandora's
box of different people, characteristics, virtues, vices,

strengths, weaknesses, that beset him and demand to be released. When he is not opening the cage door to let prowl one of his beasts, he is not 'dead behind those eyes': what we are allowed to see is the wary gaze of fear. In all his many costumes, behind all the false noses and the wads of make-up, under the wigs and beards and padding and armour, he is telling us the truth about himself. He is always himself, always naked.

EARLY DAYS

The first day's shooting had been rearranged a couple of times. He was not quite as well as he wanted to be. He needed another week or two on his autobiography. When he did arrive he was both effusively and convincingly apologetic. We set up the cameras in the upstairs room of his comfortable country cottage-house. There was a warm, early summer sun. He pottered about and settled himseu comfortably – the left leg had a tendency to swell up rather painfully, needed to be kept up, underpinned by a cushion or two. That pipe was produced with a nod and a flourish. While the lighting men coped with the sun's dazzle through the windows, Olivier and I chatted a little, deliberately off the subject. Yes, he had finished the first draft of his autobiography. It was far too long. He had discovered how extraordinarily boring he was. It had been the hardest thing he had done but he had done it and by himself. Yes indeed, it could be called useful for this filmed interview: he was all up to date with himself, too full of himself you might say, absolutely primed. And determined, he said, given the rules I had laid out for the interviews (no liberties to be taken with private matters; no holds barred on the parts and the other public work), to be as truthful as he possibly could be. It was as easy and pleasant a set-up as I had

ever enjoyed. The sun, the man, the calm, the time
to shoot. 'Action!'

It is useful sometimes to begin with a vague and
general question, more of a net than a line, a friendly
heave up, more of a handshake than a lead. On the
whole, I asked, looking back on his childhood, what
was his strongest overall impression? And into that
serene room, from the world-famous actor in his
mid-seventies who wanted to make up to us and
wanted to be truthful, came the unhesitating response.
'I was frightened. More than anything else, I was
terrified.' It was chilling.

For more than two centuries, the men in the Olivier
family elected, predominantly, for the Church.
Olivier's father was the tenth child of a parson and
after an early (quickly squashed) hope of being trained
for opera, a foray into dramatics, a short sharp lesson
in financial and academic failure, he became a schoolmaster and a cricketer of county standard; then, well
married, well set up with his own private school and
a life of Edwardian privilege, he gave it all up, in
his zeal for God, unplugged himself from material
contentment and took his family along the strait and
frugal round of bare pickings and Anglo-Catholicism.

Laurence was the third child: there was a sister six
years older and a brother about three years older.
Laurence's sister has quite straightforwardly confirmed his vivid recollections of being 'frightened'. It
appears that their father could not stand his youngest
son, could not tolerate him. Perhaps he was associated
with a bitter convulsion within the marriage, or
with the very indifferent worldly luck that came to
the Oliviers after the dramatic entry into High-
Churchmanship, or maybe there was, even at that

tender age, rivalry. For certainly it appears that his mother Agnes absolutely adored him. He made her laugh, she had hair so long she could sit on it, she was brown and quick as a gypsy, he has repeatedly said how much he adored her and how no photograph can show off her beauty. Perhaps this imp at the feast provoked jealousy in the breast of the father. It has been known. His manner, though, or his revenge, was to frighten the boy who would remember it and possibly use it for life.

It was all the more frightening because Gerard Olivier was the priest of God. To be despised, rebuked and condemned by father on earth meant, sure as eggs were eggs, that the Heavenly Father too thought you a very poor specimen. And Olivier's religiosity was early intense. There was 'Laurence's Shrine' where solitary private services were conducted by the five-year-old arrayed in a popish eiderdown. He was very vulnerable to what he could intimate as the desires of the Almighty. By the age of seven he was inside the altar rails, an acolyte to his own father-Father, terrified even more by the fear that he might do something 'wrong', misdirect the wine, forget which response came after the blessing of the bread, just think one wrong thought and the Might of the Lord would descend on him. This fearfulness is the molten core of his childhood.

Agnes his mother was bedrock. She seems to have loved him particularly: even now he talks of her with an unaffected girlish spooning. It was she who – consciously or not – took him out of the spheres of his father. She preferred a better class of church to the one her husband preached in and attended the fashionable All Saints in Margaret Street, central

London. It had a famous choir school and she placed
her elder son, Dickie, there and in 1915 – at the third
time of trying – slipped in the scraggy little Larry. It
was a sanctuary.

For five years he boarded there, lived a life of
the monastery, sang solo to expensively dressed,
connoisseur congregations, took part in the religious
dramas of Anglo-Catholicism, blotted up great scores
of choral music, great periods of Jacobean prose, great
rituals in glittering vestments. Like Richardson and
Gielgud at about the same age, he longed to be a
priest.

We went back to All Saints one afternoon after a
rather hedonistically heathen lunch at Overton's. Not
knowing what to offer a man such as Olivier, I
suggested oysters and champagne to start with which,
although he was 'not to drink much, dear boy, not
today nor any day', he diffidently accepted. A couple
of bottles later he was in fine form directing the driver
up and down the back-street mazes of central London
as we weaved about looking first for All Saints and
then for a parking space. Finally we got out and
walked: he, though an hour or two ago declaring
himself 'rather low', and indeed then looking it, by
now transformed and as jaunty as a sailor on
leave.

Inside the church he was instantly subdued in tone
but at first the bubbly style would have its say – 'the
most beautiful church', 'look at the Lady Chapel –
over there', 'most wonderful acoustics in London –
you aimed for the West wall – there – and up it went
into the ceiling', 'marvellous organ', 'here's where we
used to process – I was a boat boy, carrying the
incense'. Soon it wore off and either tiredness or too

pressing a rush of memory gradually blocked out talk.
He simply sat and looked about him.

For this was where it all started, he said. Anything
that mattered to him. He had been 'too weak a vessel'
to go into the priesthood and he was not now a
practising Christian although he kept his own faith,
but here he learnt, he knew that you had to dedicate
your life to a great purpose and with passionate conviction.

And inside the choir school that great purpose was
plain. For next to God, the All Saints choir school
worshipped the theatre. Geoffrey Heald, a teacher at
the school, put on productions with such panache that
it became the thing for some of the greatest actors of
the day – Ellen Terry, Forbes Robertson, the young
Sybil Thorndike – to go to the performances. Olivier
seems to have been an instant star. His doubting
father was one day greatly flattered to hear his son
praised in the very highest terms by one of the very
greatest actors in the land. Shrewd Ellen Terry saw
his potential at once. As did Father Heald – whose
tiny (fourteen-strong) school turned out at least three
renowned actors – who commented of Olivier's Kate
in *The Taming of the Shrew* that it was the best he
had ever seen. A comment complemented by W. A.
Darlington, who reviewed the fledgling production in
the *Daily Telegraph* and was only one of several
national theatre critics present: he praised Olivier
roundly and concluded, 'I cannot remember any actress in the part who looked better.' The performance
was put on at Stratford-on-Avon in Shakespeare's
birthday week and the fourteen-year-old Laurence
carried the wreath in the procession from the theatre
to Shakespeare's grave.

When you look at Olivier as Kate the Shrew you meet a strange expression. It looks not vulnerable but hurt and powder-ready to retaliate. The attitude of the face and the body are womanly rather than girlish: there is little skittishness in the look of this Kate. She seems drawn not from youth but from the world of older women. A world just then cut off from him by his mother's death.

Olivier has described how utterly bereft he felt.

He is also prepared to appraise the strengths such an acute loss might have given him. Not that this serves as compensation or consolation: but something came of it. In the Olivier household of genteel poverty where a chicken could be so finely sliced it could serve the family for three days, where the bathwater was shared by the three males and suits were passed down from better-off uncles, nothing was to be wasted. Or perhaps Olivier, wanting his mother's early death to stand for something more than a tragic loss, cannot bear to let her go without claiming for her one last gift. Her death might have given him, he says, that quality of detachment, that haunted quality.

Or it might, in its way, more brutally, have killed off some central root of affection so decisively that he has found nothing to replace it since: only relief in the taking on of roles. I have always found it most odd that he speaks of his attraction to Joan Plowright – his third wife – in terms of her 'likeness' to his mother: that in this younger woman he found at last or re-claimed the tie broken when he was thirteen. He was over fifty then. I accept that he is speaking the truth as he finds it. What, then, of the time between, when his character, his career, his achievements, his fame, his whole complex trajectory of life was established and so richly developed? At the very least this confession of rediscovering his mother in Joan Plowright must point to that mother having been 'lost' or repressed for an immense haul of his life. As he has declared his mother to be at the root and centre of his affection and capacity for affection, perhaps her death created an empty centre, devastating the young boy the more cruelly as he was at full stretch. And to appease that empty centre, to keep himself company or to staunch the loneliness, he turned to others: but not people. Roles.

For which people could he turn to? He was already an outsider. At thirteen a 'star', a solo boy, a pet of the famous and a name in the newspapers, he was about to be catapulted into the unknown and inhospitable territory of an English public school which he hated. They thought he was a cissy; they thought he was a show-off; they thought he was a lousy sportsman. They were right, he says, one – two – and three. 'I tried to be anonymous,' he recalls. 'All I wanted was to be like the rest.' He is convinced that he would have succeeded but for the other pull: acting. 'They had heard about the acting.' He was Puck in the school play. National reviews once again and yet Olivier is convinced that his success only filled his school colleagues with disgust.

Puck had been a release but the boy wanted to disappear into the crowd. When his elder brother Dickie set off for India for the first half of his nine-year stint, Olivier, with his father in the bathroom that night, asked when he could follow him into the Indian Civil Service. The few years at public school had unravelled all the embroidered dreams woven from the rituals and sermons of his father, the excitements and triumphs organised by Father Heald, the feeling of a wonderful, chosen life to be lived inspired by his 'darling mother' and his intense espousal of a personal God. The Civil Service was now the answer. From the pinnacle of being adored, applauded, singled out and encouraged to feel that the world could be commanded by his ambition, he had plummeted to a view of himself which insisted that he be 'like everyone else' and, to make doubly sure, as like his steady, reliable elder brother as possible.

It was here – as Olivier has often told it – that his father abruptly told him not to be silly, he was to be an actor. Olivier was not only delighted with this directive, which rekindled hopes he had held since his last years at the choir school, he was, just as importantly, 'amazed that Father had taken the trouble to think about me and to make a plan for me'. It is a peculiar scene. Naked widower priest and spindly teenage son in cold bathroom in Pimlico playing out a love scene. For it is in that tone of voice that Olivier still now refers to it. His father – the awesome, frightening, terrible Gerard with God on his shoulder – had received his son. In some way, Olivier must have felt himself blessed.

His father set out the terms and conditions for his career and, in his gratitude for the affection so long withheld and the release from the fear so long endured, Olivier obeyed them to the item and may be said to have abided by them since. There was a Miss Elsie Fogerty, his father said, who ran the Central School of Speech Training and Dramatic Art: Laurence was to go there, get a scholarship and further, win the £50 bursary which was on offer. Without it his

father would not be able to support him and there
would be no acting career. From the very first, then,
at the age of seventeen, Olivier was plainly told and
knew he had to believe that success was entirely up
to him and that earning money was part of it: what he
wanted had to be earned and in cash. Any ideals, any
vows on the cross of dramatic art, any swearing by
the sword of aestheticism was as foreign to this
enterprise as clean bathwater.

He did exactly as his father ordered.

If his mother's death had scooped the heart out of
him, thus, as it were, fancifully speaking, leaving the
space free for so many other characters to inhabit and
comfort, his father's mundane battle plan sent him
spinning into his career like a top and like a top he
whirled his way through Miss Fogerty's school of five
boys and eighty girls.

Miss Fogerty seems to have been a matriarch of
talent. She warned the young man about his brow ('a
weakness' – eyebrows too thick, hairline too low)
pointed him away from over-gesticulation and put him
through the hoops of voice training, dancing, learning
different parts, acting.

Peggy Ashcroft, an exact contemporary with whom
he shared the top prize – she Portia, he Shylock –
described him, mildly, as 'uncouth'. He looks at that
time positively in from the Bush. His hair sprouts
out of scalp and eyebrows; his complexion is almost
swarthy; his teeth are splayed and gappy; his nose
seems not so much dominating as overwhelming; his
suits, we are told, were short at the sleeve and equally
ill-fitting at every other point; his diet was buns,
buns and coffee and not many buns and his energy,
according to Peggy Ashcroft, was 'quite tremendous'.

She laughs at the recollection: even now a little appalled at the violence of it.

But he had to move fast: his mother's place had to be filled and his father's enabling imperative meant that he had to succeed. If he failed to succeed he would be landed with himself, his empty anonymous self. He needed all those other people: all those people who could neither frighten him nor die on him. And all those people he could love. Love and be. He has often said that one of the key tips in his life was Tyrone Guthrie's injunction that unless he 'loved' the character he was playing then he would never play it fully. And another tip he took firmly on board was 'all parts are character parts'. He wanted to get hold of those characters to express himself: without them he would simply be himself and that state always has and still does puzzle, bore and dull him. 'I never know what to think or say. I never know what to do.' Characters were his spokesmen.

Olivier can still execute a brilliantly mimicked memory of his early failures, malnutrition, falling flat on his face at his first entrance onto the professional stage and several firings for various crimes of unprofessionalism, most usually giggling on stage. In our interview he castigated himself at this period as 'a twerp' and laid into his twenty-year-old self so robustly that one or two critics thought he was just enjoying the knockabout. Not, apparently, so. There is much evidence of his twerpiness, of his vulgarity: wanting to rip down the backcloth on stage (during performance) because he knew 'the girls' were changing behind it and he fancied seeing 'all those bare bottoms'; calling the company which gave him his first real start playing in halls and swimming baths in the suburbs 'The

Lavatory Players'; being rescued and repaired by those old friends of the family and soon to be his own 'dearest friends', Lewis Casson and Sybil Thorndike. He seems to have whirled about like a dervish, terrified to be out of work, almost hysterical when he was in work – but work he must.

He was fortunate to go to Birmingham in 1927 – still only twenty – to join the company of Barry Jackson, who employed and often discovered and 'brought on' an astonishing number of the finest actors and actresses. Birmingham gave him exactly what he needed: work and characters. In a year he played about a dozen roles and, as we can see from photographs of Tony Lumpkin and Uncle Vanya, he was already – and the virile roughness of those early attempts is very touching – straining to do what became his life-plan: never to look the same twice. He will refer to this rather musingly, almost, even, reverentially, as a 'compulsive quest for versatility', or he will dismiss it as 'a childish desire to show off so that people coming into Birmingham one week would say, "Oh! That can't, surely not, be the very same young man we saw looking so very different last week."' Whatever mood he is in he never baulks at referring to it. And in it, he found his release and his equilibrium. From now on that was to be his life. Work, new characters to absorb, new parts of himself to display through the inventions of others. Whenever he was not working, whenever he was without a 'character', he would declare himself null and void. The only way he could be himself was to consume others.

For the title role in Tennyson's *Harold* he learnt at least 3000 lines in one week. His devotion to detail was already evident. Everything, he confessed openly, was to be used. Everything he saw, overheard, encountered, heard of, was to be used. No one was safe. He prides himself on storing away information which he can conjure up years later when he needs it. For example, when we spoke that sunny morning in the Sussex cottage which he has cunningly and appropriately made look like a mini Elizabethan residence, he told – alas at too great a length for our film – an anecdote of Shandean-shaggy-dog-story complication about a dinner he had à trois with Charlie Chaplin and Paulette Goddard. All the time he was speaking I wanted to say 'Please cut, please get there', or I was thinking 'How will it edit? What can we do with this except show it at full length but there is so little time and so much other more directly germane material.' On and on went this anecdote as Olivier amused himself – he knew, once he had become labyrinthine by accident that the wittiest course was to stay labyrinthine by design – but the point was this: Chaplin and Paulette Goddard were having a row in front of Olivier. The burden of Chaplin's complaint was not – oh no! – that Goddard had taken a fancy to another man, but that she should provoke a row in front of a guest. In his 'funny American cockney,' Olivier said, 'impossible to imitate,' he added – and then imitated it – 'Charlie kept saying that her behaviour was "an insult to my mind".'

'You see,' Olivier said, 'it wasn't enough for him that he was the funniest clown in the world; he wanted to be thought of as an intellectual. Well, I used that, eighteen years later, when I did Othello. In the first speech to the Senate, Othello speaking as one intellectual to another. You know?' Olivier smiled angelically and then either to mitigate the confession of stealing from a private conversation or of retailing the private conversation itself, he punctured his own observation instantly. 'Got a laugh,' he said. 'If you can find a laugh or two in Othello, it's very helpful.' Just the sort of anti-intellectual remark he likes to specialise in.

He stole from other actors, particularly the screen stars. At this time Olivier was swept into the general passion for matinée idols – Ronald Colman, Douglas Fairbanks. The glamour! The elegance! The style! The dash! The moustache. 'I said to him' – Ralph Richardson recalled the time when they had just met – 'I said, "What's that?" "That's my moustache," he said. "What do you want that for?" I said.' He never told Richardson that in his first flight of enthusiasm for *the* moustache he had been so impatient that he had *painted* it on. Nor would he have been likely to confess to the man who was going to become his lifelong friend, colleague, advisor and sparring partner, that he had virtually redesigned himself.

He had shaved back and plucked the hairline, at last taking notice of Miss Fogerty's comment on his 'weakness' (low forehead). His eyebrows were plucked. He took exercise to fill out the barely nourished 'wires' as he called his limbs. He dressed gaily. He went to nightclubs. He met the girl – Jill Esmond – who was going to be 'my very first wife'. He was going to be Beau Geste.

The transformation is somewhere between comic and worrying in its neat, sweet all-completeness. The rough gypsy boy with a face full of bumpkin mischief and unpredictable energy has been wiped out. Even the glowering intentness of the many roles at Birmingham have slipped quietly away into the wings. Stage front, tailored like a swell, glistening with the very latest line in handsome maleness, he presented his new self – Beau Olivier.

The Beau Geste role was to be translated onto the stage and, like every young actor in England, Olivier was after it. It is impossible to believe, looking at private and stage photographs of him at that time, that he could have been made for any other role. Ronald Colman released him into the twirling twenties. The moustache and later its memory gave him what Richardson called 'his cool: his panache'. Beau Geste was to bring him what he most wanted aged twenty-two: all the fame in the world.

He was by no means the leading contender and, refashion, reshave, remodel himself as he would, it seemed for some time that he was scarcely a contender at all.

He took a lead part in a play by R. C. Sheriff called *Journey's End*. It ran for a few weeks and, as was becoming usual, the young Olivier was picked out with some excellent notices. The cast believed in it with great conviction and when it failed to find a backer all of them stood by it – all that is, except Olivier. The author thought that Olivier had been rather reluctant to play the part of the young First World War officer – Stanhope – who takes to whisky to stave off cowardice. He was right: Olivier left to play Beau Geste at the irresistible salary of £30 a week.

Beau Geste, full of sound and fury, full of effects and acrobatics and the sight of money being burnt, flopped. *Journey's End* reopened to nineteen curtain calls, a run of 600 performances, world-wide success, a film and fortunes for all involved.

In the next eight months, while *Journey's End*

clocked up audiences, money, prestige, records and excitement to become one of the phenomena of the theatre, Olivier played alongside it in several London theatres: in the New Theatre as Prince Po in *The Circle of Chalk* – a flop; in the Lyric as Richard Parish in *Paris Bound* – which flopped; in the Garrick as John Hardy in *The Stranger Within*; in the Fortune as Jerry Warrender in *The Last Enemy*; in the Arts as Ralph in *After All* – flop, flop, flop. He went over to New York to play Hugh Bromilow in *Murder on the Second Floor*. Flop. He maintains that not doing *Journey's End* – the big hit – was one of the best pieces of professional luck he was ever to enjoy. That, anyway, is his story and he sticks to it.

His reasoning makes sound retrospective sense. While Colin Clive, the new Stanhope, had one time to shine, Olivier was constantly being re-presented to West End First Night audiences and critics who would generally find something kind or admiring to say about his performance while being lukewarm or worse about the play. And – again in retrospect – being stuck as Stanhope, Stanhope on stage, Stanhope in New York, Stanhope on celluloid, could have meant Stanhope for ever: nearly the contemporary equivalent of getting typecast in a television soap-opera. On the other hand . . . there are those who said he was more than a bit fed up. And after all, he had created the part in the first place.

Help, though, was at hand. If not the US Cavalry then Noel Coward. The darling and idol of the boulevard, lyricist, librettist, writer of comedies, actor of wit, and no mean tap dancer. He had written *Private Lives*, which he knew would be a smash hit, for Gertie Lawrence and himself. (Himself also directed, of

course.) There were two other parts, neither up to
much. The husband was fundamentally dull, a lump,
a feed, in all conscience little more than a device. He
wanted Larry in the play 'because I said I must have
somebody who's physically very attractive otherwise
Amanda would never have married him. He must have
something to give, he hasn't got much in the dialogue
way. And poor Larry never really enjoyed playing it
much. I think he enjoyed acting it with me, we had
great fun, and curiously enough it did him a lot of
good.'

It gave him £50 a week and enabled him to get
married to Jill Esmond, a young, very successful
actress from a theatrical family whose outspoken
views on marriage ('If ever the man I married behaved
decently towards me or I towards him only because
it was laid down in an unwritten marriage contract, I
should feel it was high time we parted') added another
charge to a glittering theatrical wedding – Ralph Richardson, Jack Hawkins, Nora Swinburne – graced by
aristocratic gifts including a necklace of pearls from
Princess Marie-Louise who loved the theatre, and
held in Olivier's beloved All Saints with the new
generation of choir boys aiming, just as he had done,
for the West wall.

It gave him his first West End success and an
introduction to the luxury living of success à la Noel.

It gave him a reading list. 'Noel made me use my
silly little brain.' Bennett, Maugham and Brontë were
the first three authors Coward recommended: Brontë,
Emily, *Wuthering Heights*.

It gave him the beginnings of wider fame. He was
interviewed in Manchester for example, where –
riding so high, in love, well off beyond his dreams,

twenty-three, light years away from the bit part cadg-
ing days only three years previously – he declared
that 'only fools are happy . . . I somehow can't get
that way. I always examine things so closely that
immediate pleasures are dwarfed by my insistence on
ultimate benefits . . .'

Only acting, it seemed, could reliably oust that
ever-threatening despair. And Noel Coward's final and
arguably his best gift to Olivier was, as he might have
put it, 'in the acting field'.

Olivier's giggling was an unbecoming, unprofessional but apparently incurable nuisance. It was, as
Olivier now says, a form of hysteria. The force of
energy and desire which had shocked him into action
as his father, totally unexpectedly, fired the starting
pistol, and the sense of emptiness within himself he
still felt, combined with an overspill of sheer activity
perhaps helped detonate the hysteria. Coward would
not have it. He said that he would cure Olivier of it
and he did. Night after night he would try to make
Olivier giggle on stage and whenever Olivier did so,
Coward would 'kill' him – publicly humiliate him and
later in front of the entire stage staff, dress him down.
It was a very long battle: the young actor full of
impulse and scared-stiff spirit but powerful, and the
totally detached, professional, even classical Coward,
able to wither anyone across the breadth of a stage.

Perhaps only someone of Coward's determination
and authority could have done it – for Olivier declares
that it took about seven months. But he was cured.

He was twenty-three. His new wife was to come
into *Private Lives* as it set off for New York where it
would be a sure hit. He had rocketed to stardom and
in the process apparently changed himself utterly. He

was now the complete, debonair, matinée idol about
town. To the life. He had changed himself and found
himself. Professional to the last pluck of an eyebrow.
And if Noel Coward ever dared try to make him giggle
on stage he knew – as that boat set sail for New York
– that he was now strong enough to outgun Coward
and, as the term goes, 'kill' his teacher.

FAME AND HOLLYWOOD

There is a thirty-second strip of newsreel from 1931 which 'stars' Laurence Olivier and his new wife Jill Esmond. They are posed as for an official portrait. Their attitude is that of a couple representing some Very Important Institution. Appropriately for the times, it is the handsome young man who speaks, modestly, while the beautiful young woman maintains an equally modest, supportive silence. The location was Hollywood, RKO Studios.

'Ladies and Gentlemen,' the young, double-breasted Olivier said. 'May a comparatively young English actor offer his very humble congratulations to those who have initiated this enterprise. Hollywood has set a very high standard of production but I know perfectly well that the British brains and the British capital embodied in these and other British studios will make the British Picture Hollywood's most successful rival.'

Even at that stripling age, Olivier's sense of being English – the word 'British', you feel, was a committee's cautious corrective – had been noted, was being merchandised with himself as a willing agent. This undisguised and instantly, perpetually, available patriotism is clearly felt most sincerely: it is also a part he can assume, abroad or in a crisis; a part which, once again, takes the onus off himself, the empty bore he persistently describes his 'real' self to be.

When Olivier arrived in Hollywood – predictably yanked over from the success of *Private Lives* on Broadway – he came to a film industry rejoicing in the invention of the Talkies, mad for English accents and abounding in famous exiles from Chaplin to Ronald Colman.

Olivier had made himself like Colman. He had seen him as the man who could give him the eminence he lusted for. He had made a remarkable job of turning a gauche, skinny, rough, idiosyncratic quirk of a youth – as might be a young Heathcliff – into the debonair, athletic, dewy-eyed charmer of the matinée crowd. Coward had sharpened him up. Jill had brought him firmly into Society; she was one of the best-connected, most talented, most desirable and loveliest of the young actresses. Coward was the wittiest and one of the most successful playwrights in the Western world but Colman was a universal star, and with Jill, Olivier said his farewells to Coward and set off to be greeted as a very possible second Ronald Colman. He saw the way the wind was blowing and let it take him. Colman was the key to the fame of the times.

Olivier has often said that he was 'greedy for life', that he wanted to 'eat it all up'. John Gielgud speaks with something approaching alarm of Olivier's whole-hearted, forceful, even reckless seizing of a part and 'wringing its neck'. 'Terribly brave,' says Richardson, who chose his words with considerable discrimination. 'Didn't give a damn.' Only assumed characters can get Olivier out of the dungeon of his own Beckettian bleakness. And in 1931, Ronald Colman was all a young man could want to be.

So Ronald Colman he became.

He was also in love. From accounts of the time he was, like Romeo, in love with the idea of being in love. He seems to have fallen for ladies tall, small, older and younger throughout his Birmingham and early London days. He tippled into affections like a game pup getting into trouble. He could not help it, so it seems. A kind look, a charming smile, a pretty figure and whoosh, away he went, empty as a drum, longing to be taken over and played upon.

It would be surprising if his intimate life with Jill Esmond, as later with Vivien Leigh and Joan Plowright, did not have a significant influence on his public career as an actor. It would be surprising if there were not parallels, connections and crossovers especially as all three were at the very least accomplished actresses – in the case of Vivien Leigh a world-famous film star, in Joan Plowright's case a superlative theatrical actress – all of them intelligent, all of them strong-minded enough to have careers of their own and yet delighted to act alongside their husband whom all regarded, whatever the particular colour of their respective fortunes, as the superior talent. And insights galore could be had from knowing about those private lives, no doubt. In the most quiet, two-alone times is he the chameleon king or the nonentity – anonymous? Is control in public, that unknowable but undoubtedly colossal will to succeed, to dominate, to star, to attack, to be at the centre, is that balanced by or sustained and relieved by a tormented, unjust, insecure, unreliable, petty private face? There has to be some clay somewhere; and the rumours and the gossip, the malicious memories and the posthumous revelations, all conspire to throw a murk of innuendo over what may be rather simple and comparatively blameless. For he might indeed be a rather ordinary conservative chap who in a long and unusually testing life entertained three marriages – not all that remarkable in this day and age, even among apparently rather ordinary conservative chaps.

I have no way of knowing and such speculation is not within the bounds of this essay. There are certain assumptions it is reasonable to make – insofar as they touch on his career. His love for Vivien Leigh, to take one example, encouraged him to mount a *Romeo and Juliet* with her in New York in 1940 which was a terrible flop, took all their hefty savings and turned them to actions they might not otherwise have taken. His love for Joan Plowright, to take another example, appears to have stiffened his resolve to take the new ideas, writers and mood of the late fifties with him into his pre-National Theatre run up. Anything much else would be little more than idle chat. And, who knows? Perhaps the truth of it all is that he led his patently 'driven' life in some profound way regardless of the woman he was in love with, just as he led it despite, as often as following, the best advice and against, as often as for, his own apparent best interests.

It cannot have been the greatest fun for him to realise – swiftly – that in Hollywood, Jill Esmond was widely regarded as the better bet of the handsome new English pair. Even the Ronald Colman lookalike job lasted only so long: soon his rather desperate American publicists were dressing him up in American sporting gear and attempting a repackage. In two years he made three films – none distinguished, none at all extending him – and he felt so underused that 'I

even wrote a play. No good, of course.' Jill and
he had been instantly adopted by the smart young
Hollywood crowd which swung around with Douglas
Fairbanks Jnr, a most sympathetic friend, who remem-
bers Olivier as being 'known as Jill Esmond's husband.
Naturally that didn't appeal to his sense of pride very
much and it discouraged him a great deal. He wasn't
getting many jobs.'

Lack of work stifled him. He could not bear it and
to escape it did what some of his friends thought a
very ruthless thing: 'Behaved like a shit' was one
later comment. Jill was offered a star part in *Bill
of Divorcement* by Selznick: Clemence Dane's highly
successful, controversial play. John Barrymore was
to be in it. It was the proverbial chance-of-a-lifetime.

Olivier wanted to go home and work in London.
There was a film waiting for him with Gloria Swanson
– *Perfect Understanding*. Jill went with him.

Bill of Divorcement was a smash hit, making its new
leading lady – Kate Hepburn – into a twenty-two carat
star. *Perfect Understanding* was a flop.

They resettled in London. A fashionable residence
was acquired. Normal West End life resumed as
quickly as possible.

Almost immediately Olivier received a request to
return to Hollywood to co-star with – Greta Garbo.
He accepted. Jill went with him.

The newspapers went mad: local boy made good;
Garbo's charisma and mystery, her beauty and popularity. The chilled sexy way she said the words had
made her 'world-famous'. It was as if our boy was
being sent into the lists, or, more crudely, out to
stud, so stridently did the British press proclaim their
delight that Garbo had fingered Olivier and no other.

One of the characteristics of Olivier, during our interview, was the way in which he would switch his own roles as he told different parts of his own story. Nothing very unusual about that except, of course, that in his case both the switches and the echoed roles were more than ordinarily interesting. When he talked about his teacher, Elsie Fogerty, for instance, an affectionate tone, at once lightly mocking and lightly ponderous, summed up the picture of a woman of Agatha Christie or Margaret Rutherford bulk and benign intensity, shrewd though eccentric, acute but also helplessly open. When he spoke of being stifled during those two years in Hollywood when all he picked up were three undistinguished films, he literally strained back his head, unconsciously – it seemed to me – searching for breath: truly. As if he were remembering, re-enacting a literal withdrawal of the basic substance of life. I looked at it again on the unused rushes: exactly that.

When he talked about Garbo he first of all beat about the bush. He can be and he is retrospectively quite tough on himself. Some would say cleverly too tough thus forcing you to reconsider your own toughness and ameliorate it – but he was merely searching for the clearest, simplest expression of what was a woundingly clear and total rejection of him by the Great Swede. 'I wasn't up to it,' he said. 'I couldn't compete. I was out of my league and she knew it.' Even now, owning up is not so easy. Defeats dent confidence and confidence is essential, he has said, to acting: as essential before an audience as humility is before a text. Possibly he had not yet been able to uncover a sexual self able to deal with Garbo's demands.

Brutally given the Garbo heave-ho, he went to New York and repaired some of his hacked-down ego with what was widely regarded as a blindingly brilliant performance as a homosexual in *The Green Bay Tree*. Back in London he played Bothwell in *Queen of Scots* directed by John Gielgud and then took the town by the throat at the Lyric where he gave a Barrymore-Fairbanks-Olivier display of matinée swashbuckling and audience-grabbing pyrotechnics as Tony Cavendish in *Theatre Royal* directed by Noel Coward. That made him feel better: restored the balance a bit. Time to look around. Time to take stock. Sniff things out.

Those who know Olivier well and have followed his career closely will always talk about his very sure 'instinct'. They, too, can be seen sniffing the air as they say it, associating it with animal wisdom as we all tend to do. Instinct, though, can be the intuition of an enormously wide range of information so tightly compressed and so forceful that its complexity and its urgency elide into a compulsion to act without waiting for what would be the enfeebling hesitation of analysis. We can only guess at the final powers of those who rise to the very great heights scaled by Olivier in a profession which is so volatile and finally dependent on that dark oracle called, variously, public taste, or mood, or whim, or fantasy, or even need: something like a current of air seems to bear them up. And it is part of their genius to discover it, part of their skill to ride on it, part of the age's recognition of them to seek them out in order to bear them up. It is a deep and binding pact you make with your times and maybe you have to sell your soul to get it.

Olivier had been Ronald Colman, but it had not taken him far enough. True he could command a high fee and a starring role in New York and in London; true he was still being sounded out with film studio big-dollar contract offers; true his contracts and experience were wide enough for him to consider launching into one of his openly declared ambitions – to be an actor-manager. All this at the age of twenty-eight might have seemed a good hand for most folk. But it was Olivier's undeclared ambition which now took over: the ambition to soar up into himself through the invented characters of others which he could employ for his own release and relief.

Since his marriage, the face, the character, the role, had not been greatly stretched. Though it was always addressing itself to new parts, new plays, new movies, with – judging from the reviews of the day – massive energy, with ingenuity, with exceptions, Olivier had taken on a pattern of roles woven around the matinée idol: he was the super-juvenile lead.

South of the Thames, at that time in a grubby old barn of a theatre near Waterloo Station, Lilian Baylis and, more importantly for Olivier, John Gielgud were setting out to prove to a widely sceptical and thought to be hugely uninterested audience, that William Shakespeare could be box office. By March 1935, Gielgud's *Hamlet* had recorded 155 performances, a number exceeded only by the legendary Irving. Gielgud in Shakespeare was the toast of the town.

Olivier saw what he wanted and went for it.

It meant risking a rattling good boulevard reputation: it meant a large cut in salary – particularly painful for Olivier who has never concealed his extreme carefulness with money any more than he has concealed his apparent enthusiasm to throw it around entertaining his friends or put it at extreme risk producing and backing his own West End shows which often as not crashed. He wanted Shakespeare though: he wanted the fame and he wanted the parts. In a sense, at this juncture in his professional life – the Garbo chop had been a very public, very humiliating rabbit punch: the movie world had not taken to his impersonation of a star – he wanted to go back to his professional roots, to his first success in the choir school, in those plays applauded by his mother and the fashionable theatre people of the day. Shakespeare – for him as an actor, lost, rather, in the flight to stardom – was home.

Gielgud called him in and it was with Gielgud – to the public's delight – that he was to fence. The elegant, intellectual, thoughtful and witty John Gielgud had a purity of dedication to the work he loved that had gathered about him a flock of acolytes. There was and is something priestly in him, something Roman, Jesuitical perhaps but not conspiratorial. He was over-loaded with work and wanted someone to share Romeo and Mercutio with him. Olivier was his third or fourth choice.

As Romeo, it seems, they could scarcely have been more different. Gielgud – air and spirit; Olivier – earth and passion. The critics wanted air and spirit. Olivier was not so gently panned. He was told he could not speak Shakespeare's verse. 'Me?' He literally spluttered, remembering it forty-six years later. 'Me? Not speak Shakespeare's verse? I had been brought up with it. Me? I had spoken it all my life. Me? It was ridiculous!' And there he was, in his seventies, still struggling unsuccessfully to bottle up his indignation. 'What they meant,' he said savagely, 'is that I didn't *sing* it.'

Gielgud, who cheerfully and modestly admits now that he may well, indeed he may have 'sung' the verse, added, 'He was much more natural than I in his speech, too natural I thought at the time, but now I think he was right and I was wrong and that it was time to say the lines the modern way. He was always so bold: and even if you disagreed, as I sometimes did, about his conception, you had to admire its execution, the energy and force with which he carried it through.'

Peggy Ashcroft, who was Juliet to both Romeos, has described Olivier then as 'the definitive Romeo. A passionate sixteen-year-old boy in love with love.' Ralph Richardson, the wise owl of that generation, simply pointed to a photograph of Olivier underneath Juliet's balcony – 'the animal exactness, you see. Very fine.'

Olivier slewed his life around and faced up to Shakespeare.

Here began a series of transformations as radical as those which had turned him from a gawky student into a so-smooth juvenile lead. His Romeo is indeed, as Sir Alec Guinness recalls, 'remarkably beautiful'. Guinness, incidentally, who trod the same boards as Gielgud and Olivier, was then firmly in the former's camp, dismayed, as many were, by the matinée vulgarities – as he saw them – the tricks and tones from the commercial theatre.

But Olivier was not to be subdued. His reason for doing Shakespeare was not to win the appreciation of the Few – although he appreciated that like any sane man – nor to seek the applause of the Many – though, again, he would try everything within the character to surprise and command the audience to respond. What he wanted was to act these great characters in such a way that he could believe in them. He did not want to go through any motions. He wanted himself to be moved in them, then others might be moved or not as they would. It was his own compulsion for a variety and depth of self-expression which turned him to Shakespeare. There he could and did find enough of himself to last a lifetime. Thus the extremely poised and coolly discriminating Dame Peggy Ashcroft, in considered recollection in her lovely Hampstead gardens about half a century after the event, still flashed with the memory that 'he *was* Romeo'.

Never one to miss the chance of doubling his bets, he starred in the film version of *As You Like It* as Orlando. In a tentative, unimaginative, stiff but by no means negligible movie, his light, sweetly serious interpretation stands up well. He disliked it: it finally convinced him that Shakespeare could never be done on film and helped lower still further in his eyes the status of a film industry which had failed to embrace him strongly enough. *Fire Over England*, set in the time of Elizabeth I but in prose and in full pursuit of a contemporary audience, was much more the thing that films could do. Vivien Leigh was his co-star. Her rise to national stardom had been dazzlingly swift: one night unknown, with a single small stage appearance to her credit, the next, the West End's hottest new name. She had had a crush on Olivier for some time; they fell in love in *Fire Over England*. At about the same time, Jill and Laurence Olivier had their first child, Tarquin.

In 1937, girded for the battle and wise to what he wanted, Olivier came back across the river into the Old Vic, and, to start with, Hamlet. After that he came on as Sir Toby Belch looking so radically different

that the only way you could tell that it was the man
who had played Hamlet, said one critic, was by his
teeth. Hamlet had been arrived at through careful
study with the director Tyrone Guthrie, poring over
psychoanalytical interpretations, burrowing as deeply
into himself as he dared. He was still criticised for his
speaking of the verse and there were some barbs but
overall the critics were 'fine', says Olivier. 'It was
thought to be OK. I got the worst over first.' The
public turned it into a huge hit. The beginning of what
was to become a matinée-idol following for Olivier's
Shakespeare interpretations was seeded here.

If Hamlet gave him the chance to exorcise some
demons from his own fear-filled childhood, Sir Toby
Belch let him loose once more as the joking, coarse,
irresistible, grand master Twerp of the age. The
contrast could not have been more dynamic, which is
just what Olivier intended it should be. He was running
a campaign and he was taking as few chances as
possible: which meant, in his terms, to take as many
risks as he could get away with.

The campaign was to compel Them – whoever and
wherever They might be – to know that he could and
would and should play Shakespearean roles because
he needed to and had to and was going to put himself
in a position where it was his unassailable right to play
any damned Shakespearean part he ever had a mind
to whenever he chose to do so. Henry V was next,
again directed by Guthrie, whose guiding intelligence
greatly nourished Olivier as he yoked himself to these
labours. For work it was. He did not like *Henry V* in
1937: he thought that the public might not like *Henry
V* with all the thought of war and the rumour of
war. At first Olivier appears to have attempted an

anti-heroic Henry V and we can see in the photographs
of that time little of the deeply confident, even swag-
gering, kingly qualities he brought to the role later.
But once again it was a hit. 'Do you know why you
are so good in this part?' asked Charles Laughton.
No: why? 'Because you are England.'

Jill Esmond had been with him in *Twelfth Night*.
When, at the end of the season, the company was
invited to give *Hamlet* at Elsinore, it was Vivien Leigh
who, out of nowhere it seemed, quite suddenly joined
them and was Ophelia to his Prince. At Elsinore, too,
it was a palpable hit.

He was not finished yet. He decided to do *Macbeth*
with Michel Saint-Denis: again, as people tend to be
when their talent and their boldness are united flat
out and with a single aim, he was lucky in this director
too. Saint-Denis told him to 'find the sense through
the verse'. To this day, Olivier repeats it as if it were
an incantation. Slowly, his eyes on the middle distance,
moving his shoulders as if delivering a final conclusive
line, 'You must find the sense *through* the verse.
(Pause.) If that doesn't make any sense, sorry: it's
the best I can do.' Iago was next for the operating
theatre of Olivier's seemingly relentless display of
strength and versatility and finally a Coriolanus which
at last all the critics rose to. Directed by Lewis
Casson, who had known and helped Olivier since he
was a boy, the part brought out all Olivier's commanding manliness, his breathtaking stage acrobatics, his
furious attack. He had conquered the London critics;
he had bowled over the audiences; he had taken and
was now living with Vivien Leigh; he had reached out
for air and grasped greedily at Shakespeare to give
him new lives. He was the chief lion of the pride, the

new prince of the boards. See how he stands as Coriolanus: arms crossed, face granite, the undisputed victor, the Champion.

Then he left the stage to go back to Hollywood.

He had, of course – because there was and is a cautious side to Olivier, too, a belt-and-braces Olivier and also a workaholic and I'll-do-it-if-the-money's-right Olivier – made three films while he was laying siege to the characters in Shakespeare. One of them again co-starred Vivien Leigh – with whom he was entering into a lifestyle demanding far more cash than the Old Vic could ever offer – and on the two others he worked with his old friend and advisor, Ralph Richardson. It was Richardson's advice he sought when offered the part of Heathcliff in *Wuthering Heights*. 'Bit of fame,' said Richardson. 'Take it.'

Although this is the merest speculation, it seems to me possible that the quite furious outburst of creative versatility at the Old Vic might have been ignited by his love for Vivien Leigh and her loving positive belief in him. He wanted to show her what he was made of, what a man she had on her hands. He wanted to show off. As she had – he has openly said – loved him more richly, far more richly, than anyone hitherto, and he her, so he wanted to open himself up, show her the power and the profundities, show her the glowering faults and the strength. Being who he was, he did this in the character of others and in public. No wonder those who saw those performances in the thirties at the Old Vic still talk vividly of how Olivier 'moved', 'struck', 'thrilled' them. He had opened up new cylinders.

But the call of the siren was not to be resisted.

Even though the part was Heathcliff, the producer

Sam Goldwyn, the director William Wyler, the money good, the cast including his pal David Niven, Olivier hesitated. He wanted Vivien to play opposite him as Cathy. Wyler said no. He would offer her the second female lead – which, for an English actress unknown in America, would be a tremendous start, impossible to imagine a better. No, said Vivien Leigh, she wanted the lead or no part at all. And she had already announced to some friends that she was going to play Scarlett O'Hara – the most coveted female role in the costliest film in Hollywood's short, blockbuster history.

Olivier left her for Hollywood full of conquests: Shakespeare, Vivien Leigh, London, the British cinema. After a few weeks on the set of *Wuthering Heights* he was all but crying to go home. He had been humiliated, insulted, mocked and cut off at the knees by a director who thought he was artificial, operatic, snobbish and unserious about the great new medium of cinema. Olivier confesses to having behaved very badly: he was hoity-toity and unforgivably patronising to Merle Oberon whom he saw fit to remind that she was not a 'real' actress; he called film 'this anaemic little medium which could not stand great acting'. He seems to have behaved like a spoilt and ignorant brat aping outmoded oh-so-English aristocratic mannerisms to emphasise a superiority that existed only inside his 'conceited' (his word) mind. Wyler flayed him alive, in public, daily, giving him nothing but the whip. After Take 32, when Olivier would be almost whimpering with frustration for some guidance, some note, some help, something, Wyler would pause, meditate and pronounce: 'I just want it better.' Or Wyler would mock, 'Which dimension do you think you're in now, Larry?' and constantly tell him he just didn't 'believe' in him. This, to Olivier, whose sense of his own identity depended on making himself believable, was intolerable. He became ill. He was petulant. But he listened. And he took notice.

And today he confesses that Wyler was right and that he was an insufferable snob. 'You see, we – my lot – didn't take it seriously. We loved the The-a-tre. To us, movies were just for the money. Cinema to them was the sacred art.' And from that Olivier now concedes he blindly and blithely hammed until Wyler taunted it out of him. And now he is more than generous – grovellingly grateful – to his old tormentor who 'taught me how to act in movies: taught me respect for them: taught me how to be real'. The old Olivier inner calculator had not only been ticking along to clock up all those unpalatable new truths about film acting, it had also made a couple of surprising leaps. (1) That if stage acting looked phony and affected and unreal on the screen it might well be because most stage acting *was* phony and affected and unreal. This went into the Olivier bank and from then on he says that he drew on his 'P/W' (post-Wyler) film experience to help his stage 'reality'. (2) That anything at all could be put on film if only you could find a way. Wyler, at the end of the shooting of *Wuthering Heights*, invited the hurt, humbled and still squirming young Englishman to his house to dinner to bang him over the head one final time with that parting message: yes, even Shakespeare could be put on film if you could find the way. Remember that.

Wuthering Heights was a triumph. (Doubling up as usual, Olivier had a concurrent triumph on stage in New York.) He was now, at last – in a role which, ironically, drew most from that rough gypsy boy, pre-Jill, pre-Colman, pre-Coward – a massive and important Hollywood star 'with the right kind of spotlight shining on me,' Olivier explains today, careful that you should appreciate it exactly, 'the right kind of success in the right kind of part.' When his beloved Vivien came, alone and afraid, to seek her screen fortune, he left Hollywood. In a repeat of his behaviour to Jill Esmond, he almost put a spoke in the wheel of Vivien's great fortune in landing the part of Scarlett O'Hara against enormous odds. Her long-term contract offer did not suit his purposes and he objected. He was told not to be 'a shit for a second time'.

Vivien, under the most colossal pressure and without Olivier, became an even bigger film star than he was. Ticker tape, world fame, celluloid glory.

He from his pinnacle, she from hers, they looked out for each other and tried to work together. She tested for *Rebecca*. A screen test exists and decently good as she is you can see why the producers would not buy her: she was much too sexy, lively, kittenish, mischievous for the part eventually taken by Joan Fontaine. Nor was she allowed to be in *Pride and Prejudice* – yet another distinguished hit for Olivier who now, it seemed, could do no wrong.

But they would play together. As lovers. In Shakespeare. And put all their money on it. *Romeo and Juliet* was a disaster and all their money went down the drain in Broadway.

War had already been declared. Too old to be called up in the first batch, Olivier nevertheless says, convincingly, that he hated his accidental exile, felt like a coward, felt 'ashamed, dirty, horrible'. He took flying lessons – although flying scared him – and got his licence so that he could go straight into the Fleet Air Arm – as he hoped – on his return.

His genuine and complicated guilt did not prevent him and Vivien – a newly married couple – from making *Lady Hamilton* before their return. This was to be, and proved to be, a propaganda film especially well thought of by Churchill – his favourite film, in fact – and by Stalin. (Hitler, on the other hand, was especially fond of *Fire Over England*.) Much of the reason for doing the film was to give them some money so that they could properly look after their various children and other dependents. Nelson's words were aimed as much at the Germans as at the French and his sentiments were unblushingly close to those of Olivier himself.

For his Englishness – his 'birthright' as he still calls it – never far below the surface, had swept him up, elbowing out all other acts and parts. He wanted to be back 'home', to be the Englishman he needed to be at this hour. Olivier and Vivien landed near Bristol and were driven to a bomb-shattered hotel so cold that they slept with their clothes on. It proved to have been a good idea. The sirens went in the middle of the night and they hurried for cover.

Olivier declared then and maintains now that after eighteen months of 'agony', he at last felt happy. He was 'home'.

SHAKESPEARE
AND ENGLAND

'We will go forward. Heart, nerve and spirit steeled. We will attack. We will smite our foes – and in all our deeds in this land and in other lands, from this time on our watchwords will be "Urgency", "Speed", "Courage". Urgency in all our decisions. Speed in the execution of all our plans, and Courage in the face of all our enemies. And may God bless our cause.' The unmistakable voice of the young Fleet Air Arm officer bugled through the Albert Hall; the organ played 'Jerusalem'; the ranks of British servicemen and women swelled to match the moment. Cry Larry, England and St George!

If – as I have decided to – you opt for believing everything genuine that you feel Olivier has said about himself, then he was at this time desperately attempting to be anonymous. He was also determined to serve his country. He is convinced that he succeeded in the first and indeed if one looks at the casual, almost blandfaced, stocky photograph of the quiet-seeming man in uniform you can see what he was hoping for. He was disappointed that his strenuously won flying licence enabled him to do no more than ferry air gunners around safe skies in southern England so that they could learn how to keep in touch with base. He was an erratic pilot, it seems, and more than one, more than two aircraft hit the dust too hard for their frames. But he studied to be anonymous. 'The best part I ever played,' he says.

Which, of course, leads one to an assumption contrary to mine – that you must not believe anything he says because he is always acting. I believe Joan Plowright has said that he is 'always acting'. Her authority is scarcely to be questioned. But the conclusion must be that it makes little difference to the truth of his remarks whether he is 'acting' or not. Indeed, my understanding is that he can only express the truth of himself through the acting, just as he insisted that in Shakespeare you can only arrive at the truth through the verse. He is what he seems and he always believes it: that welcomed stamp of passionate, early faith is indelible. A favourite anecdote of this time in the Fleet Air Arm was once, when eating in the Mess, a senior officer was told that the young man down the table was the actor who had played Nelson. 'Nonsense!' said the senior officer, squinting carefully at the anonymous Olivier. 'Fella doesn't look a bit like Nelson.'

It was necessary for Olivier to be anonymous in order to do his job. He felt that the only way to survive was to assume the local colouring. 'I wanted them to think that I had been called by God into the Fleet Air Arm: that there was no other station in life I could possibly in any way fulfil.'

The new part was not only necessary for his survival and to ease what he saw as his new passage – as a serviceman. It was also an essential defence. It is easy to forget how very exposed, how very much at risk actors are: and in the truth emerging through parts and tales, incidents and anecdotes about Olivier, it is useful to remember that there is also a strong conviction of the necessity for reserve, for 'no show', for very English, very public school, very stiff, emotional reticence. Olivier likes the character of the deeply shy conservative: it is always on the stand there, out in the hall, and you never know when he might not take it down and put it on. But he was well aware that in his films and in his stage performances, with those cries, those leaps, those sobs, those declarations and extremes of feeling – he had laid himself bare. Those people in the Mess knew him and he feared how very well they might know him. He went into anonymity like a turtle into its shell.

For this section of his life – the War, the roaring forties, the quasi-royal procession into the mid-fifties – I interviewed him back at the Old Vic. He was very pleased to be there. It was not one of his best days but he was well enough and he darted around backstage and on stage pointing out a feature here, cursing himself for extending the apron and 'ruining a perfectly gorgeous Victorian acoustic'. It was here that I had some intimation of just how much it takes, just how much you need. For he looked out into the empty auditorium sad and apprehensive. 'I'll never act on stage again,' he said. 'I haven't the guts. I haven't the nerve.' The risk and the insecurity of it all was all in that weary, sorrowful look.

We rarely see powerful people doing their work, which is most often that which both gives them and shows off their power. Great politicians, international businessmen, administrative mandarins, heads of departments, universities, corporations, states – all of them work largely in private if not in secret and we have intimations of their character only in gossip-column flashes or in rare moments of in-vision. One of the reasons we like our sportsmen so much is that we can see displayed before us qualities we all have but raised in them to a superlative degree and enjoyed by us because of the revelation of power play as much as for the sport itself. Even more so with actors, who test and risk their reputations and livelihoods before our eyes. Although the preparation, the thought, the rehearsal are all done before we are allowed in, nevertheless when we are allowed in we see the works. Not only the drama itself but the play of the actor in the character. And if we have been compelled to suspend disbelief, commanded by someone of Olivier's authority to believe in the truth of what he is doing, then we feel we know the man. We may be right. The man himself may – in Olivier's case fully admits it – 'give himself '. What he has given, though, if he has any range – and Olivier sought range, demanded versatility, refuses to have anything to do with the safe, predictable packaging which was so profitably wrapped around most stars – is many selves. In that range he revealed a lot that was not very comfortable. Not very nice. Not at all pleasant. More than a bit much. Best to roll into a ball of blankness in the Mess like a little hedgehog and push out all your quills: *noli me tangere*.

Yet there was a greater force and that was England. His patriotism – mistrusted by many of his friends – was freely on tap, unlike tears which, he says, he has never been able to call up. England, at this critical juncture, called on everything he had to offer. I am sure he believed in every word, every ringing intonation of the speech that opened this chapter. England, over the next decade or so, England, and his place in it, was to be the unifying factor in his life.

Olivier wanted everything, as he has said. He wanted stardom in Hollywood: got it. He wanted the praise of his contemporaries in the great roles of Shakespeare: got it. He wanted one of the world's most beautiful and prominent women: got her. He wanted money: got it. He wanted to be a dashing West End idol: got it. He wanted to maintain his personal obscurity: just about got it. He wanted close friendships: got them. He wanted to be somehow aloof at the centre of it all: seems to have got that too. Now he wanted to be England.

In the War, he was asked to introduce this, to read the commentary on that, to appear here, to act a support there, to lend a hand, a name, a voice, a presence. He took it all on, and this feeling of himself as one serving his country, and through it realising yet more hitherto unused reservoirs of character and energy, swept him into a period of quite stunning achievement.

In the twelve years between 1944 and 1956, he ran through great parts on the stage like a high-wire artist superbly teasing gravity: Richard III, Sergius, Astrov, Hotspur, Oedipus, Mr Puff, Sir Peter Teazle, Caesar, Antony, Macbeth, Malvolio, Titus Andronicus. He played with smaller parts, ornamenting them to unforgettability: the Button Moulder, Mr Justice Shallow, the Grand Duke of Carpathia. In the cinema his three Shakespearean films made history, as they say, and the cliché was apt: *Henry V, Hamlet, Richard III*. Nor was that enough: he starred in William Wyler's *Carrie*, he starred in Peter Brook's *The Beggar's Opera*, he starred opposite Marilyn Monroe in *The Prince and the Showgirl*. And moreover, with Vivien Leigh (who was Cleopatra to his Caesar and again to his Antony, Blanche in his production of Tennessee Williams's *A Streetcar Named Desire*, Sabina in his production of Wilder's *The Skin of our Teeth*, Antigone to his Chorus) he went into management and ran the St James's Theatre, having been ousted from the Old Vic, a company which he, Richardson and Burrell built up to world standards as a repertory company fit and ready to be the launching pad for the dreamt-of National Theatre. We are not finished yet. There were projects he started and despite even his energy failed on – the film of *Macbeth*; there was a midnight birthday dinner party given him by Churchill; there was a knighthood and a tour of Australia where he and Vivien Leigh took a 'royal' salute. Fans lay out all night in the streets in the rain to see him: he was mobbed after performances of classical power and integrity; he was the greatest actor, they said, married to the loveliest star in the whole damned world, and then he took on Marilyn Monroe. And that was not the end of it. He got himself Notley Abbey – against advice from Vivien and most of his friends – and set himself up in this twelfth-century Augustine monastery with seventy-five acres and a full, belted, high-style English landowning nay aristocratic county life complete with house parties, digging out clogged-up ditches and a model farm. He lived the lives of many men then and it was England which both released him and kept him together, which unloosed his greatest versatility, which at times seems to have made him incredibly arrogant, overweening, power-seeking, autocratic, dictatorial, ruthless and at other times ushered in a pastoral and patient tenderness. Shakespeare was the pivot.

'As far as I was concerned it may as well have been the first Shakespearean film. So far as I was concerned it *was* the first Shakespearean film.' *Henry V.* So far as the public is concerned he is right: it is the first Shakespearean film.

In his constant battle to stave off boredom – which is a kind of death – Olivier employed many tactics: one was the surprise attack. He went out to surprise his audiences with the histrionic leaps, the sudden falls, the great cries. He constantly and often alarmingly surprised his fellow actors. 'It's like being on stage with a cage full of lions,' said Anthony Quinn. Most of all he yearned to surprise himself. And so after William Wyler and Carol Reed had been approached and been unable to direct the film, Olivier decided, in 1944, to direct this expensive, difficult and important film himself. He had never directed a film before. He would also produce it. Oh, and he would take the leading part. And, moreover, do the adaptation, take work of William Shakespeare and take it on himself and cut it down to size. It would all be very surprising indeed.

Olivier, though, at that time, doing something for his country which, however obliquely, he knew was in some way what his country needed, was on song. Again and again in *Henry V* Olivier's ideas, Olivier's control and Olivier's ambition thudded into the bull's-eye. He was worried, for example, about the 'unreal', 'unnaturalistic' Shakespearean verse in a medium seemingly – at that time – bound eye and tongue to naturalism, to realism. His answer was brilliant. He would give the film an opening – in, as it were,

Shakespeare's old Globe Theatre – of such High, even Camp theatricality and artificiality that when the cameras swung away into real landscape, the relief of getting out of that theatre would cushion the equal artificiality of verse spoken in natural surroundings by men acting in a realistic convention and mode. Throughout the film, whenever possible, the scenic effects are highly theatrical, even fantastical, not unlike the illustrations in *Les Très Riches Heures de Duc de Berry* which Olivier consulted: and, he hoped, that heightened background would deflect attention from the foreground making it easier on the ear of conventional forties cinema-going expectation.

But that was just the beginning. He made the fights look like fights, the battle look like a battle, he opted for a way of shooting a long monologue which went directly against the prevailing wisdom – i.e. the camera pulled further and further out as the verbal intensity grew whereas the Commandment until then had said the camera should go further and further in. He shot the open-field sequences in Ireland and some of his most self-enjoyed anecdotes are about that time and his tussle with the Irish farmers who brought their own horses for £3 10s. a day, who wore the chainmail knitted by blind nuns and challenged 'Mr Oliver' as they called him to show them the way to do all the acrobatic bits, which he did and badly sprained an ankle, dislocated both elbows, bruised this, jolted that. He charged around the Irish acres either waving a sword at the head of an army or pointing a megaphone, in charge of a film crew. Like all highly successful men in what are basically cooperative ventures, he took great care to surround himself with expertise and loyalty. Reginald Beck advised him on technical matters; Dallas Bower, who had already done a script of *Henry V*, was brought in as associate producer; Robert Krasker was the cameraman; William Walton did the music; good and reliable actors filled the major roles; and the whole enterprise was nursed by an extraordinary little Italian co-producer, Filippo del Giudice, who adored Olivier, was unshakable in his belief that a masterpiece was being created, shielded his man totally from the slings and arrows of outrageous backers and was the eventual recipient of Olivier's special Oscar. 'Without you, dear fellow,' Olivier said, '*Henry V* would never have been made.' There was never any lack of style.

Henry V was a success in England and a triumph in America. It made money. It gave Olivier a unique place in the cinema's pantheon of great actors. It introduced many, many people to the work of Shakespeare. It was excellent propaganda. And still today it stirs the blood while Olivier – who rarely allowed himself more than a single take even for the longest of speeches – comes across with unfailing heroic conviction. 'We happy few . . .' indeed: those who made it.

If *Citizen Kane* is rightly reckoned the most astonishing first film ever made, *Henry V* has a serious claim to run it second.

But Olivier was basically an actor and before *Henry V* was released he took on another high-risk venture. He was to co-direct at the Old Vic alongside Ralph Richardson and John Burrell. And he would take on the big roles. He had glamour enough from *Wuthering Heights, Rebecca, Pride and Prejudice* and *Lady Hamilton*. Now he wanted the glory.

To loosen up a bit, he and Richardson took *Arms*

and the Man out of London. Olivier was playing Sergius. When Tyrone Guthrie complimented him on his playing, Olivier retorted angrily. How could he be expected to play such a stupid, unlikeable fool as Sergius. 'You have to love him,' Guthrie said, 'or you'll never be able to play him.' Olivier has several times mentioned that this struck him deeply: certainly he went on to play Sergius to huge acclaim. At last, Olivier has said, he understood something both profound and practical. Yet it seems to me he had always known it. It's curious. For the same thing had happened to him in the thirties with Henry V until Richardson had gently led him to love that blatantly heroic king. And again and again Olivier had difficulty in actually liking, much less loving, the people he was expected to play. His dislike, even hatred, of them was often expressed in the fulminating, rather blustering language of the public-school dormitory – what beastly awful rotters they were, what dreadful chaps, really! It was as if he could not admit anyone into his inner being unless he loved them and yet he could not give what he wanted to the act of playing them until he loved them. Once admitted, he could feed them. But it was a jealously guarded cave, that empty centre still full of terror and loss, still desperate, compulsive for another life to appease it or anaesthetise it. Anyway, Sergius was a hit.

He had begun his second career at the Old Vic with the shrewdly modest little part of the Button Moulder in *Peer Gynt*. This was a great triumph for Richardson, who was also in his greatness as an actor and fully able to stand firm against the torrents of his old friend. It was very nicely calculated. There he was, the great film star, the great patriot, the great idol of the London stage of the thirties – and oh, look, he had taken on such a very little part so as not to stand in the light of the great beams coming from Richardson. Then Sergius – totally different – a transformation so complete that, were it to happen in Hollywood today to one of the current film actors, there would be an international conference called upon to admire it. Olivier did it, business per usual, without fuss. His audiences knew him now: his differences were their pleasures.

Then came Richard III, Shakespeare's crookback, since mourned and criticised by fervid companies of scholars who declare that a great poet did great injury to a great King: but the play survives and Olivier was one of a long line of English actors who, through the centuries, came to *Richard III* as full of expectation and apprehension as he himself came to Bosworth Field.

Olivier's use of make-up has often been remarked on. In his quest to be different he must have slapped pounds, even tons, of putty and greasepaint onto his features. The nose is what he tends to go for. His principle is that it is better to change one thing radically than attempt an overall reshaping: and the nose is the easiest game. He has never stopped changing his looks and, incidentally, changing his shape; heavy exercise at last released his reborn limbs to the air and in some photographs he looks quite musclebound – once again a feat of will for a man whose metabolism and inheritance leans decidedly towards slightness. The nose in *Richard III*, though, became, through the portrait by Salvador Dali, through the photographs, through the film and the *réclame* of the part, almost a character in its own right with an existence of its own, a Gogolian, monstrous nose. But it was only the start.

There was the limp. A limp given unwarranted help during the filming – ten years later – when an arrow fitted with a warhead and intended for the flank of a steel-plated and protected horse instead went through Olivier's calf. Then there was the humped back. And the voice – a thin, donnish reed was selected from the quiver of possibilities, partly because it was far away from the sound of Donald Wolfit, whose Richard III, well received, still surged about Olivier's senses, partly because the donnish reed seemed so far away from the full-blooded evil of the man.

The 'look' of Richard III illustrated yet another aspect of Olivier, and one which he speaks of defensively. That is, his admission that he builds up a character through externals. He is always accused and humbly accepts that he is the epitome of the anti-Method. One clear source of inspiration, it seems, for Richard III was the American theatre producer, Jed Harris, 'the horridest, vilest, cruellest man I ever met'. Jed Harris had directed him in the *The Green Bay Tree*. Harris seemed to provoke virulent dislike in many quarters: even the Big Bad Wolf was modelled on him.

All those easy explanations and relaxed analyses were in the future, however, when Olivier faced that first night as Richard III: the renewal of his life-giving struggle with Shakespeare, a basic embrace/conflict which he has been engaged in now for almost seventy years. He knew – because his antennae catch all the messages on the wind – that the audience and the critics out there were waiting for him. And, in his dressing room, he feared that he was cracking up. He did a most curious thing. He called in a friend, John

Mills, whom he knew was in the audience and told him that he could not remember the lines, that he could not get the character, that he was going to give one of the worst performances of his life and would he, John Mills, please go around and explain and apologise to his friends for this terrible mistake and disaster that was going to happen in about ten minutes.

If my notion has any truth in it, then what was happening was Olivier's realisation that he would have to show the nastiness that was in him. And to do that he would have to live the crook-backed, evil man. If it is true that he allowed himself no real character of his own but sought to piece it together through the creations of others – just as he himself pieced his characters together through the observation of others – then he was having the greatest difficulty swallowing Richard. He knew that on the other side of fear lay relief – for at last that particular part of him would be given life – but he was also creating monsters out of himself and perhaps there would be not only relief but a permanent addition to his character. If Henry V left him in some way forever heroic, might not Richard leave him malevolent? He has spoken about this, lightly but keenly.

'You probably have some venom in you . . . you may be a venomous character to a certain extent, probably I am . . . I may have all sorts of vices, in fact I'm sure I have, but through the medium of acting you can get rid of an awful lot of that . . . and I think it's absolutely permissible in acting terms . . . it's like a confessional almost, you're confessing your sins, which is a great relief to the soul . . . you're using your performance . . . I think that's alright.'

Richard's malevolent, power-seeking, cutting,

crippled, cruel vision of life was there, in him, to be called on and he was almost hysterically afraid to summon it up. But by the time he had limped onto the stage, ten minutes after the confession to John Mills, that profound metamorphosis had yet again taken place, and Olivier gave a performance which dazzled and stunned the London audience.

He was to live with that Richard III on tour and then in the film for about the next ten years. It could be argued that its effect on his own character was more disturbing than anything else that happened to him during that time.

He decided to film *Hamlet*. Once again he would do everything – the script, the directing, the acting and all the stunts, including the longest sword fight in screen history (over 300 mostly vicious passes). Olivier never gave an inch in fights: you went for him or he went for you. 'The only way to make it look real,' he said. 'And you have to have a gift for it. You have to enjoy it.'

He set himself an entirely different set of objectives in *Hamlet*, filling it with the artifice of the camera, glooming it in atmosphere, in the process having to exclude one of the key monologues. An old friend who worked on it with him observed at the time how definitely Olivier snapped in and out of roles: at a certain time of day he was the producer; then he was the director; then he was the actor; then he was the script consultant; then he was the editor. On the set he seems to have had no time for discussion: he knew how he wanted every movement, every inflection, every rhythm and the job of the crew and the company was to do as told. *Hamlet* brought him even more *réclame* than *Henry V*.

The English critics – once their textual qualification had established their literary credentials – purred: the American critics swooned. Even Sam Goldwyn rhapsodised. Crocodiles of children were once more trailed through the streets to see Shakespeare in their favourite context. Hollywood laid out four Oscars. Olivier got his knighthood. Richardson already had his. We are told that Olivier was furious that Richardson beat him to the honour. We are told that Richardson rang him up, when offered his, to assuage any natural jealousy and that Olivier congratulated him warmly. Whatever and what matter about all that, the knighthood gave Olivier very great pleasure: he still prefers Sir Laurence to Lord Olivier. As a knight of the realm and the Prince of Denmark, he and Vivien Leigh had become theatre royals. From Mayfair to Melbourne, from country house to country lass, the glittering brilliant talents, seen to be a smiling charming couple who had begun in an enviably risqué manner as lovers but redeemed all by marriage, international success and stout war effort, were now idolised . . . they were an ornament to the nation.

Meanwhile, down at the Old Vic, Olivier continued to plunder himself for a series of varied parts. As Astrov in *Uncle Vanya* he 'found' the character in a pince-nez. As Hotspur in a ginger wig he had a death scene so dramatic that there were those inclined to discount the whole of *Henry IV*, Part I in anticipation of that spectacular fall. He was by all accounts a most athletic and terrific Harry Hotspur, a lad fit for war and fun. As Mr Justice Shallow he was all but unrecognisable, an old maid of a man, so full of business that he threatened even the unrolling majesty of Ralph Richardson's mighty Falstaff.

Richardson spoke of his Shallow with great affection. 'Laurence said – why don't I keep bees? I said – good idea – Shallow lives in the country – let him keep bees. Well, that was all very fine but I would be saying something and – slap! – a bee would sting him and – slap! – there would be another one and – well! – buzzing about everywhere. Now look here, I said, we can't have you going on like that. I have a lot of plot to get through here. If you carry on like this I shall just – bumble off. And he smiled his sweet smile and said, OK Ralphie, I'll bee-have. And he did.' And then he was a thundering King Lear.

On one double bill his versatile virtuosity glowed out like a pair of Chinese dragon eyes, facing out of a cave, daring challengers to come in and challenge. He played Oedipus in Sophocles' *Oedipus Rex* and, having left the stage with bleeding eyes and a howl based on his imagined reproduction of the pain a fox felt with its leg caught in a steel trap, he reappeared fifteen minutes later as the ridiculously liveried, powdered and pomaded, flighty and sparklingly superficial Mr Puff, to be hoisted and shot and cannonballed around the stage like a rag doll. 'It was vulgar,' he says now, 'showing off.' As box-office it was, yet again, bull's-eye.

For Olivier was now doing something quite extraordinary. To the classics and to a company of serious actors, he was drawing the numbers and enthusiasms of a matinée crowd. When he took the Old Vic Company on a tour of Australia and New Zealand in 1948, the send-off in London and the reception down under were both fan-filled; show-biz – front page!

In Australia he led a company through a most

exhausting and difficult tour. He remembered every
birthday. He attended every laid-on cocktail party. He
made pro-British speeches. He took the salute at a
march-past. He played his great parts to astonished
audiences and his wife batted alongside him blow for
blow. Just as the Old Vic, with its unexpected, Lilian
Baylis, uniquely theatrical Englishness provided the
right setting for his burgeoning as the greatest actor
on the English-speaking stage – Gielgud, with enormous and characteristic generosity had handed over
to him Edmund Kean's sword for his Richard III – so
this tour of Australia was to be the training ground for
the future National Theatre Company. For that was
what Olivier had his sights on and that is what he was
moulding. Indeed that is what it was, in all but name,
as the tour swept through the cheering colony and
the crowds slept out in the streets.

Then he was fired. Right then, in the middle of the
tour, between performances, on the other side of the
world, he got a letter saying that he, Richardson and
Burrell were fired. Olivier even today can't quite
believe it. He still laughs with astonishment. 'I mean
– we'd built it up. We'd made it what it was, the three
of us. You know – I think they were jealous.' It appears
they thought that Olivier and the others had got above
themselves, were too much the stars, were using the
Company for their own ends. That action probably set
back the opening of the National Theatre by ten years
– more – and what a National it would have been if
Olivier and Richardson had led their young troops –
most of whom, since then, have made great reputations – into that battle.

Still, he was fired. Not that it took effect right away:
no, he had to come back and do another stint at the

Old Vic, during which he transformed a deficit into a thumping profit.

By now Vivien Leigh had clearly found herself the resources to take on major roles and the strength to stand up to her husband on stage. She had scored a remarkable success as Sabina in Thornton Wilder's play; she was Lady Teazle to his, unusually subdued, Sir Peter, and then she was Antigone. Olivier directed and played the Chorus in what became a very unexpected success. They were flying in their professional lives, although rumours were afoot that their private life was under great strain. Vivien Leigh's health was certainly under strain and when Olivier agreed to direct her in *A Streetcar Named Desire* there were those, like her friend John Gielgud, who feared for her in such a role.

'You see, it was so very like her, in a way. It must have been a most dreadful strain to do it night after night. She would be shaking and white and quite distraught at the end of it. Perhaps it was unwise to let her do it.' She had tuberculosis and suffered from mental strain. She drove herself remorselessly.

But it seemed the two of them were employed in a perilous game of urging each other on to greater and greater tasks, higher and higher risks, their mutual and independent ambitions now intertwined, now opposed, driven on, both of them, from different roots, by different demons, to burn up the moment. They were locked in some extraordinary sorcery of play, competition and lust for incandescent experience in drama and perhaps in life. Jilted by the Old Vic, they determined to remain the royal pair of the London theatre and went into management at the St James's with a dash and extravagance that made a mockery –

was it intended to? – of Olivier's widely confessed and often noted meanness. He was still trying to build a great company, still had visions of leading it into a National Theatre, lost money regularly and recouped only when he and Vivien came into the bullring together. They were Caesar and Cleopatra, they were Antony and Cleopatra, and although the critics in London were far from totally enthusiastic – and Kenneth Tynan said some penetratingly wounding things about Vivien Leigh, even accusing Olivier of chivalrously bringing down the standard of his acting so as to make hers seem better – in New York they enjoyed unalloyed praise.

With all this, Olivier was still ample enough to pursue his rediscovered Englishness in less intense ways. He had a small part in *The Magic Box*, for example, as a baffled London bobby, in which he showed himself the personification of all the good old London Gilbert and Sullivan bobbydom in the world. He scandalised the serious-minded by taking on, leading in and directing *The Sleeping Prince*, but he loved Terence Rattigan and he could see a boulevard smash hit when he saw one, old hand at that, and it was. He spotted new talent in Peter Brook whom he encouraged to direct *The Beggar's Opera*, disappointed only that Brook's singlemindedness did not let him contribute enough. But he played and sang and rode to the hilt (so violently that he gave his horse a heart attack) and did not sulk when what had seemed a lovely spry project turned into a dark commercial disaster. In Australia he spotted Peter Finch and took him up and took him on board and in the maze of private intimations and manoeuvrings may well have known fully what he was doing.

Above all, though, there was, throughout this period, Notley Abbey. It was here that the many lives of Laurence Olivier came home to roost. Douglas Fairbanks Jnr was a regular house guest. 'I suspect he envisaged himself riding in and out of it in full armour . . . the place had such romance, almost theatrical romance, like a set.' And Gielgud found his friend played many parts. 'One day he was the landowner, one day he was the squire, one day he was the gardener, one day he was the great host. I was always rather fascinated. He does enjoy playing a number of roles off the stage as well as on, I think.' And what fun it must have been for him. Though the compulsion might often be strangulating in its demands, there must be days when the faculty of being multitudinous must be something to revel in: such a sweet revenge on the mean trick of this one life we are given and given in such a way that the more we learn how to live it the less time and energy we have to do so. At Notley he planted his colours – the Englishman for all seasons.

There was at the end of the forties, early fifties, more than a murmur of criticism which accused Olivier of being too technical. James Agate articulated a prevalent anxiety when he wrote, 'When I look at a watch it is to see the time and not to admire the mechanism. I want an actor to tell me Lear's time of day and Olivier doesn't. He bids me watch the wheels go round.'

When we were filming the profile of Olivier, almost all the actors we spoke to referred to his technique. All praised it. All, at the same time, seemed to suggest that it covered a certain emotional void. In as polite a way as I could, I put this to Olivier, who did not take it at all well. We left in the film much of what became rather a wrangle – with him winning hands down of course and eggs streaming down my face by the dozen. But we left it in for two reasons. Firstly because it provoked into life a side of Olivier which we had seen nowhere else – a tetchy, defensive, even angry, even crushing side. For whatever it's worth, we thought it worth showing. Most people would – and did – blame me for the mood anyway and besides there are miles of him being, as he is, charming, funny, as Agate also said 'a comedian by instinct . . .' (the sentence completes itself '. . . and a tragedian by art'). Secondly, though he had denied any especial cleaving to technique, he went on to confess that his resentment at the line of questioning came because he had so often been criticised for his technique being a substitute for feeling. And he was most vehement that he did feel, he felt all he did, he felt it as strongly as he could and, looking around, as strongly as anybody else. But his job was to portray the character for an audience and in order to build up the character he collected and used effects, that was the only way he knew how, that was his method but it was all in the service of the truth of the character.

Looking at the scene again I find it rather distressing and almost wish we had cut it out. Because, I think, we were quite near the bone; also because he was by no means on top form that day, off balance a bit through fatigue; and partly because he wanted to protect the method which had been so flaringly successful in his professional life. To suggest that there was 'nothing inside' was to hit very hard and to seem to score. For the one actor who did not refer to Olivier's technique, perhaps the actor who knew, appraised and loved him best, Ralph Richardson, had a commanding grasp of Olivier's 'great greatness' as he called it, but would point to a photograph and after a paean of affection point further and say 'totally bored'; or end an excursion on a series of great parts by saying 'he didn't give a damn'. He knew the fear of emptiness at the centre. But he also knew – as I believe – that it is the fear of emptiness and not emptiness itself, and that when Olivier protests that he feels as much as anyone, he is right. Indeed he feels as much as everyone he plays, for all of them were summoned in to take him out of himself.

As if realising that a great span of awesome achievement were coming to an end, with the instinct once again which marks him out, he swung his forces around in the mid-fifties. In 1955 he went back to the scene of his first triumph, back to the fount of his many characters, to the mould of his many masks, Stratford-on-Avon, where he played Malvolio, a titanic and shattering Macbeth and a Titus Andronicus which horrified audiences so much that nurses were called to stand by. As if marking some as yet undrawn line in his career, he did an extraordinary thing at the end of the last performance of Titus – a massive part which, alone, would have totally drained most actors. He stepped forward and thanked the company and all the technicians, by name and denomination, ninety-seven of them.

And then came Marilyn. The Knight and the Garter. *The Prince and the Showgirl* – a reworking of Rattigan's *The Sleeping Prince*. It was a publicist's and press paradise and a producer's hell. Olivier was the producer. Marilyn Monroe became the sex symbol extraordinaire, an angel of sex, an unexpectedly gifted comedienne; the American way of life, gushing up from squalid poverty through soft sex, celluloid and a sporting hero – Joe DiMaggio – to screen power and the netting of the intellectual playwright Arthur Miller. Marilyn Monroe was well known to be delicious, wonderful, box-office; rare; and a director's nightmare. Olivier was the director. Her rows with her studio, her sudden but real ambition to educate herself – into acting, thinking, culture, the works – rode badly on her body-perfect-public-sensational-sensuality. She insisted on her own dramatic coach, she would go for take after take after time-wasting, money-wasting, spirit-wasting take until she got what she wanted. She seemed to like to begin by wearing down her leading men. Olivier was her leading man. She operated entirely by a tight-shut inner motor which let her and her alone into its secrets. Olivier expected things to be done on request, on command, even the spirit could be conjured up by the will. Leave her alone, said his oldest friend and wisest mentor, Sybil Thorndike, who was also in the film; she knows what she is doing. But Olivier wanted to exercise his control. For many years now he had honed it and strengthened it and practised it on himself and others and it had worked again and again resoundingly. He brought into play all his considerable patience, all his immense courtesy, all his incontestable charm, but he still wanted her to do what he wanted her to do when he wanted her to do it. She insisted. She too was fighting with her life.

She won.

It marked the end of surely one of the grandest chapters in the career of any actor.

'THE ENTERTAINER' AND
THE NATIONAL

By a fluke I have four key views of Olivier's next major move – which was to take the role of Archie Rice in *The Entertainer*. One from Arthur Miller; one from the author, John Osborne; one from Joan Plowright and one from Olivier himself.

While Marilyn was filming in England, she and Miller were virtually trapped by the press. This may have accounted, in some way, for her own 'unprofessional' behaviour on the set. It was all but impossible for them to move out of their rented country house without running a gauntlet of flashbulbs, leading a Keystone Cops steeplechase of press cars through the country lanes of England, and ending up with a night-out blighted.

Arthur Miller wanted to go to the theatre. To get Marilyn Monroe to a London theatre without causing a traffic jam and a riot in the foyer seemed impossible. And he wanted to see this new play *Look Back in Anger*. Firstly he liked the title. Secondly he looked down the list of plays on in London and all the rest seemed 'that awful English polite stuff' or revivals of classics. And finally, when Olivier told Miller that he, Olivier, had seen *Look Back in Anger* and loathed it 'because it was an affront to England', that clinched it: an affront to England was precisely what the weary, besieged husband of Marilyn Monroe most wanted to see.

Olivier fixed it. Cars roared out of different exits at the same time with lookalikes prominently installed. The press hared about after the decoys while, as in the very best thrillers, the real car with the real people sped out quietly when the coast was clear. The Royal Court had been most discretely pre-warned. Three seats were kept empty in the back row. The car circled Sloane Square with Marilyn bending her head as if scrambling for a contact lens and Olivier waiting for the start time to pass.

Curtain up was held for a couple of minutes and while the punters coughed nervously in the dark, the three musketeers slipped in the back. Similarly at the end of Act One the house lights were held while the three of them scampered away to have a private drink with George Devine and so on until the end when they met Osborne himself.

Miller greatly admired the play. Olivier greatly admired Miller. During that little drink after the show, a most diffident Sir Laurence – pillar, column, monument of an Establishment on which Osborne's play poured vitriol for its hypocritical, empty, gutless, nerveless shams – gave the young playwright to understand that if ever he should come to have a part that he might think that he, old Larry here, might be able to tackle, then he would be very obliged to be given first refusal, very obliged indeed. Miller is very pleased to tell that story: it is part of his evidence that Olivier is the only actor he has ever known who 'matured'.

'It was a remarkable thing to do,' says Osborne. 'Quite remarkable at the time. People don't remem-

ber. There were those who warned him against the
risk. And it was a risk. The part of Archie Rice seemed
to go against everything he stood for – and certainly
I did and certainly the Royal Court did. But he came
along and did it. It was very brave. He was far and
away the first of all that lot to notice that something
was going on.'

'We thought that to act you had to wear jeans,' Joan
Plowright said. 'Anybody very well groomed or too
well dressed for their own good – we suspected all
that.' The Royal Court was self-consciously, confidently and successfully radical. Olivier's arrival was
regarded with some misgivings. 'But as soon as he
rolled his sleeves up and started working with us it all
fell away,' Joan Plowright went on. 'You can't argue
with someone who can act you off the stage whenever
he feels like it. You just can't argue with that sort of
talent.'

'I was in a stew,' says Olivier, 'and I needed a
change. It was big classic stage part, film, big classic
stage part, film; I was boring the public, I was boring
myself, I was predictable as hell, and it was a wonderful, wonderful part.'

There are those who think that he has never been
better than he was as Archie Rice, the failure, the
lecher, the empty clown, the song-and-dance man full
of tired public gags and exhausted private pain. Olivier
loved the part, he researched for it in the music halls,
he found himself in it: 'I could have been Archie Rice;
I could have joined a chorus and called myself Larry
Olivier and been as happy as a lark at first.' He dazzled
even its author at rehearsals with his cornucopia of
inventiveness. In one bound he entered the New
World of British drama and refreshed himself mightily.

But another failure further helped to define his position. He tried with all his considerable powers to acquire the comparatively modest sum required to finance a film of *Macbeth*. Despite the artistic and box-office successes of *Henry V, Hamlet* and *Richard III*, despite his success in other films and his proven popularity on the stage, it was no go for the Scottish play. Olivier's greatest declared pleasure – to produce, direct and act in a film – was now put behind him. That game was up. From then on he increasingly took cameo roles or small parts, like Crassus in *Spartacus* or the third lead, General Burgoyne, in *The Devil's Disciple* – in both cases, however, stealing the reviews from the expensive Hollywood muscle employing him.

And he was not going to let anything go. In 1959 Peter Hall directed him in a *Coriolanus* that had the critics racing for their most burnished superlatives and audiences again turning to the black market for tickets. He had one foot planted firmly in the new – in the same year as he played Coriolanus he filmed *The Entertainer* – but he kept a hold of his classical nurse just as he kept a way open to the American purse. He always did want everything.

The awesome thing is that, to an outsider, he very nearly seems to have got it. Most people whose talent or luck imposes its image strongly on the world have a brief shine of it, or fix themselves in a predictable firmament holding onto what got them there in the first place. Olivier's lustre seems never to diminish and never to stand still. When you look at a list of his credits, his roles in the theatre, his parts in film and on television, the plays he has directed, the films he has directed, the plays/films/television he has produced, the companies he has run, the business careers he has had, the public service career he has had, the private lives, the long friendships . . . there cannot have been his like.

He has said that Joan Plowright was the woman he found to replace his mother who died when he was twelve. He was almost fifty when he met Joan Plowright, already then an outstandingly accomplished young actress whose dedication to the theatre and steady sense of the radical movements of her own generation put her in a unique position: a complete pole apart from Vivien Leigh it might seem. They married a few years later when both their divorces were through.

If he had needed any encouragement to apply himself to the new course he saw opening up before him, then Joan Plowright was there to give it. There is a sense in which, by marrying her, he united the two most powerful factions in the British theatre: his own – the knight of the old glamour, the War, great roles, household names and honours galore; and that of John Osborne – young artists turning to the theatre to practise their art and display their genius but also to force society to listen to them, to make the stage into a pulpit as much as a playground. A new morality was loose and Joan Plowright was one of its most distinctive representatives.

The course he saw before him was based on two families. His own, with Joan Plowright and a house in Brighton, young children waving at the window as he went off to the station, a regular household just like the one he used to know as a child. Family snaps now capture Olivier as the new family man. And he wanted a theatre family. He had brought one into existence two or three times: now he was going to rear a family which would have a permanent existence as the National Theatre Company of Great Britain.

But he would not cease from the endless life-giving compulsion to surprise and to activate himself through taking on other characters. After Coriolanus, he swung through 180 degrees to play M. Berenger in Ionesco's *The Rhinoceros*, directed by Orson Welles. Another hit. You look at him as the bloodlusting warrior, you then look at him in Ionesco and you wonder anew at the dynamic which was still sending up such forceful pulses for renewedness. And then to Anouilh's *Becket* and from that subdued almost inscrutable fanaticism to the whisky-stinking priest in Greene's *The Power and the Glory* for American television.

His first step in front of television – in 1958 as John Gabriel Borkman – had been attended by the sort of press coverage given to a world cup football final and the thunder throughout the land of television sets being turned off. Needed more concentration than anything else, he concluded, this newfangled television business. Needs fullest possible attention. So *The Moon and Sixpence* for NBC irradiated the American screen and sprayed him with raves and another new public. Nor was his mischief any less active. When Anthony Quinn left *Becket* after playing Henry II to Olivier's Saint, Olivier instantly grabbed the Henry II role and gave it such a seeing-to that the critics squealed with delight and, unfairly, pointed up Olivier's quicksilver versatility by contrasting it with the plodding interpretation of the departed Mr Quinn now gnashing his teeth in fury as he addressed himself to Barabbas. Olivier played Henry II in the biggest theatre in New York to packed houses while through the days he rehearsed and shot *The Power and the Glory*.

In 1961 he married Joan Plowright and was appointed Director of the Chichester Festival Theatre. That a very small county town most inconveniently situated for London should decide that it could sustain a theatre was rum enough: that it enticed the world's leading actor and a host of master players to come down and get it going was more than rum. It was to be a practice run for the National.

The trouble was it leaked. Or rather, it was announced that this Chichester team was going to be the basis for the long, long awaited National Theatre, and all the fun and sympathy that Olivier and his glittering troupe might have expected from this gallant country enterprise was swept aside as the microscopes bore down on the embryo that dared threaten to become the full-bodied National Theatre at last.

It's an odd world when something we are so provenly good at as a nation and something which gives pleasure to millions, employment to hundreds, exports well, brings in foreign capital and visitors, is precisely what we need to be doing in this post-industrial day and age, should have to batter its way through an ignorant and philistine government and bureaucracy as if it were an importunate outcast. Out to serve his country as he was, Olivier was to spend the next twelve years being a battering ram, a butt, an object of scorn sometimes and suspicion too often: but he did it. He hauled the National into existence and despite his final failure to lead his troops into the South Bank HQ itself, no one doubts that the National is perhaps his most enduring monument.

Not that it seemed much of a prospect in 1961,

especially as the first two (of three) productions were slammed. Fletcher's *The Chances*, which he directed, and *The Broken Heart*, in which he played Bassanes, brought on the 'Is this what we are to expect from the future director of the National Theatre?' and drove out the Chichester audiences back, back into the pastures from which they came. Chekhov rescued him. Chekhov, Michael Redgrave, Joan Plowright, Joan Greenwood, Sybil Thorndike and Lewis Casson – his guardian angels – and himself as Astrov in Uncle Vanya. 'Perfection.' 'A wonder.' 'A masterpiece.' A cannonade of praise drowned the earlier cries of anxiety. After a bit of a wobble, he was on his way.

Meanwhile he clocked up two parts which showed his devotion to the new mood of the time: the wrongly accused schoolmaster in *Term of Trial* and Fred Midway in David Turner's *Semi-Detached*. Neither was well received. Neither was enjoyed by Olivier. Neither gave his sharpest critics much comfort about his judgement.

He asked the sharpest critic of all to come and join him. Kenneth Tynan, international apostle for hedonism, theatre critic extraordinary, taste maker and reputation breaker, had given Olivier some of his finest notices and some of his most wounding criticisms; he had mauled Vivien Leigh and hurt her feelings badly; he had championed John Osborne and was champing to find a battleground where he could clash prominently with prevailing attitudes which were, as he saw it, ridiculously puritanical, restrictive, ill-bred and hypocritical. It is typical of Olivier's sense of what was right for the purpose in hand that he was persuaded – he gives Joan Plowright the credit for this – to take on board the flag bearer of the New. It

is a further tribute to Olivier, as much as to Tynan,
that the younger man accepted. But then, as Peter
O'Toole and scores of others have attested, when
Olivier wants you to do something, he is hard to
resist. Tynan was on board, which meant that the
fledgling National Theatre would have range, it would
have intellectual justification for what it did and it
would have controversy. Olivier may well have given
himself the shot in the arm he needed by employing
Tynan: it could also be argued that it was Tynan's
influence which crucially allowed him to lose his power
base inside the company hierarchy and, in an apparently gentlemanlike fashion, be shown the door when
he was owed, and in bucketfuls, much better treatment than that.

And so in 1963 the National Theatre centre of
operations moved to its final staging post – a Nissen
hut beside the Old Vic. Olivier brought in the hot
young Peter O'Toole to secure the maximum bums
on seats for *Hamlet*: he himself gave his Uncle Vanya
and took a small part in *The Recruiting Officer*, thus
demonstrating that he could be absent, dominant and
supporting. Treble top. A very politic opening and a
good season. *Vanya* was filmed as an increasing number of his stage performances were to be from now
on. Though the quality of those films varies, they are
never dull and at best seem to provide a good record
of the production.

In 1964 he took on 'the impossible one': Othello.
He had long thought it unplayable. Orson Welles had
just got near it, he thought (in a production Olivier
had presented in London), but 'he lacked the breath'.
In a controversial career (controversial, that is, as
well as everything else: it was also a classical career,

a career of majestic unfolding, a conservative career in some instances, now and then an erratic career, in some ways a supremely purposeful career) this was to be one of his most disputed roles. Even his faithful Sybil would have none of it. To others it was the very summit of artifice. To those who played in it with him it could be devastating: one dazzled night they lined the narrow corridor behind stage and applauded him back to his dressing room. He slammed the door on them. But why, they asked, when you were great? 'I know,' Olivier said, 'but I don't know how I did it, so how can I repeat it?' Zeffirelli said that the performance summed up 300 years of acting.

He took exercise. Weights. Jogging along the Brighton sea-front. Voice classes to get a whole new octave. Make-up taking three hours. Made discoveries of vanity in Othello, of intellectual pretension, of visceral jealousy. Loped like an African hunter, played up the African, an outsider still now in a white European society, and had to shield himself from plaudits and brickbats both.

In the same year he swung north to Halvard Solness in *The Master Builder*. It is quite tricky to think up a bigger contrast. It was to prove Olivier's most frightening role.

That dressing room he retired to was also his office. One of his leading actresses was also his wife in a full and happy spate of breeding and rearing a family. The workload he was giving himself beggars belief. Only someone who could lead several lives simultaneously could hope to survive it. Olivier seems to be a man whose energy feeds off energy, whose strength is given voltage by powerful achievement. The danger is that if you miss a beat, miss a footing, reflect on the peaks you are scaling so scarily, then the abyss and the attraction of the abyss can open up to suck you into it.

It happened for Olivier on the first night of *The Master Builder*. His throat clenched, the audience – including Noel Coward, Kenneth Tynan, John Dexter, Bill Gaskill, the press, friends, fans – went round and round ('anti-clockwise: why is it always anti-clockwise?'). He could not remember the lines. Even now, when he reinvokes it, something of the panic is clearly visible, clearly branded on his memory. He walked back, he got out one line, he thought of coming to the footlights and apologising 'Ladies and gentlemen, I am very sorry but I am rather ill and . . .', but there were those out there who would never forgive him and never let him forget; nor would he, he was convinced, ever act again if this terrible blankness, this sudden nothingness were not to be filled with something.

His third child had been born. He had everything he wanted.

Maybe it was here, after the colossal strain of Othello which drained every gram of his forces (and remember, he maintained it was 'impossible to play', yet he played it); after the great happiness of the third safe child; after the cruel over-activity of running the young National but the great feeling of knowing it was on its way; maybe it was here that he relaxed and, for the first time since the terrors of abandoned adolescence, looked plainly into himself, the Master Builder. And found a most terrible, terrifying void.

He got through the performance, but for the next seven years it was liable to strike at any time.

Strategies were employed to help him. He could not bear to be alone on stage and so in Othello's great monologues, for example – for the disease raced through all – his Iago had to stand in the wings where Olivier/ Othello could see him or he simply could not do the part. When he felt the black about to strike he would summon the company and beg forgiveness for his unprofessional attitude but ask them not to, never to, please not to look him in the eye because if he caught a glance direct he would be finished. He fought it with the weapons of a man in an African village fighting against the fell judgement of a witch doctor. At the same time, he started on what was to be a long and grave run of physical illnesses.

But he went on. He took the Company to Moscow and, dressed as a steward, welcomed them all on board the aeroplane. He took the Company to Berlin and, as always, after an exhausting performance, stepped forward to thank the audience in the language of the land. He directed Arthur Miller's *Crucible* and O'Casey's *Juno and the Paycock*. As Tattle in *Love for Love* he pulled out a circus bag of slapstick and as Captain Edgar in Strindberg's *The Dance of Death* he delivered a performance of such force (recorded on film) that, for example, Gielgud considers it his finest non-Shakespearean role. He directed a *Three Sisters* memorable for its intense unity of style and for Joan Plowright's radical and realistic performance. He took a small part in *A Flea in Her Ear* because among the other thousand and one things he had to show – 'if you are an actor or a boss you have to get out and prove it' – was that he could be a good Company man. And every night of his life he was stalked by the terror of that black and bottomless pit which could open like a trap door and leave him silently howling and straining against the force of nothingness.

In 1967 he became involved in a bitter, wounding and draining fight with his own Board. Kenneth Tynan wanted to put on *Soldiers* by Hochhuth. It was an attack on Churchill which claimed, among other things, that the death of General Sikorski in an air crash in 1943 was an act of sabotage against the Free Polish leader, an act connived in by Churchill. No evidence was produced for this. Lord Chandos, Chairman of the National Theatre Board, a member of Churchill's War Cabinet and a friend of Churchill, would not have it. In his bones, in his background, in all his speaking for England, you feel that Olivier himself would not have it either. But he backed his man Tynan and he fought for his right to have complete artistic control. The correspondence, the passions and the injuries were all considerable. Olivier showed quite exceptional nerve and loyalty in working against an Establishment he adored and cherished. He lost and perhaps he was unwise to put so much into a battle which he surely knew he could not win. But he was someone who led from the front and went on until he won or dropped.

In the same year Vivien Leigh died.

It was also in this year that a cancer tumour was discovered. With quite foolhardy recklessness he insisted, at first, in having his heavy treatment as an out-patient while still holding up his Atlas-load at the National. But his health broke down.

Typically he turned his attention and his will onto the cancer to 'beat the bastard'. He succeeded. The tumour died away.

His greatest roles during this period were perhaps

off stage: the administrator and the family man. The administrator can be seen in any number of photographs, with co-suited colleague administrators. The building of the South Bank theatre dragged on. His one five-year term was to turn into a second five-year term – all the time being forced to show how commercial he could be, how grand he could be, how National he could be, how bureaucratic he could be. Whenever they were attacked – which was often enough – Ken Tynan would always point to the record: in their joint time there they had more and, it could be argued, a higher quality of successes than any other theatre in the United Kingdom. Olivier planned and waited; paddled in the sea with his children; scooted off now and then to make good his extremely modest National salary with a film or two. He took part in *Bunny Lake is Missing*: so equally regrettably, did Noel Coward. He was the Mahdi in *Khartoum*: that was more like it. And Premier Kamanev in *The Shoes of the Fisherman*: that was not.

So bent to the great wheel of the National was he that his best performances on film were either in the recordings of the stage productions (*Dance of Death*, for instance, is electrifying) where he had already worked over and worked through the part; or in cameos (Field Marshal Sir John French in *Oh What a Lovely War*, Sir Hugh Dowding in *Battle of Britain*, Creakle in *David Copperfield*, Count Witte in *Nicholas and Alexandra* or the Duke of Wellington in *Lady Caroline Lamb*). In all these cameos he offered something definite: just to look at that particular gallery of cameo faces is to appreciate the singularity of each characterisation, the effort made to get it right and get it different. It is possible that the cameos were so much better than the longer parts precisely because of his integrity. He could not bring all he wanted to the longer roles and so delivered muted, disappointingly unlively portraits. For the sprint of a few minutes' screen time he could group his forces effectively: and strike off a likeness.

His working day was from 10 a.m. until midnight. Its book-ends were the London–Brighton trains. In his ten years at the Old Vic, there were seventy productions. He appeared in nine of them and directed eight – not much evidence of greed there. He was forcing himself to be a Company man. Yet it has to be said that the parts he took on were generally very big and tended to figure regularly in the rep. This made financial sense. He was the best box-office the National had and when a deficit threatened or happened, an Olivier lead would fill up the till. But much of his time was committees, architects, planners, local government, unions, craftsmen, estimates, budgets, designers, bills, hirings. In his hirings he seems to have followed the practice of young Prince Hal when he became Henry V: old pals from around the camp fires of the old days, the great old Shakespearean movies, the grand old times of the thirties and forties Old Vic, all the old faithful were not invited to the National party. He was starting afresh.

There were those – Tyrone Guthrie was the most prominent – who mourned this immersion in bureaucracy, seeing it as necessary for someone to do but possible for many to do, whereas Olivier acting in full maturity was something unique and to be cherished. There were others – John Osborne was the most articulate – who regretted Olivier's wasting his time on anything so museumbound as a National Theatre and further regretted seeing him deliver himself into the ideas of Ken Tynan whom Osborne accused of 'intellectual spivvery'. There were good men who left the National and good men who did not try too hard to join. Yet, taken all in all, it is very doubtful whether anyone else could have done a better job. More to the point, it is highly unlikely that anyone else would have been given or been able to do the job at all. Olivier made his calculations, as he always did, as he did, his elder sister said, from a very early age, before he uttered any opinion. He saw his great role as that of the actor who conjured up the National Theatre. Nobody else had done that. Done once, nobody else could do it again.

On stage he played both A. B. Raham in *Home and Beauty* by Somerset Maugham and took the part of Chebutikin in *Three Sisters* which, with *The Beaux' Stratagem,* he took to Los Angeles in 1970.

In the same year he became the first actor to become a peer of the realm. Lord Olivier. He has never liked the ring of it, but he does like being a Lord: just as he loves having a railway engine named after him.

And in that same year he played Shylock in a nineteenth-century setting of *The Merchant of Venice* and the following year let rip in a gigantic *Long Day's Journey into Night.* As in *The Entertainer,* Olivier found much in himself for James Tyrone: it was an elegy to someone else he might have been and a roar of pain at the thought of that damnation. As Antonio in *Saturday Sunday Monday* he romped through a production which saw Joan Plowright yet again command the applause of critics and audiences and finally, with all the irony available, he came to play his last stage role in *The Party.*

Trevor Griffiths' play about the schemes and principles, the paranoia and desperate politics of the far Left had as its hero John Tagg, a man who was civilisations away from Olivier, and yet he took on the long, taxing part at a time of great personal stress willing, to the end, to demonstrate that he was as committed to the new as the old, to the political as to the passionately private, that his National Theatre could contain multitudes.

He relinquished his post in 1973. He resigned. The theatre was not yet completed and he would not have the glory of taking his Company into their home. It was a cruel disappointment and, one thinks, more than a bit mean and small and lacking in generosity of all those concerned that they could not find a way to enable him to carry the torch those last few symbolically clinching steps.

But it is there. He more than anyone else put it there. A splendid auditorium bears his name. He rarely used to go. His last work there was in 1974, when he directed his wife in a play by J. B. Priestley – *Eden End*. It could have been an epitaph.

SOLDIERING ON

The next eleven years, which provide the shortest chapter, were probably, in many ways, the most anguished and slow, drawn-out time of Olivier's life. He became critically ill, recovered and then ill again and again. He had lost the nerve and the guts to act on stage ever again – very hard, for someone who had fed and fed off a live public since boyhood. He considered that he had failed his greatest test – taking a Company into the National. He had a young family to look out for and a world of hire and fire staring him in the face with no institute to shield him and no guarantee of health to support him.

He has often been criticised – several times over the years for taking unworthy parts in poor films, particularly in this period which saw, some would say alas, *The Betsy, The Boys from Brazil, Dracula, The Jazz Singer* and others. Olivier will always defend his acceptance of cameo roles and now he needed to service other characters more than ever before, perhaps. For his own essential physical character seemed to be breaking down: 'It was a kind of uproar in the cells,' Joan Plowright has said, 'and a sort of nervous breakdown, I suppose.' It threatened and broke, withdrew, regathered force and hurled itself on him again like the physical manifestation of that vertigo of stage

fright which might well have been the advance mess-
enger.

If – as seems possible – he lived many of those years
in the shadow of death then there is a supplementary
explanation for those roles: he wanted to leave his
young family properly provided for. The money at the
National had been sufficient for a quiet life but scarcely
enough to leave an overflow for securing the future
of young children. And despite Olivier's undoubted
carefulness, even meanness, about petty savings,
there are also many proofs of his generosity. When
there is that sort of fear the need to ensure as
cushioned as possible a future for your dependents
must become urgent. He was looking after his own.

In amongst all that, because the man is and always
will be a surprise and a star, he did some films which
no one need be ashamed of: most of the world's actors
would give their eye-teeth to have been half as good
as he was in *Marathon Man*. While in *Sleuth*, as
Andrew Wyke, he pulled off such a succession of
tricks and tributes, such a 'Comstock Lode of experience' said Joseph L. Makiewicz, the director, that he
had seen nothing to equal it in forty years. Most actors
would have rested up for the remainder of the decade
on the strength of it.

One of the many fascinating things about Olivier is
that whenever he seems remotely to be typecast, or
cornered, or in a rut, a pattern, a slide, he will see a
way out and quite suddenly pounce on it. Now, unable
to force himself back onto the stage and unhappy with
the roles he could command on film, he swung his
attention around to television. In America he enjoyed
Love Among the Ruins with George Cukor and Kathar-
ine Hepburn. But it was in Britain, at Granada Tele-

vision, that he found a home, a substantial base and one worthy of him. He was given a brief to make a selection from great twentieth-century plays, to produce them all and act in whatever he chose. This resulted in some quite marvellous work, especially his performance with Alan Bates in Pinter's *The Collection*. Once again, Olivier seized on a centrally contemporary playwright and funded the character with such richness that you catch yourself smiling throughout at his delight in himself, in the part, in the man he is showing you he is.

Nor was he afraid – was he ever? – to challenge comparison with others, as when he took on Big Daddy in *Cat on a Hot Tin Roof*: he had not the heft of Burl Ives, perhaps, but he was a Big Daddy all right.

And he was Nicodemus in Zeffirelli's *Jesus of Nazareth* and a wonderful bicyclist in *A Little Romance*. In many of these later roles he seems, usually sportively, to be trying on different versions of old age for size, rather as he might be trying on different suits. What sort of old man shall I be? Spry? Ugly? Mean? Sanctimonious? Ever so humble? A little vicious? Lovable? Unrepentant?

In 1981 he appeared in two huge British television hits. As Lord Marchmain in *Brideshead Revisited* he bided his time until he came to the scenes preceding his death when he exploded with a wonderful personal gaiety, raising the quick memories of Coward, the clipped playing of the twenties, the dash of the old matinée idols. 'When the time comes for my own death,' he said, 'I should be very good at it. I seem to do one rehearsal after another these days.' In *A Voyage Round My Father* he got to perfection the

stern, playful, moving, incisive eccentricity of John
Mortimer's blind father without ever listing into
sentimentality. When he has his breath and a part
he wants and the time to prepare it as he wants,
he can still stun you so that you wake up and
believe in him: even though it has got harder for
him, and for us, through the years as our memories
and his many roles have encrusted themselves on
our pupils so that we see him through wrappings
of other times, other characters, other days. Yet
his capacity to compel belief remains: even through
all that, even through a legend which could have
put him in a straitjacket.

While we were making our film he was sometimes
ill. On one extremely worrying morning we arrived
only to clear out half an hour later as he took a bad
turn. He had been through long, arduous and punishing
assaults of treatment. There was the thrombosis,
there had been the huge spread of cancer, there was
that 'uproar in the cells'.

Yet again and again he warbled like a lark, shone like
a star. After the first day's shooting – two three-hour
sessions plus all the setting up and sorting out –
he had champagne for everyone and, seeing how
awkward and shy most of us were in the presence,
so to speak, of someone we all admired intensely and
feared we had overtaxed that day, he rolled out a
barrowload of stories, voices, self-mockery, mimicry,
giving them to us with easy generosity. We felt as if
we had been given 'going away presents' after a party.
He likes a drink, people would say.

One day we bowled along to Brighton to do some
filming with John Osborne. Olivier announced that he
had given up drinking 'forever'. It affected the

memory, he said, adversely, and he had taken the odd
one, or two, and maybe even sometimes three or
could it be four in his time, but all that was in the past.
Did we know how bad it was for the memory, the
liver, the this thing and he forgot which other thing
but it didn't do any good at all? No. Seventy-five was
an age to take a grip on yourself, sort a few things out,
stop wasting your life with fripperies, with damaging
fripperies like drinking.

Osborne was sipping champagne.

'Well,' said Sir Laurence, 'just a glass, just the one
mind you, so as not to insult my old friend John
Osborne here, can't have him drinking alone, oh –
wonderful to be in Brighton again, marvellous thank
you, thank you very much, you'd better leave the
bottle just in case old Johnny might need another
glass, you never know.'

And on we went with this supposed, and genuinely,
very sick, worn-out old man – an hour or so later
roaring through a splendid, full and sufficiently al-
coholic lunch ending up, in his case with two puddings
and a final, but final little glass of that bubbly stuff.
Out onto the promenade for the interview, parading
down it like a guardsman, delighted with Osborne's
affectionate wit.

Or we were at a party to which he had been invited. He had come although he was very ill and indeed he was. He sat quieter than quiet, eyes closed
some of the time, seemingly willing himself out
of the room, out of the company. He was no one
and wanted no one to etch a mark on him, wanted
to be left to his anonymity like some forest bird
seeking the retreat most safely suited to its
camouflage.

Yet at that very time he was in training to do King Lear.

'In training' meant the usual combination. He gave himself voice lessons every morning, banging away at the piano, pushing his voice down a note at a time, yelling out the notes with uninhibited force and no tunefulness at all. The object was to extend the vocal range.

Then, the physical exercises. Ill as he had been and could still be, he made himself swim about a quarter of a mile every morning. This would give him the stamina and strengthen his arms. He wanted to be strong enough to carry Cordelia.

And, as at all times when he has taken on one of the great roles and wanted to use every minute of rehearsal time to fullest advantage, he learnt the part in its entirety before the very first read-through. And, as with Othello, as on so many other occasions, word came down, eventually, from Manchester, that the assembled cast had been stricken when, at what they thought was a chummy, first-get-together read-through, Olivier had blazed off his part all guns firing.

I asked him if we could come into the rehearsals, knowing the answer. Even a read-through? Not a chance. That was all too private business. It was there that the hunt was on, the pursuit into himself for that man he could have been, and the building up of the external mask which would tell the naked truth.

We were in the garden of his country place for that last interview. A mild English summer day. He had shown me proudly and expertly around the garden which he had so artfully laid out. He had always enjoyed designing gardens. He pointed out the little paths, the surprise views, the bowers and secluded sunny spots. How would he describe this garden? 'Oh, very vicarage,' he said, 'which is just as it should be.'

EPILOGUE

If only by being a thousand others could Olivier be fully himself, then that personal compulsion has also been the means of giving millions of people pleasure, terror, delight, awe, feelings of splendour, ripples of fun, other lives by courtesy of his great, great talent. If it is true that the enemy was blankness, that the goad was avoiding boredom, that the fear was his own death forever ready to claim him unless he took a life in his hands and escaped it, then his victories have not only saved his life but enriched ours. I am sure that a score of people would give you a score of characters and all of them would be right. But despite the huge presence of that giddily exceptional gift, he has worked for others, brought up children, cossetted friends, entertained all manner of troops, brought on talent and knocked off unnecessary lights to save on the electricity bill. Taken all in all we will not . . .

He is fearless or makes himself seem so even though he constantly confesses to being frightened to death. Not only the many feats of physical daring, often crazy. Fearless in his determination. At William Walton's Memorial Service in Westminster Abbey with the music, the fine singing, the large crowd of friends, the sophisticated society of music – Olivier went up into the pulpit, limped up, almost, looking

tired and not at all well that day and then, starting
softly, growing slowly, rolled out the great speech
from *Henry V* which Walton worked on with him,
loosed it like a quiverful of arrows to all the corners
of the Abbey so that we would thrill, with him, to
remember his friend through great language.

When Olivier made *Hamlet*, there were many
scenes which had to be cut. 'The rule in editing
Shakespeare,' he said, 'is to lift out whole scenes. If
you trim here and trim there, all you have left is a lot
of loose ends.' This is the first part of a soliloquy he
hated leaving out: he did, because the film needed it.
But he sorely missed the chance to say it:

> *Ay, so God buy to you! Now I am alone.*
> *O, what a rogue and peasant slave am I!*
> *Is it not monstrous that this player here,*
> *But in a fiction, in a dream of passion,*
> *Could force his soul so to his own conceit*
> *That from her working all his visage wann'd;*
> *Tears in his eyes, distraction in's aspect,*
> *A broken voice, and his whole function suiting*
> *With forms to his conceit? And all for nothing!*
> *For Hecuba!*
> *What's Hecuba to him or he to Hecuba*
> *That he should weep for her? What would he do,*
> *Had he the motive and the cue for passion*
> *That I have? He would drown the stage with tears,*
> *And cleave the general ear with horrid speech;*
> *Make mad the guilty, and appal the free,*
> *Confound the ignorant, and amaze indeed*
> *The very faculties of eyes and ears . . .*

Bon voyage, and thanks.

PRAISE FOR *THE KARMA OF SUCCESS*

'Liz Tran has the striking ability to bring out best selves within reach.
Equal parts a spiritual journey and a pragmatic guide, *The Karma of
Success* will be a treasure for anyone who is ready to unlock the true
potential of their lives.'
—TRINITY MOUZON WOFFORD, cofounder, and CEO of Golde

'Ambitious people often twist themselves according to what they
think the world wants to see. *The Karma of Success* is a welcome reminder
that our own voices are the best guide – and a step-by-step playbook to
listening to and caring for your own intuition.'
– KIRSTEN GREEN, founder of Forerunner Ventures and
investor in Glossier, Ritual, and Hims & Hers

'If you're ready to break free of the limiting, stagnant world of
traditional career advice, then this is the book for you. Instead of
giving us prescriptive instructions on how to play by the rules, Liz
takes a beautifully holistic approach that creates room for us to succeed
as our fully unique and individual selves. I wish I'd had this book
when I first started out in my career.'
– KIM PHAM, cofounder of Omsom

'This book is a must read for anyone who cares about building a
successful and truly meaningful career. Liz is just the visionary we
need as we reimagine the future of work! She shows us that work
can be enriching, enlivening, and exciting when we approach it
with care and intention and reminds us that the best thing we can
do for our careers is to invest in ourselves.'
– PIERA GELARDI, cofounder of Refinery29 and
founder of Wild Things World

The Karma of Success

SPIRITUAL STRATEGIES TO FREE YOUR INNER GENIUS

Liz Tran

RIDER

1

Rider, an imprint of Ebury Publishing
20 Vauxhall Bridge Road
London SW1V 2SA

Rider is part of the Penguin Random House group of companies
whose addresses can be found at global.penguinrandomhouse.com

First published in Great Britain in 2023 by Rider
First published in the United States of America in 2023 by Portfolio/Penguin,
an imprint of Penguin Random House US.

www.penguin.co.uk

A CIP catalogue record for this book is available from the British Library

Graphics by Tessa Forrest
Book Design by Tanya Maiboroda

Some names and identifying characteristics have been changed
to protect the privacy of the individuals involved.

Trade Paperback ISBN 9781846047503

Printed and bound in Great Britain by Clays Ltd, Elcograf S.p.A.

The authorised representative in the EEA is Penguin Random House Ireland,
Morrison Chambers, 32 Nassau Street, Dublin D02 YH68

Penguin Random House is committed to a sustainable future
for our business, our readers and our planet. This book is made
from Forest Stewardship Council® certified paper.

*This book is dedicated to
every person who believed in me
before I knew how to believe in myself.*

CONTENTS

Introduction: Intuitive Work   ix

THE FOUR EXPANSIONS

1. The Changing Self   5
2. The Authentic Self   10
3. The Joyful Self   20
4. The Intuitive Self   26

Synthesis: The Expanded Self   35

SPIRITUAL STRATEGY #1
INQUIRING INWARD

Interlude: Goodbye, Book   39

5. The 3 S's   43
6. What's Your Type?   51
7. Sizzle and Steak   61
8. Ego vs. Inner Genius   70

Synthesis: Inside and Out   79

SPIRITUAL STRATEGY #2
MANIFESTING MINDFULLY

9. Advice from Sam   85
10. What You See Is . . .   91

11. $2 Coffee Rich   100
12. Confidence Bank   111

Synthesis: Journals Past and Present   121

SPIRITUAL STRATEGY #3
ENRICHING YOUR ENERGY

13. The Three Treasures   132
14. Easy Cleansing   141
15. Playing Defense   151
16. Bigger, Brighter, Amplified   161

Synthesis: Forty-Eight-Hour Energy Reset   171

SPIRITUAL STRATEGY #4
BECOMING BRILLIANT

17. The Gentle Way   179
18. Reverse Golden Rule   185
19. No Timelines Allowed   193
20. Let Your Struggle Be Your Making   204

Synthesis: The Genius Truths   219

EPILOGUE   In Two Words   225

Acknowledgments   229
Notes   231

Introduction
INTUITIVE WORK

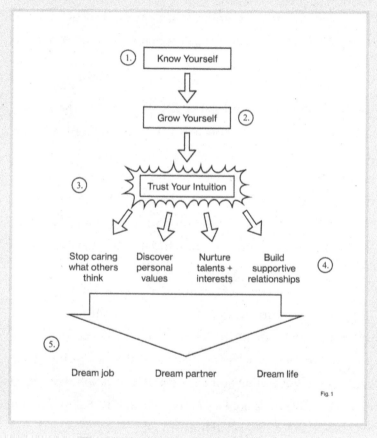

1. Know Yourself
2. Grow Yourself
3. Trust Your Intuition
4. Stop caring what others think | Discover personal values | Nurture talents + interests | Build supportive relationships
5. Dream job | Dream partner | Dream life

Fig. 1

Fig. 1 | The Intuitive Work Process

We are taught to chase after achievements without giving much thought to our inner world. This is a fallacy. The best results come from the inside out.

very great work of art, science, or knowledge in this world can be traced back to a flash of intuition. Georgia O'Keeffe followed her intuition to leave New York City and her circle of artist friends for a new life in rural New Mexico. There, she made her own clothes, ate from her own recipes, and, for today's equivalent of $165, bought a ruin of a house that no one else wanted but she loved.

Ignoring the critics, she painted the harsh landscapes, adobe buildings, and animal skulls she found in the desert, a dramatic departure from Abstract Expressionism, then the obsession of the art world. By simply focusing on what mattered to her, she generated the best work of her life, paintings that now hang in the Met, MoMA, and the White House. "I always had to be willing to stand alone," she said. When it came to both her work and her life, she listened to no one except her inner voice.

Whether you call it your inner voice, instinct, gut feeling, or inner truth, we've all experienced intuition in our lives. It's the moment in the shower when you finally untangle a problem, or the brilliant idea that drops into your lap. It's the gut feeling you have about a situation that's later confirmed to be true. Psychologists Martin Seligman and Michael Kahana described it as "rapid," "not conscious," and "often made with high confidence." Put simply, intuition is knowing something without knowing how you know it, and the only difference between the ordinary and the genius is the amount of time we spend nurturing our intuition.

I first started trusting my intuition in the mountains of Northern India. This was ten years ago, and I was studying yoga at an ashram a stone's throw from where the Dalai Lama lived. One day, I heard of an Irishwoman giving healing sessions for fifteen dollars. I was lost in my career, unhappy in my marriage, and desperate for direction. Without knowing what a session would entail, I reached out to her. When I got to her room, she asked me to lie on the floor and close my eyes for a guided meditation. The session began with her voice ushering me down a set of stairs, through gardens, and into the mysterious rooms of my mind. Soon I was in a deep trance. Then she told me that she wasn't going to give me the answers I wanted. Instead, I needed to provide them for myself. "Use your intuition," she said. "And ask *yourself* for guidance."

Still in the trance, I followed her instructions. "I'm lost," I said. "I have no idea what to do with my career or my relationship. Intuition tell me the path to take." Two sentences came into my mind right away. I heard them clearly. The voice in my head sounded like me, but stronger and more certain. There, on this stranger's floor, my confusion dissipated, and I knew exactly what to do.

After we finished our session, I left the healer's room to walk home and was drawn to an unmarked trail through the woods, and I soon found myself completely turned around. I didn't have a cell phone, so I walked and walked while the sun changed positions in the sky. I scanned for signs of life, but there was nothing. No people, no buildings, no slivers of road. I was lamenting my choice of path when a sudden noise cut through the quiet of the forest. My head spun to the left, and I held my breath as I waited for the sound to reveal itself. It was, of all things, a wedding party, winding its way through the woods.

Forty revelers in bright colors filled the forest with music. Their instruments sang and their cymbals crashed as the bride and groom, looking happier than I knew people could be, sat atop a dais carried by their loved ones. It was a moment unparalleled in beauty or magic, and I knew I needed to follow them wherever they went. Eventually the procession led me to a road, and when I looked around I realized that I was only steps away from home. I had followed my intuition down an unknown path, and even when I felt lost and uncertain, I was exactly where I needed to be. The symbolism couldn't have been clearer. Just as the healer said, I could trust my inner guidance.

Before that day in India, I'd only done the opposite. I constantly compared myself to my peers and copied the most successful ones. I sought out mentors and did everything they suggested to a T. I was perpetually accumulating data and information that would help me in my career, but despite my best efforts, my work in HR and recruiting was unhappy, unremarkable, and unfulfilling. I'd also married young and quickly to someone who seemed great on paper, but just like every other choice I made because it seemed like *the logical thing to do*, the relationship wasn't working. I had put all my trust into external sources of knowledge and given none of it to myself.

The two sentences my intuition told me that day in India were simple, but they changed the trajectory of my life. It said this: "Don't worry about your career or your relationship, but instead, put your focus on *your inner world*. There are years of evolving to be done, and the time to start is now." When I got back to New York City, I threw myself into exploring who I was on the inside. I found a therapist, joined a Buddhist group, and studied meditation, astrology, and a form of Japanese energy healing called Reiki. As I did that day with the healer, I asked myself over and over again what wisdom my intuition had for me as I navigated divorce, family challenges, and my new spiritual journey.

I was more surprised than anyone to find that my career blossomed while I was focusing on my inner world. It turns out my intuition had been right. When I stopped paying attention to the outside world and started caring for myself, the chaos of work and love that I'd always known somehow resolved itself. A few years after that trip to India, I was working as the only female executive at a prestigious venture capital firm with more stability and money than someone like me, who had never met her father and was raised by an absent mother in low-income housing, could ever have imagined. No matter how "impractical" or "illogical" people told me my choices were, I kept on following my intuition, even when it meant leaving that lucrative job to start my own company, Reset, where I now coach the CEOs and founders of the world's fastest-growing companies and host a podcast about spirituality that reaches a passionate audience around the world. In following my intuition, I've created even more stability and financial abundance than I ever thought possible before that session in the healer's room.

I see so clearly now how success finally arrived for me, not *in spite of* my spiritual practices, but because of them.

As I explored my inner world, I was generating the Karma of Success, which is when wins and achievements come through an intuitive and spiritual path. The idea of Karma dates back thousands of years, and the essence is this: Karma is the personal destiny you earn based on your actions in this life and past ones, and we can generate good, positive Karma when we live in alignment with our values, authenticity, and intuition. Thus, your investment in your spiritual life is not a time drain or a diversion from work but rather the essential soil from which all your greatest achievements will grow. The Karma of Success refers to the inevitable *external* success you find once your *internal* world is in alignment.

Another important concept we'll explore is that of the Inner Genius. Just as everyone on this planet has their own Karma, that specific destiny they're meant to fulfill, every person is also born with an Inner Genius. Think of it as the best version of yourself. It's the part of you that's infinitely smarter, wiser, and more creative than you realize. Your Inner Genius always knows what to do, even if you consciously don't. It's the force that moves your fingers across the keyboard, canvas, or kitchen counter whenever you create something brilliant. When you connect with your Inner Genius, not only do you generate your greatest work but you also do it in a way that is easy, enjoyable, and energizing.

Inner Genius, Intuition, and the Karma of Success. They are the harmony, rhythm, and melody of the same song. Your Inner Genius is the part of you that brings your best ideas and creations to life, and your Intuition is the language you use to communicate with it. The Karma of Success emerges when the first two are engaged and activated. As you explore your inner world, all three—Inner Genius, Intuition, and the Karma of Success—work together to bring your greatest dreams to life.

As you make your way through this book, you'll notice that much of the knowledge here comes from Eastern philosophy and ancient sources of wisdom like Buddhism, Zen, and the Tao. We need their guidance now more than ever. So many of us are overworked, burnt out, and unfulfilled, and none of this is made easier by the modern obsession with productivity and accomplishment that asks us to work longer hours, network harder, and sacrifice more. I call this default approach to our careers Mechanical Work, because like robots, we follow the instructions we're given by our peers, colleagues, and society, and we forget how to decide for ourselves. It's how I spent those early years before I connected with my intuition.

The opposite of Mechanical Work is Intuitive Work, and it's what you'll learn in this book. It's the ancient art of tuning out the external world and listening to your inner voice. When you practice Intuitive Work, your options are no longer restricted by your résumé, your network, or what other people think of you. Instead, you stand out from the crowd as brilliant insights and breakthroughs become a regular part of your day. You free your Inner Genius and, thus, generate the Karma of Success.

There are four Spiritual Strategies in this book that will

help you switch from Mechanical to Intuitive Work and create positive Karma for your career. They are:

1. Inquiring Inward
2. Manifesting Mindfully
3. Enriching Your Energy
4. Becoming Brilliant

You'll get to know the ancient wisdom behind these strategies and hear stories of people who practice them, and, most importantly, you'll be on a journey to understand yourself more deeply than ever before. This book, at its essence, is about finding success in your career, but it's also about happiness and fulfillment in your personal life, too. One important thing I've learned from my own journey and from coaching others is that our work selves and our home selves are not separate beings. Professional happiness feeds personal happiness, and the same is true in reverse. You are a complex, unique being, and my goal is to support all of you, the holistic you, and as you take care of yourself you'll also take care of your career.

If you picked up this book, it means that you are ready. Your intuition guided you here, and deep inside you know that you want a more meaningful career and a more meaningful life. The time has arrived to employ the wisest mentor you've ever met: your Inner Genius. I am simply here to be your coach and encouragement. You and your intuition will lead the way.

The
Karma
of Success

THE FOUR
EXPANSIONS

✴

※

FOR MOST OF MY CAREER, I'VE BEEN ON THE receiving end of well-intentioned advice, telling me how I need to change in order to be successful. Here's some of what I've heard:

> You can't be so emotional when it comes to work.
> You need to be more polished and professional.
> You should dress differently if you want to be taken seriously.

What about you? What have you been told about who you are? How have you been asked to edit yourself? At first, I believed the advice I was given, and I followed it, but as time went on I grew frustrated. I sensed that it was meant to erase the uniqueness of my personality and turn me into someone more predictable and conforming. Plus, the advice didn't even work. Trying to be someone different wasn't making me more successful. In fact, the more I lost track of my true self, the more disconnected I became from my Inner Genius.

That's why, unlike in other books that want to force you into some outdated mold of professionalism, you won't find any rules here. Instead, what I offer in these next chapters are Expansions. They are encouragements to help you reconnect with your unique self and activate the Inner Genius within you. There are no guidelines to follow or principles to memorize. Your only work now is to become reacquainted with the boldest, truest, most alive version of you.

✳

CHAPTER 1

THE CHANGING SELF

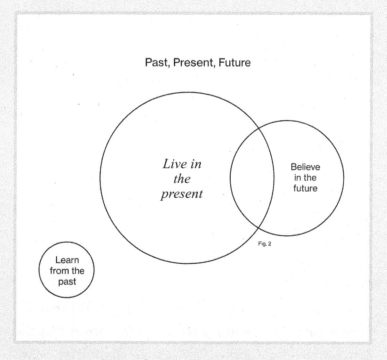

Past, Present, Future

Live in the present

Believe in the future

Fig. 2

Learn from the past

Fig. 2 | Past, Present, Future

If you are open, present, and aware in this moment, everything and anything becomes possible.

D on't worry too much about what's happened (or not happened) in your career so far. The past doesn't matter. None of it is relevant to where you're going. The only thing you must do is choose to see yourself differently from how you've seen yourself before. What you've thought of yourself in the past has gotten you to where you are today. So it stands to reason that if you want something else, something different, something more, you'll have to see yourself in a new way, too.

> **EXPANSION #1** | *I can change. I allow these changes to be easy and natural.*

Shunryu Suzuki Roshi, a Sōtō Zen teacher, was once asked if he could explain Buddhism in one sentence. The audience laughed. How could a 2,500-year-old spiritual tradition be reduced to a few words? Suzuki Roshi, however, was unfazed. Without skipping a beat, he replied, "Everything changes," and he moved onto the next question.

Change is the fundamental premise of life. The only difference between a dead flower and a live one is that the dead one no longer grows. We must keep growing or we perish. If we knew what was good for us, we'd wholeheartedly embrace change, but boy, do we resist it.

We hold onto the good parts of our lives, intent on ensuring they persist. We even grip tightly onto the not-so-good, unsatisfying parts. We'd rather continue on with a bad situation than risk the uncertainty of the amorphous unknown. Buddhists call this *attachment,* while psychologists call it *loss aversion*, the human tendency to feel loss twice as deeply as the equivalent gain.

Loss may seem like a strange word for your career, but it's apt here. You will lose and change many things when you pursue the Karma of Success. You'll lose the old parts of yourself that are no longer working for you. You'll say goodbye to stale beliefs that pin you to the past. You will shed everything that has held you back from becoming who you deserve to be.

There is a story about a rich and powerful man who wanted to learn from a wise Zen master. He went to the Zen master, full of conviction and used to getting his own way, and said, "I have come today for you to teach me about Zen. Open my mind to Enlightenment." "Let's discuss this over a cup of tea," the Zen master said. He set down a cup for the rich man, started pouring and didn't stop. Even when the cup had overflown, he continued to pour. He poured and poured and poured, and even when the tea spilled off the table and onto the rich man's robes, he kept going. "Enough!" the visitor shouted. "Can't you see the cup is full?"

The Zen master finally set the pot down and smiled at his guest. "You are like this cup of tea. So full that nothing can be added. Come back to me when the cup is empty. Come back to me with an empty mind." This story is my inspiration for how I choose the clients I work with. I don't pour tea on them, but I do want to know if they are able to begin with a fresh slate. In the hour we spend vetting each other, I don't ask anything about their achievements or successes—those things don't matter. The only thing I care about is if they are ready for change. It is the only factor that defines whether they will succeed.

The same holds true here between you and me—in our pact as reader and writer. Before we go any further with this work, I invite you to ask yourself: Am I ready to change?

Say yes, emphatically and easily. Remember that you're actually changing right now without realizing it. Your hair is growing, your brain is adapting, and your skin is shedding as you finish this sentence. Every cell in your body is making its way through a life and death cycle. White blood cells live for a year; red blood cells are gone in four months. In seven years, every single cell in your body will have turned over, and you are effectively brand new. We gain and lose memories, change our preferences, and become the people we swore we'd never be. Despite our best efforts at stability, we still change. Imagine where you would be if you stopped fighting and embraced it.

Snakes spend over 10 percent of their lives in an intense state of change called ecdysis, also known as shedding. It's an unpleasant endeavor that involves the snake going blind for a few days and rubbing itself against hard, painful surfaces to try and get the old skin off. Snakes will hide themselves and stop eating during this period because they're so irritated and vulnerable. The whole experience is excruciating, but you would never, ever see a snake reject the process. There's simply no alternative. Snakes shed, birds migrate, and the grass grows. Notice the ease with which all this happens. The grass doesn't "try" to grow, and the snake doesn't force himself to shed. The same applies to you, too. Forget loss aversion. Let go of attachment. Get out of your own way and allow what is already happening to happen.

Your intuition led you here because you're ready for something different now. Your Inner Genius wants you to evolve into the best version of yourself, and now you've arrived at the moment to empty your cup. Your first opportunity is right here, and all it takes is embracing the First Expansion.

> **EXPANSION #1** | *I can change. I allow these changes to be easy and natural.*

As we work through the lessons of this book, any time the idea of change feels overwhelming, just picture the grass growing, the sun rising and setting, the ocean tides lapping the shore, and remember that you were born ready for change. You're already changing, and change is simply a part of your true nature.

CHAPTER 2

THE AUTHENTIC SELF

How to Be Yourself

Share your
unfiltered self
with the world

Listen to
your intuition

Know that "fitting in"
is overrated

Quit comparing yourself to others

Appreciate and admire what makes you unique

Fig. 3

Fig. 3 | How to Be Yourself

For many years I was afraid I wouldn't be accepted if anyone knew the real me. Everything changed once I understood what embracing myself truly meant.

f you were to tell anyone who knew me in my younger days that I now advise CEOs and am passionate about spirituality, they'd laugh. There were a dozen places I should have ended up, and none of them would have been considered a success. For my first three decades on this planet, I didn't know about the concepts of Karma or Intuition, and I certainly didn't trust who I was.

Since before I could read, I considered my lack of money to be the root cause of all my problems. As a little kid, I remember days without lights in the apartment because the electricity bill hadn't been paid and feeling embarrassed to tell my teacher I couldn't finish a third grade science project because I didn't have the supplies. The money issues and chaos only got worse as I grew older. In my teens I would scream at my mom, telling her that it was her job to feed us and take care of us. One day when I was fifteen, after one of these fights, she decided once and for all that it wasn't. The next day, I was sent to live with my aunt and uncle. At my new high school, I lied to the friends I made, telling them that the adults I lived with were my parents.

I couldn't have articulated this then, but I was sure that I was broken and deficient. My mother and father had both decided individually that they didn't want me, and I felt ashamed, believing it must be my own fault. It was a self-destructive time. I did well in school, but I skipped classes to drink malt liquor in parking lots, shoplifted from department stores, and developed unrequited crushes on people who got me into even more trouble. There were no benevolent forces in the places I hung out, and by the time I left for college, I was cynical, jaded, and an atheist, and I saw capitalism as my only road to salvation.

In my mind, poverty and chaos were intertwined, and I was determined to make enough money that I'd never experience the turmoil of my childhood again. I moved to New York City when I was twenty-three and worked as a cocktail waitress while I looked for an office job. I was a state school liberal arts major with a mediocre GPA and no connections, looking for work during the worst days of the Great Recession, so I cast my net wide, without considering purpose, fulfillment, or even personal interest. I accepted the first job I was offered, ran with it, and turned it into a career, and that is the entirely random reason why I dedicated a decade of my life to the tech industry.

Five years later, things were going well from the outside. I'd come a long way from the empty fridges and housing projects of my youth. I was an HR director at a fast-growing startup and married to a talented filmmaker. I was finally out of debt and financially comfortable. Yet still, I wasn't happy, and neither was my husband. We'd gotten engaged just three months after our first date, and the endorphin rush of the honeymoon phase was already gone. We were itching and restless and recently disappointed by our respective jobs, so we decided to take our savings and leave Brooklyn for a yearlong travel sabbatical. Our dream was to make a film together and coauthor a book. In our minds, this trip would not only rocket our careers, but also bring us closer together.

Halfway through the trip, we faced reality and decided that spending a month apart in different countries might do us good. He went to Thailand, and I headed to India for the yoga teacher training where I'd eventually meet the Irish healer and begin to trust my intuition. The monthlong program was serious work. The day began at five thirty a.m. when I'd walk down the hill to the yoga shala and ended at eight p.m. when I'd walk back up. I was learning at a faster rate than I ever had. Every day was filled with five hours of physical yoga practice and two hours of chanting and prayer, with the rest of the time studying topics like the history of yoga, the Bhagavad Gita, and Ayurveda.

During meals and breaks, I bonded with my classmates, soaking up learnings from their spiritual seeking. Because participation required taking a month away from "real life," the ashram attracted a certain type of person. Every single yogi in the class was in the midst of a major life crisis. Over dinner one night, we counted. Half of the people in the room had just ended a relationship, and the other half were transitioning careers. I was a bit of both. It was liberating to speak so freely and openly with these strangers about the dark questions that loomed in my mind, thoughts I'd never even shared with my brother or my best friend, and to be met with empathy and mutual commiseration.

No one had any idea who I was outside of the ashram. No one knew rebellious-teen Liz, HR-tech-company Liz, or married-to-the-guy-she-met-a-year-ago Liz. Free from any social and societal expectations, I didn't have to hide who I was as I'd been doing all my life. Not only could I be myself, I was even free to go deeper and ask myself who I *really* was.

From the other yogis in the group, I heard about whole new systems I could explore. For instance, there was Human Design, a new age personality index that asserts that every person in the world fits into one of five energetic profiles. I learned that I, like 20 percent of the population, am a Projector, and therefore extremely sensitive to the energies of others. When a Projector is around other people's challenging emotions like anxiety, sadness, anger, or self-consciousness, they feel it viscerally, as much as the person who first felt it, and it becomes amplified in their body unless they take time to expel it through rest, sleep, and alone time.

I think I'd always sensed this about me, but I denied my need for rest, chalking it up to laziness and pushing myself to work even harder. Human Design let me reframe this part of myself from an embarrassing shortcoming to a valid aspect of my selfhood. I finally felt permission to set boundaries and become the introvert I always was but didn't think I deserved to be.

Along with Human Design, I also became fascinated by astrology, and that was how I found myself, a couple weeks into the trip, huffing my way up a hill to see Dharamshala's preeminent Vedic astrologer. Before this, my experience with astrology was relegated to reading monthly horoscopes online or in the back of magazines. I didn't know it then, but this experience would kick-start my yearslong deep dive into astrological study. Over the next few years,

I'd read hundreds of charts for others and consult the planets for all my big decisions. All this richness began with just 4,500 rupees, or roughly fifty-five US dollars, and thirty minutes of astrological insights that introduced me to the second expansion.

> **EXPANSION #2** | *I can be my authentic self. I let my full self lead the way.*

Astrologers say that every one of us is born with a unique astrological chart that is calculated using the time and place of your birth. The resulting tapestry represents the placement of the celestial bodies in the sky at the exact moment you were born. The pop-astrology of magazine horoscopes only ever focuses on one of these planets—the Sun. But to fully understand who you are, an astrologer must examine all ten planets, their signs, their exact locations, and the angles they make to one another. With all these variables, there are at least 13 octillion (as in a billion, billion, billion) possible birth chart configurations. There have been only 107 billion people on this planet, and therefore you and me and everyone else in the world is each one of a kind. One in 13 billion, billion, billion to be exact. Earth has never met anyone like you, and the Karmic destiny you're meant to fulfill is just as unique. You can't know your fate until you get to know yourself first. The two are facing mirrors. So, getting to know you, all the fascinating crevices and crannies of you, is the foundation of a happy human experience (and career).

"It's not enough," the astrologer said to me when I asked

him about my destiny in the world. "You must go deep, and you must be alone. Everything you ever make with someone else, even your husband, will always fail." How had the astrologer known that I was working on a film and a book with my husband? I hadn't told him anything about our lives. I sat quietly outside, overwhelmed with confusion. I had no clue what to even think or feel about the astrologer's words. I was still too early into the process of getting to know and embrace myself to understand what he had meant.

My friend Kim Pham is someone who has always known herself. No matter what, she can't help being anyone but herself—a queer, sex-positive domme, and the daughter of Vietnamese refugees whose career goal is to bring joy and freedom to communities of color. On a day-to-day basis, this means running Omsom, a food company that Kim co-founded with her sister, Vanessa, to reclaim and celebrate the multitudes in Asian flavors. Since Kim had worked in venture capital before starting Omsom, the sisters knew more than most first-time founders, but even so, it seemed that their business could have been over before it even started. Despite nonstop hustling, they could not get anyone to say yes to investing. It was frustrating. They were doing all the right things to be seen and understood by the rooms of white men they pitched for funding, including diluting their activist messaging. Worried that investors might think that AAPI consumers weren't a big enough market, they pitched Omsom as a brand for everyone.

They got no after no after no, and finally Vanessa decided that it was time for a change. "If we're going to get rejected," she said, "it might as well happen with the real company we want to build." They tried again, this time with their original vision of Omsom as a loud and proud brand for Asian Americans, created by Asian Americans, and they quickly raised their pre-seed round from a dream group of investors. In the first two years of business, Omsom found a devoted customer base, partnered with Disney and Instant Pot, and was featured by national media outlets including *TODAY*, *The New York Times*, CNN, and *Bon Appétit*. Now you can find the Phams' products on the shelves of Whole Foods and Target. As Omsom has grown, Kim has experienced more and more pressure to edit her external persona, but she continues her commitment to authenticity and living a fully integrated life.

On her public social media accounts, Kim posts Omsom updates in between educational content for those new to BDSM, fetish, and kink. With her profile rising, Kim has done the opposite of what many would do—she is louder about her experience as a domme and as a member of the BDSM community, in hopes that it will help others feel seen and accepted no matter their sexuality.

Omsom is successful because Kim is 100 percent herself, not in spite of it. Kim Pham, the person, and Kim Pham, the founder, are both bold, courageous, and proud of who they are, and the world can't help but take notice. Kim's authenticity and the success it has created are perfectly captured in a glowing *Wall Street Journal* profile of Omsom where Kim is depicted in all her quotidian majesty, wearing space buns and a leather bondage collar.

What's your version of a leather bondage collar? Meaning, what do you feel pressure to hide from the world in order to be taken seriously, respected, or allowed to belong? For me, it's my love of all things spiritual, including astrology. For most of my career, I was sure that if people knew my spiritual practices, they'd never respect me as a businessperson. I worked in a world where numbers and spreadsheets were dogma. How could I admit that I believed in scientifically indefensible forces like the tarot, Feng Shui, and Reiki? We all have aspects of ourselves we cover up because they don't fit into the stereotypical picture of success. We think we're helping our chances, but really, we're doing the opposite. When you hide what makes you *you*, you also bury your brilliance. You block the Karma of Success from coming into your life. Like Kim Pham, just imagine all the good you could do in this world if you stopped worrying about what other people think and instead, directed that energy to being fully yourself.

EXPANSION #2 | *I can be my authentic self. I let my full self lead the way.*

That same wayward year I went to India, I also made my way to a small town in Japan called Beppu, nestled between an eastern bay and volcanic mountains. The small town's lively geography accrued to something magical—over two thousand hot springs across just forty-eight square miles. The ritual bathing process in healing water was exactly what my stress-laden body craved.

One day, out of the blue, my old boss called. Since I happened to be in Japan, she wondered, how might I like building out the Tokyo team for the company? I said yes, incorporated an LLC, sent over my first ever consulting proposal, and that was the beginning of my career as an independent consultant to tech startups. From there, I helped that same client hire teams in Hong Kong and Brazil, and by the time I returned to the States, I had set up shop as an HR and recruiting whiz who consulted for the hottest tech companies.

I can't help but think of the astrologer's guidance that day in Dharamshala: "You must be alone. Everything you make with someone else . . . will always fail." It turned out he was right. I had to stop hiding behind my husband's dreams and discover what my own were. The trip that many of my friends and family saw as a frivolous break in my career actually wound up being the best thing that ever happened to it. The film and the book with my husband didn't work out, and neither did we. Those were crushing, unyielding times, but I found my true self in the process, somewhere between India, Japan, New York City, and disappointment.

That was the unique and winding path I had to take to find my way. Your own Karmic path is equally specific to you. You are a one-in-13-octillion person, unlike anyone that has ever existed. Your mission in this world belongs only to you and luckily, all you must do to uncover it is to be yourself. As you work through the spiritual strategies later in this book, always remember that you are carving a singular path for you and you alone.

> **EXPANSION #2** | *I can be my authentic self. I let my full self lead the way.*

THE
JOYFUL
SELF

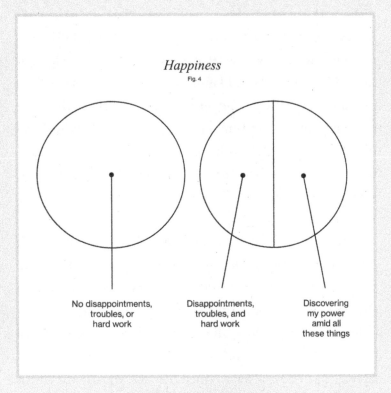

Happiness
Fig. 4

No disappointments, troubles, or hard work

Disappointments, troubles, and hard work

Discovering my power amid all these things

Fig. 4 | Happiness

If you are waiting for life to be free from problems so you can be happy, then you are waiting for a day that will never come. Happiness is available right here and right now, no matter the circumstances.

lbert Einstein, one of the most brilliant thinkers of our time, is my role model for infusing work with joy. First off, he slept for ten hours every night, which is a fact I often remind myself of when I forget that I'm a Projector and feel guilty for having slept in late. I tell myself, "Einstein did it. I must be a genius, too!" On top of those ten hours, he also napped every single day. Sleep, which is unfortunately considered a distraction from productivity by many in our society, was Einstein's way of tapping into his most groundbreaking, innovative ideas.

He'd make himself comfortable in an armchair, ready for his nap with a spoon in hand and a metal plate below. He'd bring his thoughts to what most confounded him as he set off to sleep, and right when he drifted off, the spoon would fall from his hand and clang onto the plate, and he'd wake just in time to recall the solutions his sleeping brain unearthed for him. "We cannot solve our problems with the same thinking we used when we created them," he said. The Theory of Relativity came to him in a dream about cows. Yes, cows. Einstein knew that his research and hard work, while important, were nothing without these playful journeys through his inner world. Through joy, he generated the Karma of Success.

EXPANSION #3 | *I can be happy. Joy creates better outcomes than fear.*

Long nights of sleep and five-minute naps are powerful tools for connecting with the genius within. The same is true for daily walks in the fresh air and playing a musical instrument just for fun, which were also tools Einstein used to get in touch with his Inner Genius. For him, the answers were never found in working harder. They made themselves known only once he was able to back off, let go, and enjoy himself.

The same applies to you, too. The more you release the heavy, grinding feeling of Mechanical Work and embrace the lightness and levity of Intuitive Work, the closer you'll get to connecting with the genius inside you. The best advice I can give to clients who feel lost, confused, or in the midst of a challenge is to remember that the path of ease is the fastest route to all solutions.

Of course, finding joy isn't as easy as snapping your fingers, especially in our reality of economic inequality, rampant discrimination, and environmental uncertainty. There is much to mourn, and that is especially why we must look for pockets of happiness where we can. Poet and author Ross Gay said, "It is not at all puzzling to me that joy is possible in the midst of difficulty." He named this experience "adult joy," which is the act of holding both the sorrowful aspects of life and one's happiness equally. They coexist.

Happiness is not the absence of joy or struggle as we've been led to believe, but rather, our ability to find joy in spite of it. Of course, we should not ignore the hardships in the world that are happening to ourselves or others, but we also can't wait for life to be perfect and problem-free before we give ourselves permission to enjoy it. Whenever I struggle to find "adult joy" and need inspiration, I think of the Dalai Lama, who, despite being the spiritual leader of a people who have experienced decades of occupation, exodus, and suffering, is able to hold massive hardship and joy simultaneously.

In fact, the Dalai Lama laughs all the time. He laughs while giving advice to world leaders. He's hilarious during spiritual talks for very serious audiences, and he chuckles while explaining complex topics like universal consciousness. On days when I am especially blue and it feels tough to find joy, I first think about everything the Dalai Lama has experienced, and then I take five minutes to watch YouTube compilations of him laughing. Seeing his eyes crinkle and hearing his unfettered laugh always reminds me how spirituality, at its essence, is joy.

In his book *My Spiritual Journey*, he reflects on his commitment to humor in the face of hardship. "When people ask me how I have the strength to laugh," he writes, "I reply that I am a professional laugher." Can you become a professional laugher, too? Can you sit with the sadness that abounds in the world, while also connecting with humor, ease, and lightness?

Imagine that you are driving down a winding road to deliver a very important package. You could approach the trip with seriousness, brow furrowed and hands gripping the wheel, or you can cruise that same stretch of road with the windows down, singing along to your favorite song on the stereo. Either way you choose to drive, whether anxiously or joyfully, you get there, but the latter is far more enjoyable, and according to psychologists, also more effective. The Yerkes-Dodson law states that taking your endeavors too seriously actually works against you. Of course, you want some healthy tension, enough so you feel focused and motivated, but psychologists know that your ability to think, create, and problem-solve drops significantly once you cross over into the "distress zone" of anxiety, fatigue, and burnout.

Simone Biles, the four-time Olympic gold-medal gymnast, withdrew from the 2020 Tokyo Olympics where she was regarded as the strongest contender. Surrounded by her beloved teammates in front of a crowd of reporters, she explained her decision with clarity. "I just don't trust myself as much as I used to. I feel like I am also not having as much fun," she said. "This Olympic Games I wanted it to be for myself. I came in and felt like I was still doing it for other people. That just hurts my heart that doing what I love has been kind of taken away from me to please other people." We all have once-joyful areas of our lives that have been robbed of their lightness. For some of us, all of life, work included, feels more like a never-ending to-do list rather than an adventure. The steady uptake of seriousness happens to us all. Take this startling fact: children laugh about one hundred fifty times a day, while the average adult laughs fewer than twenty.

What was your count today? When was the last time you laughed so hard your stomach hurt? When did existing start to feel like a chore? In Sanskrit, the word lila means "divine play" and is a way of describing the true nature of reality. It asserts that everything in this world springs from spontaneous, lighthearted energy. I think about this whenever I'm coaching a client who is going through a challenge. Instead of meeting them in that stressful place and reinforcing their negative mood, I remind myself that play is at the center of reality, and with a lighthearted touch I guide them into shifting out of the Yerkes-Dodson "distress" zone and into a flow where they can see solutions more clearly.

Oftentimes the challenges my clients face are so unexpected or ridiculous that when you zoom out, they're actually hilarious. So, I help them acknowledge the humor in the situation, and sometimes, like the Dalai Lama, we can laugh about it. I also prompt them to comb for any silver linings or teachable moments, steering them away from frustration, regret, or guilt, and toward gratitude for the possibilities of the present moment. Then, just as Einstein said, the problem can be solved with a different way of thinking than what was used to create it.

> **EXPANSION #3** | *I can be happy. Joy creates better outcomes than fear.*

To generate the Karma of Success, you must go easy on yourself. This is your formal invitation to sleep in, take naps, become a professional laugher, and never, ever beat yourself up when you accidentally slip back into the heavy and grim. Your happiness and your joy are of the utmost importance for the Intuitive Work at hand, so roll down the window, feel the breeze as you drive, and remember that nurturing your own happiness and joy is the most serious and important work of all.

CHAPTER 4

THE
INTUITIVE
SELF

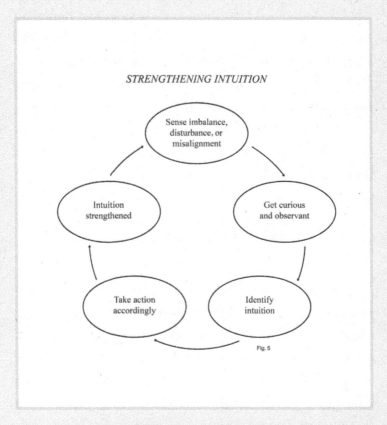

Fig. 5 | Strengthening Intuition

Intuitive decisions are even more effective than the ones we make from logical reasoning. Just like a muscle, the more you use your intuition the stronger it becomes.

The two-year period after my travel sabbatical was a blur of highs and lows. Most of my energy went into navigating the end of my marriage, and the rest went to nurturing my nascent consulting practice. It was a moment of simultaneous destruction and creation. One day, when the divorce papers were freshly signed but not yet stamped by the court, I got an email from a former client with an interesting proposition.

The client was the founder of a tech company, and one of his investors was an up-and-coming venture capital firm that was looking for someone to build and lead their talent team. If hired, I'd design a strategy to help the hundreds of startups they'd invested in with their people-related projects. It was a small, young fund that had notched notable early wins. The partners were wunderkinds, millionaires before thirty with a magic touch. My client thought the work I'd done for his company was similar to what the firm needed and asked if I'd be open to an introduction. I said yes and began my research.

Scrolling through the employees on LinkedIn, I noticed that everyone had Ivy League degrees and gold star pedigrees. I wasn't like that. I'd worked for a bunch of companies that no one had ever heard of and spent the past couple years as a freelancer. It felt like a tremendous stroke of luck that I was even considered to interview. My first two conversations went well, with an easy and energetic rapport. But the third one left me questioning how golden this opportunity actually was.

To start, the person interviewing me was ten minutes late, and when he finally joined me in the small conference room, his eyes never left his phone as he read and replied to emails and texts for our entire conversation. On autopilot, he peppered me with short quantitative questions as if my career only amounted to the number of software engineers I'd hired. He half-listened to my responses, and when the interview ended, he rushed off. I didn't think he was a bad person. In fact, I kind of felt for the guy. He seemed harried and burnt-out, an overachiever with fifteen back-to-back meetings every day. He had simply looked at his calendar and decided that mine was one that did not require his full attention. I had no hard feelings, but in my earlier decision to focus on my inner world, I'd intentionally left behind the world of Mechanical Work. This interview made me wince at the thought of returning to it.

As I walked home, the two competing parts of my personality began a debate. The first, the logical and practical one, knew what a rare opportunity this was and wanted to continue interviewing. The other part of me, my intuition, knew that no matter how impressive any role might be, nothing mattered more than living in alignment with my work. The two sides wrestled back and forth. My Intuitive Self was clear that I should remove myself from the process. It needed no other justifications other than how I'd felt during and after the interview.

On the other hand, my Practical Self was afraid, scared that I'd never get another opportunity like this. It had done the calculations. It knew that working in venture capital would be a major game changer to my résumé and my financial situation, and would surround me with people who, according to my Mechanical Work self, were in a different league. My Practical Self worried about missing out, while my Intuitive Self was sure there was something else, something better, on the other side of no.

That day, I chose my Intuitive Self and wrote an email to one of the partners letting him know that I was respectfully removing myself from the process. It was a seemingly small decision, just a few sentences, but the choice was significant in what it symbolized for me. Before I learned to trust my Intuition, I had always made calculated, seemingly rational choices about what was most likely to generate the best outcome. It's why I leaned into a recruiting career I never asked for and why I pushed to get married so young, believing that both were smart choices for getting the stability I'd craved since childhood.

Now here I was, making a big decision without any logic behind it, seemingly at odds with my desire for security. I didn't need to know where my conviction came from. I simply hit Send with no regrets and assumed it would be the end of my relationship with the venture fund. I'd keep doing my thing, and they'd move onto the next person in an endless queue of eager candidates. Then, in a twist that I couldn't have predicted, the partner wrote back and asked me to reconsider. He apologized for my experience and clarified that he too wanted more for the role. I liked his openness and authenticity and decided to keep interviewing.

When I initially decided to trust my intuition and withdraw from the process, it seemed like I had ruined my chances of working in venture capital, but in reality, it did the opposite. In asserting my boundaries, I built a stronger relationship with the partner and a precedent for direct communication between us. A couple of months later, I got a job offer despite dozens of other candidates with much more impressive backgrounds. Then I worked there for a few happy years, my longest time ever working for someone else. That role was a pivotal step in my journey. It's where I learned about executive coaching, built up my professional confidence, and cultivated lifelong relationships. None of this would've happened if I hadn't followed my intuition.

> **EXPANSION #4** | *I can trust my intuition.*
> *The wisdom it provides is real.*

It's funny how things work out. The choices I made practically, like marriage and tech recruiting, were always with a specific end point in mind. There was always something *else* that I really wanted, like money, or stability, or happiness. If I do *x*, then I'll get *y*. I thought I was making calculated bets on how my future would unfold through a careful analysis of possible outcomes.

Of course, I was sorely disappointed time after time when these outcomes didn't pan out. It was only when I took the opposite tack, and traded logic for intuition, that I was always satisfied with my decisions. Even though these intuitive choices were never made with an end goal in mind, never trying to fulfill some need or desire, somehow they always led me down the right path.

Making decisions from practicality is about control. It's thinking that you know the levers to pull for the outcome you want. The Karma of Success is the opposite of control. It's admitting that you yourself don't consciously know what will happen, but there is a part of you, your intuition, that does know and is wiser than you can even comprehend. Your whole world will open up once you acknowledge that your Intuitive Self is not only a valid way to make decisions but also infinitely better at guiding you than the limited, unimaginative Practical Self.

It took Alua Arthur almost a decade before she learned to follow her intuition. After graduating from college, she wasn't sure what she wanted from her career, so she made practical choice after practical choice. Before long, she was a deeply depressed yet highly accomplished lawyer. Alua tried to shake her apathy by making more practical changes. She switched industries to work on topics she cared about, she moved from for-profit to nonprofit, and later switched to part-time, but none of these straightforward solutions helped with her depression.

Alua needed a new way, so she began following her intuition. She meditated. She asked questions, and she became open to direction from impractical places. One day at the library, she saw a man carrying a bag that read CUBA TE ESPERA—"Cuba Awaits You." Alua was taken aback. She had just been thinking about that very same country that morning, specifically about a Cuban boy named Elián González, who had been in a heated immigration controversy a decade before, and Alua, wondering where he was now, had come to the library just to research him. The co-incidence of it all was the nudge Alua needed, and she bought a plane ticket right away.

Once Alua got to Cuba, her intuitive guidance flowed. After a series of curious coincidences involving kind strangers, a speeding car, and a near-death accident, Alua found herself sitting on a bus next to a woman with late-stage uterine cancer. She and her new friend had an hours-long conversation about death. It was the first time the woman had ever spoken so openly about her end-of-life experience with anyone, friends or family included. Then and there, Alua knew that she wasn't a lawyer anymore. It would be her work in this world to help others navigate the process of dying.

The average person might believe that it is impractical and illogical to make decisions like this—to book a trip to Cuba based on a message on a stranger's bag, or to choose a new career after a conversation on a bus, but these intuitive choices allowed Alua to free her Inner Genius and create deeply meaningful and successful work. Today, she is the founder of Going with Grace, an organization that has trained over two thousand death doulas, supported thousands more people as they've passed, and redefined the cultural conversation about death.

Alua still relies on her intuition every day to hire staff, train teachers, and design the courses. Even though it's tough to imagine any line of work more suited for her, there were no career coaches or mentors who would have ever suggested that she quit law to become a death doula. In fact, many people in her life couldn't understand why she'd want to immerse herself in death every day. But her Intuitive Self knew that this was her calling. Alua's stream of success shows us something magical—the decisions we make through intuition are far more effective than the ones we choose with our practical mind.

Know that this is true for you, too. When you listen to your intuition, you aren't making a silly, unfounded, immature choice. You're actually tapping into your Inner Genius, which has more wisdom than our human minds can comprehend. So, trust yourself. Know that you don't need data behind every choice. You are credible on your own. You don't need to prove or justify what you know or how you know it. Your Intuitive Self is far more powerful than logic.

> **EXPANSION #4** | *I can trust my intuition.*
> *The wisdom it provides is real.*

How connected are you to your intuition right now? When was the last time you had a gut instinct or an immediate sense of knowing? What insights have dropped into your lap recently? Even if you're not comfortable with listening to your intuition right now, that's okay. We'll devote all of the next section to understanding your Intuitive Self. You'll learn how to recognize and interpret your intuition, separating it from the voices of practicality and ego. You'll become so adept at trusting yourself and your choices that you'll soon wonder how you ever navigated life before.

The Expanded Self

ALWAYS LISTEN TO...
Fig. 6

YOUR
DREAMS

YOUR
INSTINCTS

YOUR
MIND

YOUR
SENSE OF
WORTH

AND IGNORE...

Other people's
negativity

Fig. 6 | Always Listen To . . .

Never forget that when it comes to your life, you know better than anyone else.

magine yourself glowing brightly like the sun, lit from the tremendous energy of your Inner Genius. This is what happens when you tap into the Four Expansions and give yourself permission to be the truest, boldest, most alive version of yourself. When you own who you are and do so without apology, you've set your foundation for the Karma of Success. Now you have what you need for your next adventure as we explore the rich world of Spiritual Strategy #1: Inquiring Inward.

THE FOUR EXPANSIONS

✳

EXPANSION #1
I can change. I allow these changes to be easy and natural.

EXPANSION #2
I can be my authentic self. I let my full self lead the way.

EXPANSION #3
I can be happy. Joy creates better outcomes than fear.

EXPANSION #4
I can trust my intuition. The wisdom it provides is real.

INQUIRING INWARD

❋

Goodbye, Book

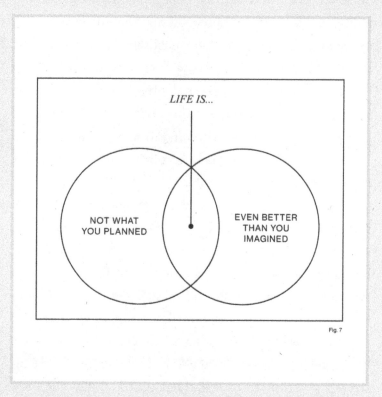

LIFE IS...

NOT WHAT
YOU PLANNED

EVEN BETTER
THAN YOU
IMAGINED

Fig. 7

Fig. 7 | Life Is . . .

We can plan and plan all we want, but our efforts will never change the delightful unpredictability of life.

When I first started writing this book, my plan was to focus on the intersection between spirituality and entrepreneurship. As I wrote in my book proposal, it would be "The Spiritual MBA for the multi-hyphenate, the solopreneur, and the side hustler." After signing the contract with my publisher, I had nine months to write the manuscript. I chugged along, typing and typing, but no matter the effort I exerted, every day felt like driving a car with the parking brake on. I put in many months of long hours and had almost nothing to show for it.

One night, with six weeks left before my deadline and most of the book still unwritten, I went to my friend Carla's house in California to write with her and two other authors. All of us planned to publish our books around the same time. I cleared out my work meetings and began each morning with yoga and meditation. I wrote barefoot outside in the desert and allowed myself breaks to watch the cottontails run across the yard. At night, we gathered around boxes of takeout to share our secret dreams for our books and our careers. Since we were all writing, I had long stretches of time to myself. That solitude, plus the pure nature around me, meant that the conditions were exactly right for my intuition to be heard.

The fourth night at Carla's house was also the night of the full moon. While my friends slept, I tossed and turned despite following my normal bedtime routine. I suspected it might be my Inner Genius keeping me up, so I willed my mind to be receptive and still. Within a few minutes, I had an insight that would change the course of the book. I needed to scrap the old title and theme, release the months of writing I'd done, and begin again from scratch. Instead of writing about the intersection of entrepreneurship and spirituality, I knew I had to write about the exact thing that had saved me so many times in my life and career. This book would be about intuition, the inner world, and how to connect with your Inner Genius. I spent the next few hours awake sketching out an entirely new structure for the new book.

The next morning, I woke up hungover from the late-night thinking and began to second-guess myself. The book had been sold with a concept my publisher liked, and now I was blowing it up just a few weeks before my deadline. Was this truly my wise Inner Genius, or was it actually self-sabotage? Was it even possible to write a whole book in a matter of weeks? Lost as to whether I should trust this insight, I returned to the Four Expansions. Was this guidance asking me to change, to become more authentic, more joyful, and intuitive? The answer was a clear yes on all counts. My intuition was demanding that my book evolve, and it was my job now to meet it with trust.

As soon as I chose to trust my Inner Genius, the blocks within me burst open, and I dropped into the flow state that had eluded me for seven months. Writing in the midst of a renovation project on my house, with little furniture and even less internet, I worked anywhere I could find quiet. I typed in a cheap tent that quickly became inhabited by a family of daddy longlegs, then I worked in the grass until I couldn't take the mosquitos anymore.

Other days, while the inside of the house was being painted, I sat on the floor of the quietest room, legs side-saddle, hunched over the computer that rested on my knees. I'd sit in that uncomfortable position for hours and get up only when my legs went numb. I wrote like a woman possessed, leaving the glare of the screen only to do yoga, meditate, or eat frozen pizza. Six weeks later, I finished the book. Despite throwing out half a year of work, I still hit my deadline. I owe this book, which I love very much, to the act of trusting my Inner Genius.

Over the next few chapters, we'll go deep into the process of how to free your own Inner Genius to generate the Karma of Success. You'll learn about the four Spiritual Strategies that allow you to work faster, better, and with more inspiration than you've ever known. Perhaps you've felt this brilliant state of being before. It's the hours of work that fly by with joy. It's the clarity and confidence to do something hard. It's you at your best, unencumbered by self-doubt. These moments of genius are usually few and far-between. This book will show you how to make them an everyday occurrence.

The first Spiritual Strategy we'll explore is called Inquiring Inward. In the following chapters, you'll learn how to create the right conditions for your intuition, how to tune in to its wisdom, and how to implement its messages into your daily life. In the process, you'll stop cluttering your life with noise and worries about what other people think and instead focus on your spectacular, transcendent inner world.

CHAPTER 5

THE 3 S'S

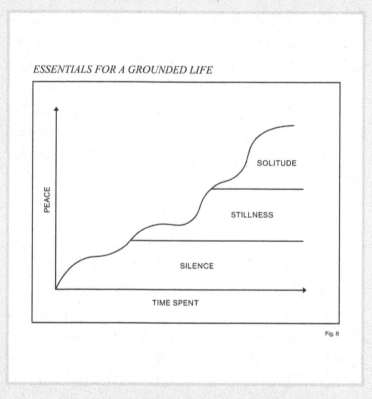

Fig. 8 | Essentials for a Grounded Life

Use silence, stillness, and solitude to ground yourself amid the stress, frenzy, and chaos of modern life.

once had a coworker who replied to every email in under three minutes, even late at night. Thinking he did it because of the pressure from work, I tried to convince him that it didn't matter. "Three minutes or three hours. What's the difference?" I said. "I don't do it because of work," he replied. "I just don't know what else to do when I'm home. I can't just sit around and do nothing."

My friend was uncomfortable in stillness. He was unable to just be. This impacted his life in many areas. He hated his job but couldn't bring himself to leave. He loved his long-term girlfriend but was ambivalent about their future. He had always wanted to live abroad, but not once had he explored other countries. This very smart and externally successful person buried his existential issues under an avalanche of action. As long as he stayed busy, he could stop the questions from overtaking his mind. Even so, he suffered. With no stillness, no solitude, and no silence, there was no way for him to find the answers he so needed. You see, when you turn up the noise in your life, it becomes impossible to hear your Intuitive Self.

In martial arts they say that the mind is like water. It can be peaceful and serene, clear and calm. But when your thoughts are racing, when you're overwhelmed, distracted, or compulsively checking email, the water becomes muddled and choppy. There's too much turbulence, and therefore no way to connect with the wisdom within you. How is your mind today? Is it a crystal clear pond or is it muddy and polluted? Is there calm and quiet? Is it a place where your intuition wants to settle down?

The 3 S's—silence, stillness, and solitude—are the home where the Intuitive Self lives. And they don't help with just your intuition. They are also crucial to your overall well-being. In just two minutes of silence, your whole body relaxes. Your blood pressure goes down and more blood flows to your brain. Focus and creativity also increase with silence, and, in fact, the 3 S's may even make us smarter. In 2013, a study that was intended to test the effects of various sounds on the brains of mice had a more important breakthrough, revealing that only the mice who had two hours of silence a day were able to grow new brain cells.

None of this is revolutionary. We all intuitively know that we crave the 3 S's. Think of Henry David Thoreau, our favorite writer-hermit, who inspired generations of seekers to find their own Walden Pond. Then, there's John Francis, who chose not to speak for seventeen years. He thought he'd try it for a day as an act of protest and then found it so transformative that he kept going.

During his time in silence, John Francis walked across the country and got his PhD. Now his TED talk is one of the all-time most popular. We're intrigued by stories of people who quit their jobs to become monks, take up homesteading, and live on the fringes of the Earth. Somewhere, deep down, we all want a break.

In Buddhism there is a concept called Noble Silence, which is different from normal silence. The latter, as you and I know it, is the absence of noise. You are silent when you don't speak, and the world is quiet when there's no sound. However, Noble Silence is a loftier goal. It is the achievement of quiet *within*. It is the clear pond they speak of in martial arts and can be achieved only when there is calmness inside of you. When you go on a silent meditation retreat, you commit to both Noble Silence and the silence we know. And it was there, on my very first silent retreat, when I came to understand just how different the two concepts really are.

I was at Insight Meditation Society, one of the oldest Buddhist centers in the United States. In addition to no phones, no computers, and no speaking, we also weren't supposed to read, write, or nap. Essentially, participants are meant to avoid any activities that might be distracting to the mind. It was even suggested that we meditate at mealtime; every table in the cafeteria had instructions for mindful eating. When you're on retreat, the goal is to spend fifteen hours a day committed to meditation. As a natural introvert, I did the normal silence part well. I was energized by the lack of social interaction and thrilled for a break from my devices. The Noble Silence part came harder.

Among meditators there is something known as the Vipassana Crush: when you are on a meditation retreat and your mind convinces you that you have fallen in love with someone else on the retreat. In the absence of normal forms of entertainment, your brain creates some drama of its own. You have fifteen waking hours a day to make up stories about this person, how wonderful they are, and why you're perfect for each other. My brain went another route. I developed Vipassana Enemies.

There was the man with a cold who sneezed and sniffled on his cushion, ruining the silence for me morning and night. There was the woman with brightly colored socks—a different pattern each day. What point was she trying to prove? I cursed the person in front of me in the salad line for taking the last olives. Surely, they didn't deserve to be a Buddhist. By the end of the retreat, the majority of my thoughts were petty and surly. I hadn't said a word, but Noble Silence was nowhere within reach.

If the 3 S's are so good for us and a prerequisite for the Inner Genius, then why are we so bad at them? Why can't we, as my coworker said, sit and do nothing? What is it about the quiet that we fear? Stop right now for a moment. Are there cars rushing past your window? How many notifications are on your phone? Do you have an endless vortex of emails and texts to respond to? The modern world is a precarious place for the 3 S's to thrive, and for the sake of your Inner Genius, it's more important than ever to get them back.

Despite my less-than-noble showing at that first meditation retreat, I kept going. Over the years, I went on more than a dozen retreats in addition to keeping up with my regular home practice. I wish I could say that I got better. That I stopped making Vipassana Enemies and my mind became a peaceful pond. But it's not true. In fact, some of my most recent retreats were even harder than the first, but I am never disappointed by this. One of my meditation teachers who I admired greatly and had been teaching for twenty years told me that she still has bad days all the time. She'll sit down for meditation, as she has thousands of times before, only to find that her mind refuses to cooperate. Instead, she'll get distracted and ruminate over something said to her, or stress over a nonissue. Her mind can't seem to focus on anything except not meditating. This knowledge cheered me, as I realized that the point of meditation is not to be perfectly peaceful at all times but rather to recognize when the pond has become muddled and make the effort to dredge it out. Pema Chödrön said it best: "Meditation is just gently coming back again and again to what's right here." Coming back again and again. It seemed like a pretty good goal to me.

Your life doesn't need to be absolutely quiet with no interruptions in order to make friends with your intuition. The only thing to do is to notice and try. Notice when the noise and commotion, both internal and external, have gotten out of hand, and then try to do something to cultivate silence, stillness, and solitude. You simply make the choice to come back again and again.

For silence, my phone is set on Do Not Disturb for most of the day. For stillness, I give myself permission to do nothing whenever I want. Sometimes this means lying in bed for no reason. Other times it means pausing with my feet in the grass. My favorite of the 3 S's is solitude. It recharges me more than the others. Every month, I find a way to spend at least twenty-four hours away from people, phone calls, and text messages so I can remember what it feels like to be utterly alone.

Aviva Romm is a master when it comes to preserving her stillness. She is a doctor, midwife, and bestselling author, and when she is creating, whether designing a new course or writing her next book, she prioritizes creating the right conditions for her Inner Genius. She lives on seven acres of land in the country, has zero notifications on her phone, and answers email only at predetermined times that won't interrupt her creative process. It's certainly easy to corral the pesky distractions we don't like, but Aviva's made harder choices, too. She's turned down prestigious advisory board roles to make more room for her Intuitive Self. "I'm committed to spending as much time in the internal as the external," she said.

Her ability to retreat from the world, to build a boundary, has actually meant that she's more successful. She's had some of the greatest eureka moments for her business while taking extra-long showers, weaving, or drawing. By preserving the liminal space of her life, the luscious moments of in between, Aviva's creativity can come through. "Nothing interrupts my showers," she said.

I have a client who meditates for sixty minutes every morning. A couple I know spends forty-eight hours each month not speaking to anyone. That is what works for those people, but we all have our own unique limitations of time and life, and there is absolutely nothing wrong with starting wherever you can. Perhaps you can't take a full day in solitude each month. That's okay; just thirty minutes a day is equally rejuvenating. Your Inner Genius doesn't care how impressive your actions are. It just needs little bits of time every single day when your mind is a clear pond to drop in and give you the wisdom you need. What will you pick? Perhaps you want to meditate for five minutes in the morning or take a vow of silence for a couple hours this

Saturday. The incredible thing is your intuition will actually tell you exactly what it needs from you. Let's invite it in right now so it can guide you toward a new habit.

INQUIRY EXERCISE #1

✳

Go into a quiet room and set a timer for two minutes. Close your eyes and sit in silence until the timer goes off. Let the stillness bathe over you. When you are done, ask quietly or aloud, "Intuitive Self, what should I do for more silence, stillness, and solitude?" Go with the first thing that pops up. That's the message your Inner Genius needs you to hear.

CHAPTER 6

WHAT'S YOUR TYPE?

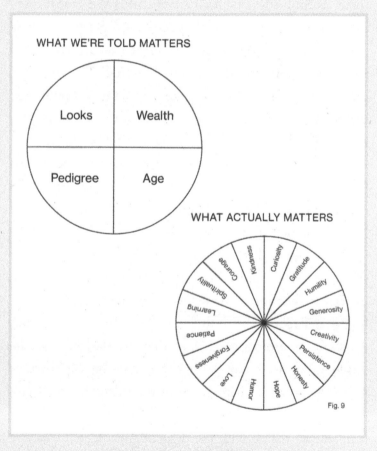

Fig. 9 | Personality Wheels

You are far more interesting than you give yourself credit for. There are endless facets of your personality that deserve to be explored.

begin with two prying, intrusive things when I first start working with a client. First, I send a list of ten highly personal questions for them to answer in writing, including, "What's your biggest disappointment in life?" and "What dream of yours is still unfulfilled?" Then, I send them a link for a personality test called the Hogan Personality Inventory. When they're done, I get to see their personality expressed in twenty-eight traits, each scored somewhere between zero to one hundred. The Hogan is quantitative. That list of questions is qualitative. I pour over this mountain of data to understand my clients' strengths, weaknesses, and motivations in the present moment.

The ability to really know a client, with all their complexities and contradictions, is the most important skill a coach can have. When I tell people what I do, they often say "Wow, you must give the best advice!" The truth is that my work isn't nearly that impressive. My job is simply to understand. I lob question after question at my clients, then listen intently to their responses without offering my opinion, trying to understand them. In the process, they begin to understand themselves, too. Once they do, they have all the wisdom they need to solve their problems on their own.

In the previous chapter, we learned that the Inner Genius requires the right home to be heard, and that environment is created with the 3 S's of silence, stillness, and solitude. Your Inner Genius also needs *Self-awareness*. If you think of your Inner Genius as your coach, then just like me with my clients, your Inner Genius has to really know you.

It needs to transcend past the superficial layers of what you've done or how you appear to others and get to the meat of you. It's hungry for the juicy bits—your dreams, fears, insecurities, and shadows—and it always wants to understand how you are changing and transforming in the present moment. The historical facts of your life are unimportant. The soulful parts are what matter, and they must matter to you, too. Before the Inner Genius can know you, you must know yourself.

When someone is described as "self-aware," it means they have a conscious knowledge of their own character, feelings, motivations, and desires. They look at themselves. They ask questions. They wonder how they got to being them and ponder whether they should keep doing it. How self-aware do you think you are?

In a study exploring how the self and others are conceptualized, social psychologist Richard Nisbett and his colleagues had university students describe themselves using the options in the table below.

Then they were asked to do the same for their best friend, their father, and finally a popular television personality. I want you to try it now, too. Take a look at the choices

1	Energetic	Relaxed	Depends on the situation
2	Skeptical	Trusting	Depends on the situation
3	Quiet	Talkative	Depends on the situation
4	Intense	Calm	Depends on the situation

and choose the descriptor from each row that best suits your personality. Then do it for your best friend and then a parent.

Nisbett discovered that the students tended to answer "Depends on the situation" more frequently for themselves than they did for other people, even strangers they'd never met before. It seems that we are often more sure of who other people are than we are of ourselves. We can easily define the people around us but have a much harder time when it comes to the self.

It's a funny thing. You spend so much of your time, actually all of it, with yourself. The Self, which is made up of the body, mind, and spirit, is the only constant companion we'll have in life, so why is it that we spend so little time thinking about it? When in school or at work are we ever encouraged to learn about ourselves? We are given opportunities to study every subject under the sun, so why aren't we empowered to explore our inner lives, too?

Imagine you have the lifelong dream of sailing around the world. Would you do it in a boat you weren't familiar with? Think of how chaotic that would be. Something small would go wrong and you wouldn't know where to go to fix it, what materials you have on board, or how long you could stay out at sea before you ran out of supplies. You can't sail around the world if you don't know the vessel. The same is true for our lives. You certainly can't find success if you don't know yourself.

What makes you better than other boats? What type of weather and wind do you fare best in? It can be tough to describe ourselves. Doing so feels indulgent and like navel-gazing. Plus, the primary way we're taught to understand ourselves is through other people. You know you're good at math because your fifth grade teacher told you so. Your parents call you creative, so you must be. By the time you grow up, your whole sense of self is a smorgasbord of things other people have thought about you. Carl Jung said, "The world will ask you who you are, and if you don't know it will tell you." You deserve to be the one who defines yourself.

For the first three decades of my life, I had no idea who I was. My greatest goal was to be liked, so I conformed to what other people wanted both at work and at home. Because I had quit my job to start consulting, gotten divorced, and grown apart from my friends all around the same time, it felt like the scaffolding of my selfhood disappeared overnight. I suddenly had to define myself, alone, for the first time. My therapist suggested I go on a weekly "Me Date." So, every Saturday, I'd set aside three hours to do some activity by myself. It had to be something I always thought I enjoyed (like going to the movies), or something I believed I hated (like CrossFit). The goal was to get curious about my interior world, see myself anew, and discover what my true self actually preferred.

There was once a distraught young woman who sought out a Zen master. "Please help me," she said. "I am confused and don't know who I am. Please show me the nature of my true self." The Zen master looked away and said nothing, leaving the young woman to wonder if he'd even heard her, so she tried asking again. Still no response. The woman stepped up closer, right up to the Zen master's face, and repeated her request. When he again looked away and continued to ignore her, she turned around to leave.

Just as she walked away the Zen master shouted, "Hey, Anne!"

"Yes!" Anne replied, ready for his wisdom.

"*There it is*," said the master.

There it is. Here you are. The path of learning yourself is not complicated. It is, in fact, your nature to walk it, and it has been waiting for you all this while. An easy place to start, since you happen to be reading this book right now, might be with the ten questions I first send my clients.

1. What are you proud of?
2. What has been your biggest disappointment?
3. What words describe how you feel about your career?
4. What is the compliment or acknowledgment you hear most often about yourself?
5. What dream of yours is still unfulfilled?
6. What accomplishments do you think must occur during your lifetime so that you will consider your life to have been satisfying and well-lived—a life of few or no regrets?
7. What words describe you at your best?
8. What obstacles or roadblocks keep you from being at your best?
9. What are you most uncertain about in the present moment?
10. What are you most sure about in the present moment?

You can do them now or wait for a moment when there's more time to answer thoughtfully. It might also be fun to dig into some personality tests. The Myers-Briggs Type Inventory[*] and the Enneagram[†] are two solid places to start. On the spiritual side of the house, I recommend exploring Numerology[‡]. For all three of these systems, there are many free online tools that help you learn your type and understand what it means. I come back to Numerology over and over again[§], because unlike MBTI and the Enneagram, which say that your profile is forever fixed, Numerology acknowledges that people are constantly changing.

According to the system, we all cycle through a series of Personal Years, numbered from 1 to 9, and where you happen to be in that cycle depends on your birthdate. Each of these years has its own theme, including corresponding benefits, challenges, and lessons. For instance, if you're currently in a 1 year, your focus is on fresh starts and new beginnings, so you might be changing jobs, making new friends, or moving to another city. Then, on your next birthday, you transition into a 2 year, a time that is focused

---

[*]This is my go-to free MBTI test: 16personalities.com/free -personality-test.

[†]After you find out your Enneagram type at enneagramuniverse .com/enneagram/test, learn more about your type here: enneagraminstitute.com/type-descriptions.

[‡]To calculate your Numerology Personal Year: karisamuels.com /personal-year-numerology.

[§]My favorite Numerology book is *Zillionz: Titania's Book of Numerology* by Titania Hardie (London: Quadrille, 2000). I learned Numerology from this book and its pages are dog-eared from years of reference.

on love and partnership, so you might be nesting and deepening your connection with a partner. As the years go on, who you are as a person evolves with the corresponding Numerology themes. Not too long ago, I had my 4 year, which was an unsexy, stressful time that required hard, grinding work as I built a new foundation for myself.

The end of the cycle is a 9 year. It's the last one before you start back at a 1 year again. 9 years are about endings, grief, and completion. They require you to let go of anything in your life that isn't working, no matter how entrenched it may be. These 9 years are very challenging because they uproot your life in a meaningful way. I remember how supportive Numerology was for me when I was in this phase. Simply knowing the task at hand helped me face the jarring changes with more ease.

Like Numerology, the Enneagram also works with a set of nine numbers. Each of the nine types has a basic desire and a basic fear that motivates them. The desire and the fear are two sides of the same coin. Take my type for instance, 7, the Enthusiast. My greatest desire is to be happy, and I am most afraid of pain, which expresses itself in jumping ship whenever things get hard. The Enthusiast hates negative emotions, so as soon as they start to feel any, they move on and run away.

When I started studying the Enneagram, I immediately saw how often that basic fear played in the decisions of my life. I was someone who was always looking for the next best thing. I had never stayed at a job more than two years and had moved apartments ten times in a decade. There are ways of expressing each Enneagram type in healthy and unhealthy ways, and for me to grow and become a healthy Type 7, I learned, I would have to stay put a day, a week, even a year longer than I was comfortable.

When I got my job offer from the venture capital firm, the numbers, the title, everything looked great. Except, they said, knowing my background of jumping from job to job, I'd have to commit to at least three or four years in the role. I'd be building trusted relationships with founders, and it wouldn't be fair to abruptly leave after a year or two. Three or four years might seem insignificant to most people, but being an Enneagram 7, it terrified me. On top of that, I had never worked in finance before. What if I didn't even like the job and I was stuck for almost half a decade? When I remembered the Enneagram, my answer was clear. I'd take the job. Commitment was a positive growth step for someone like me.

Did I say yes because the Enneagram told me to? No, but it helped me understand that the decision was about more than just a job. It was also an important opportunity for me to grow. Personality tests don't define who we are, but rather they give us a path to become the best versions of ourselves. No matter what personality tests you explore, remember that none of what you learn is gospel. The only authority who can define your character is you.

When I first started Reset, I had some stationery cards printed so I could send thank-you notes and little gifts for the many people who had helped me. I spent three whole days debating what I should put on the back of the cards when I should have been doing much more important work. It had to both represent my work and be something I knew in my bones to be true. I finally decided on a quote, one of my favorites, from Thomas Merton, a prolific writer, philosopher, and Trappist monk. In big, bold font, the back of the cards read, "My Greatest Ambition Is to Be Who I Already Am."

There it is. Here you are. You have already arrived.

INQUIRY EXERCISE #2

＊

Pick a personality test to take online. Tune into your Inner Genius and write down the descriptions of your personality that feel most aligned. Then write down the parts that don't feel like you at all. Take a moment to relish how incredible you are.

CHAPTER 7

SIZZLE
AND STEAK

THE BEST DECISIONS COME FROM...

Your Intuition

Experience

Data

Fig. 10

Fig. 10 | The Best Decisions

Logic, experience, and data are helpful for making decisions, but their wisdom is limited. Always trust your intuition.

I t was Cheri Maples's seventh year as a police officer, so when she arrived on the scene of a domestic dispute, she knew what to do. The situation involved a recently separated man, his ex, and their daughter, with whom he did not want to part. He was agitated, angry, and at least a foot taller than Cheri. He wasn't yet violent, but both the little girl and her mother were scared. Any other time in the past, Cheri would have done the obvious thing and arrested the man on the spot. This time, however, something stopped her. Instead, she spoke to him from her heart. He listened when Cheri asked him to hand back his daughter, and within five minutes he was weeping. Cheri saw that he was in incredible pain.

Three days later, Cheri ran into the man at a store near her house. She was off-duty and not wearing her uniform, but he recognized her right away. The man rushed in, scooped her up, and said, "Thank you. You saved my life." Breaking free from what she'd always done, Cheri had listened to her intuition, and it had worked. Just a week before that call, Cheri had attended her first ever meditation retreat. "What happened to me is my heart started to soften and kind of break open for the first time," she said. The retreat was a bridge to her Inner Genius.

Cheri's intuitive plan of action could be called instinct, gut feeling, or impulse. Now, we'll give it our own name. We'll call it a Higher Hunch—the experience of knowing something clearly without quite knowing how you know it. That night with the distraught man wasn't Cheri's first

Higher Hunch. It was actually a flyer at a chiropractor's clinic that led her to the retreat. That tiny choice to tend to her back had beautiful consequences. Cheri would go on to teach mindfulness to thousands of police officers, criminal justice professionals, and prisoners over the course of her life.

In the last two chapters, you learned how to create the right environment for your Inner Genius using the 3 S's. Now you'll learn how to tune into the profound Higher Hunches it wants you to hear. Your Inner Genius is constantly sending you a stream of messages. Sometimes they are as large as Cheri's decision not to make the arrest, or as small as the urge to call a friend. We can't predict these hunches, but we can learn how to harness them.

Scientists have their own way of explaining Higher Hunches, describing these intuitive hints as the influence of nonconscious information from the body and brain. Essentially, the brain runs a query through everything it knows, processing much faster than our rational minds can. Take chess players for instance. When one first starts learning the game, they have to assess move-by-move, breaking down every possibility. The best chess players don't need to do that. They immediately know all the options with a simple glance at the board. Novice chess players analyze. Master chess players intuit. Of course, this can happen only after countless hours of dedicated practice. Our miraculous instincts still need data to comb through.

I believe what science says, *and* I also believe that intuition is connected to the Inner Genius. No doubt, there's a subconscious part of my brain connecting the dots faster than I can. After all, our bodies and brains do an infinite number of amazing things like breathe, pump blood, and grow babies without any intentional thought. I assume there must also be good thinking going on in the background, too. However, this explanation feels limited when we consider unexplainable moments of inspiration, like Alua Arthur's vision for her new vocation or my certainty that I had to start all over with my book. We all receive inspiration from a source that is greater than all of us.

Whenever I'm coaching, I operate in a fully intuitive state. In every session, I get several Higher Hunches telling me what questions to ask. When I first started coaching, I didn't trust these hunches. I thought the questions they proposed didn't make sense or were too awkward, so I'd ignore them. But the hunches would persist. They'd repeat themselves over and over until I finally acquiesced. Not a single one, no matter how surprising, has ever led me astray.

I'm not saying that all you need is your Inner Genius and its Higher Hunches. Remember, I also believe in science. And, as science says, before the brain (and the Inner Genius) can do their lightning-fast processing, they also need data. Yes, I follow Higher Hunches when I'm coaching, but those hunches are rooted in deep experience, including spending fifteen years in tech, coaching hundreds of CEOs, and logging thousands of hours in sessions. Cheri Maples's decision not to make the arrest was intuitive, but she had been in the force for almost a decade and would know what to do if the situation turned. We all need both experience *and* hunches to make our decisions. We need the steak *and* the sizzle.

The steak is the diligence you put into your choices. It's the research, the data, and understanding all your options. The sizzle is your Higher Hunches—the rapid creative processing we all do. While the sizzle is fun and efficient, note that it can only happen *after* you've procured your steak first. Sometimes I think my entire job is navigating this interplay between steak and sizzle, the rational mind and the spiritual one. You know I love using the Hogan assessment to understand my clients, but I must also become familiar with their nonrational inner worlds. During many sessions, I squint at spreadsheets—budgets, projections, and pro formas—but my real job is to intuit how that data impacts my client's state of mind. It's not just me. Being successful at any job is about mastering both sizzle and steak. Unfortunately, we usually tend to be better at one or the other.

Are you a steak person or a sizzle person? Remember in the fourth expansion, we discussed how there is an intuitive and practical self within each one of us. It's your job to figure out which is in charge, then give the other one some attention, too. If you're a sizzle person, the answer is simple. Get better at making steak. Do your diligence. Log practice hours, collect data, conduct research, and try, try again. If you're a steak person, the rest of this chapter is for you. Maybe you're not used to listening to your Higher Hunches. Perhaps you don't even know what they sound like. That's okay. You just need to spend more time befriending your Inner Genius, and there are many wonderful techniques you can use for beginning that relationship. Here are some ideas:

If you're feeling confused about an issue in your life, go to the Self-Help or Business section of your local bookstore or library and skim the first book you're drawn to for insight about how to proceed.

If you're stuck on a work project, do what Einstein did and take a nap or a long walk. Or make something with your hands as Aviva Romm, who we met earlier in chapter 5, does. Do something fun, enjoyable, and purely irrational. See what pops into your mind during your adventure.

You could also try out divination tools like the tarot or oracle cards. This was my favorite way to befriend my Inner Genius when I was early in my relationship with my inner self. Most tarot and oracle decks are easy to use right away because they come with a booklet explaining each card's meaning. I would simply think of a work or personal issue that I needed clarity on and choose one card. Reading the symbolic advice from the card encouraged my Inner Genius to start speaking.

Another favorite tool I use when I have to make a yes or no decision comes from the physical self. First, I jump into the 3 S's. I sit alone for a couple minutes in complete silence. I close my eyes and picture myself doing the "yes" version of the predicament, and see what emotions come up in my body. Do I feel excited in my heart or nervous in my stomach? Did my energy drop or expand? I then do the same for the "no" version. What do I feel when I imagine myself *not* making that decision? Which is more evocative, yes or no, and were either clearly positive or negative? Our bodies always know what we want, even if we don't realize it.

Dreams are another fertile place for messages from your Inner Genius. When I first graduated from college, I decided to apply to law school because I had no better plan and my mom had always wanted me to be a lawyer. I got an entry-level job at a law firm and started studying for the LSAT. Soon, the nightmares started. Every evening, I had the same dream of driving a car with no brakes. The experience was terrifying. I'd be careening through a busy city without any ability to stop my fast-moving car, wrenching the wheel from side to side as I narrowly avoided collisions and pedestrians. I woke up each night sweating and sometimes screaming from this dream. The meaning from my Inner Genius was clear: I was not in control of my life. As soon as I made the decision to give up on law school and move to New York City, the nightmares disappeared.

You can find direction in your dreams, too. If you're new to it, first focus on writing down your dream as quickly as you can when you first wake up, so it doesn't disappear. Then analyze it on three levels. The first is *literal*. What actually happened?

The second level is *emotional*. How did you feel in the dream? Likely, your dream world emotions are ones you're also experiencing, but burying, in waking life. In my car nightmares, I was terrified and powerless. The same was not untrue for my real life.

The third level is *symbolic*. Think about the major aspects of the dream and what they metaphorically represent to you. Use your imagination, applying symbolism to the events, objects, and people in your dreams. My nightmare was obvious. The car was my life, and I was on the precipice of a catastrophic crash. My Inner Genius wanted me to know that law school was not a fruitful path for me.

Don't limit yourself just to what I've suggested here. Higher Hunches come from everywhere. It might be a song you hear, or a book your coworker mentions. I receive mine most often while I'm journaling, lying in the grass, or reading. I also hear many in the last hour of the day before I go to sleep. Yours will be unique for you. Start with the places and activities in which you feel the most relaxed.

When it comes to big, life-changing hunches that you're not sure if you can trust, I follow the rule of threes. When you hear the message the first time, pay attention. When you hear it the second time, take some time to consider it. Finally, when you hear the message a third time, take action. I have a client who was struggling with a decision to let go of an underperforming employee. His wife, not knowing the situation, mentioned a colleague at the office who was let go that day to a positive outcome for everyone, including the colleague. Then a friend sent him an article about terminating employees with empathy. Finally, when the employee underperformed yet again and mishandled their work, even after repeated feedback, my client knew it was time.

No matter what techniques you try, what matters most for your Higher Hunches is simple. They just want you to follow them. You'll hear more messages when you start taking action on the ones you're already getting. No one, including your Inner Genius, wants to waste their breath giving advice to someone who doesn't want it. If someone you knew consistently disregarded your wisdom, you'd probably stop trying to help them, too. The Inner Genius wants you to realize the Karma of Success. It is hanging around in the background waiting to be heard. Start listening and enjoy as your life starts to sizzle.

INQUIRY EXERCISE #3

※

The next time you hear a Higher Hunch, act on it right away. Like Cheri Maples, trust your instinct and do what you believe to be right. Then repeat. Note what happens when you begin treating your Higher Hunches with the respect they deserve.

CHAPTER 8

EGO VS.
INNER GENIUS

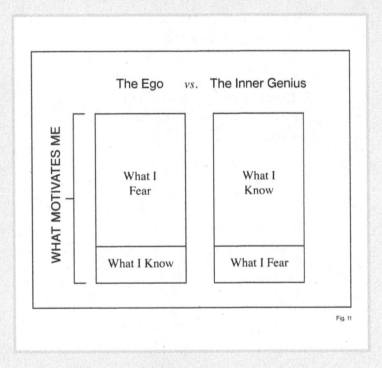

The Ego *vs.* The Inner Genius

WHAT MOTIVATES ME

| What I Fear | What I Know |
| What I Know | What I Fear |

Fig. 11

Fig. 11 | The Ego vs. The Inner Genius

Fear is the foundation of the ego, while trust is the foundation of the Inner Genius.

After three productive years of working in venture capital, I became agitated. That July, at the company retreat, I was so angry that I burst into tears, became ill from how upset I was, and spent the rest of the retreat brooding in bed while my coworkers bonded. I promised myself and my two work friends who witnessed my breakdown that I'd quit and be gone in six months or less.

Looking back now, I understand that I wasn't angry at the company or even the job itself, though that's what I firmly believed back then. Many years later, I now understood that the person I held anger for was myself. I had deferred my own dreams during this decade of working in tech, pursuing some fictional idea of financial accomplishment. My Inner Genius was tired of waiting.

But was it my Inner Genius, or was it my ego? After all, it was three years on the job, exactly one year longer than my personal record for staying put in past roles. Was this the shadow side of my Enneagram Type 7 kicking in? Was this just me, being immature and running away from the inevitable annoyances that come with a fast-growing company? Was this self-sabotage or spiritual connection? How was I to even know if this was the ego?

To understand how the ego works, imagine that your life is a movie. You are the lead with a cast of supporting characters who follow the unfolding drama of your life. Your ego is the film director who wants their work to be important. The ego thinks, "Okay, for this movie to matter, I need to win a lot of awards and make money, and for it to be seen by as many people as possible. I want it to be a blockbuster." So, the ego writes the script with the goal of winning audience approval. It amps up the drama, casts some celebrities, and adds in some impressive action sequences.

In real life, when the ego is in charge, the same thing happens. The ego wants one's life to matter, so it orients around receiving approval from others. It amps up the drama, obsesses over celebrity, and buys into status symbols. It does whatever it takes to make one's life, different, better, and unique. In a word, it wants to be *important*. Anything we do that increases the importance of "Me!" is the ego in action.

We see this so clearly at work. You all know the ego-driven colleague who won't admit when they're wrong, can't take feedback, and doesn't listen to others. Left to run amok, the ego leads to poor people management, bad decisions, and the inability to admit when something isn't working. In tech, the rapid boom and bust cycles can lead to giant inflated egos that eventually collapse. One company I worked for early in my career received an acquisition offer for $750 million. Because the founder believed that he deserved a billion-dollar offer and had narrowly missed one with his last company, he said no, just as the industry turned. Many years later he managed to scrape together a sale at $150 million—far less than what he'd taken from investors. He and his ego flew too close to the sun.

If the ego wants to turn your life into a blockbuster, then the Inner Genius is on a very different track. It's making a documentary to capture the wonder of the world. There's no script and no cast of characters. You appear in the film sometimes, but the plot line doesn't revolve around you. The Inner Genius doesn't care if the project is a success or not. Rather, the Inner Genius patiently waits to see what unfolds as filming progresses. It doesn't care about awards, accolades, or money. What matters is the learning, discovery, and creation.

In real life, when the Inner Genius is in charge, it does the same thing. There is no rushing, proving, or comparison at play in one's actions. The Inner Genius calmly waits for the events of life to unfold organically. It is neither a hero nor a victim. There's no drama or betrayal. There's no need to justify one's specialness and uniqueness. Anything we do that dissolves the importance of "Me!" is the Inner Genius in action.

Think about some ways you see the Inner Genius play out at work. Have you seen colleagues be collaborative, trusting, and supportive? Have you ever seen a workplace that is committed to psychological safety? Have you and other employees been encouraged to be their authentic selves? The Inner Genius in the office says things like, "You might be right," "Thanks for the feedback," and "What can I do to empower you?"

Here are some ways to think about the fundamental differences between the ego and the Inner Genius.

The Ego	The Inner Genius
Head-based	Heart-based
Fearful	Joyful
Rational	Intuitive
Reactive	Patient
Wants to be right	Wants peace
Constructed identity	Authentic identity
Needs control and certainty	Accepts the unknown
Afraid to change	Knows change is natural
Afraid to fail	Learns from failure
Me-focused	Connected to humanity
Cares what others think	Cares about truth and goodness
Agitated	Calm

Notice how the Four Expansions—Change, Authenticity, Joy, and Intuition—are qualities of the Inner Genius. Whenever I am in a situation where I'm unsure which part of me is calling the shots, I do just as I did when I changed the foundational premise of my book. I think about the Four Expansions and see if my decision is in alignment with their essence. If I'm still confused, I run through this broader list to see which column my choice dominates. I wish I'd known this when I was bursting with agitation and ready to quit my job in venture capital.

There is a story about how the Buddha traveled for many days to a small town to speak with the villagers. While the Buddha would often embark on such trips, this particular one was different. When he arrived, one young man in the crowd was very angry with him. He shouted at the Buddha, but the Buddha ignored him and continued to speak to the otherwise happy audience. This angered the man even more and he stood directly in front of the Buddha and yelled, "You're an imposter—a fake! You have no right to be here teaching others!"

The crowd was very angry at the young man, too. By now, everyone was yelling. The man screamed at the Buddha, while villagers yelled obscenities at the young man. Everyone was agitated. That is, everyone except for the Buddha. He turned calmly to the young man and asked him, "If you buy a gift for someone, and the person doesn't take it, to whom does that gift belong?"

The young man was caught off guard, but he thought about it quickly and soon the answer was obvious. "Of course, the gift would belong to me," he said, "because I bought it." With love and affection, the Buddha looked at the angry young man and said, "Correct. This is the same situation with your anger. If you become angry with me, and I don't become agitated in return, then it falls back on you. All you have done is hurt yourself." The young man, no longer angry, paused, looked down, and with a small bow to acknowledge the truth of the Buddha's words, went home.

I was that young man when I decided to quit my job. My ego was upset and certain that I had been wronged. I was the blockbuster director, creating massive drama in the movie of my life. I had cast myself as the sympathetic protagonist and the company I worked for as the evil villain. I was seething over everything I had taken offense at, when in reality that anger was only falling back on me. The company had treated me well and simply wanted me to stay. I had constructed these reasons to be angry as a way to justify my desire to leave. I couldn't take responsibility for my own choice, so I found a way to make it someone else's fault.

My own personal struggle with the ego has mostly been about the fifth characteristic on the table—wanting to be right. I can become dogmatic and label others as villains when they don't meet my expectations. My Inner Genius is helping me learn to release this unwanted gift of anger that keeps falling back on me. I am learning how to make room for peace in my life.

I did quit within six months of the company retreat, but I was able to do it in a mindset of appreciation for my three years at the firm. My company asked me to stay on for a year, and I tried as best I could, eventually leaving eight months after the day I gave notice. I wish I could say it was neat and clean because I allowed my Inner Genius to guide me through this uncomfortable transition, but it wasn't. Sometimes my ego was in charge; other times my Inner Genius broke through. I am grateful to now have the vocabulary and awareness to ask myself who is in charge, so at least I am aware. Now you do, too.

If it ever seems that the ego has been around for too long and you are yearning for your Inner Genius, a great way to connect to your inner wisdom is by writing yourself a letter from the perspective of your Inner Genius. This is an effective antidote for when we are consumed by egotistical thoughts or lost on the path forward. The steps are simple:

1. First you activate the 3 S's and find a quiet, comfortable space alone. Light a candle.
2. Reconnect with the qualities of your Inner Genius by reviewing the table on page 74.
3. Tune into your intuition and ask your Inner Genius your most burning question.
4. Using stream-of-consciousness writing, respond as your Inner Genius. Anything you write—no matter the content, no matter the message, how long or short—is perfect. It is exactly the message you need.

INQUIRY EXERCISE #4

✳

Think about a person or situation that aggravates or annoys you. Now imagine what would happen if you asked your ego to address the situation. Next, do the same for your Inner Genius. If you're having trouble connecting with your Inner Genius, try this. I ask myself WWDLD— What Would the Dalai Lama Do? I think about his easy, forgiving, and generous nature. Then, I'm in the right mindset to access my Inner Genius.

Inside and Out

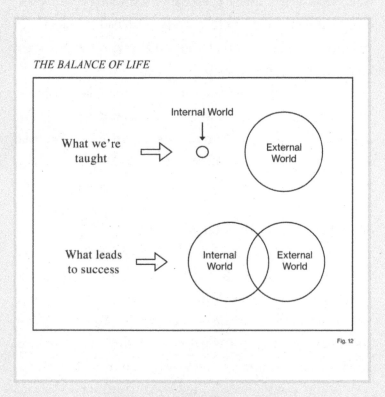

THE BALANCE OF LIFE

Fig. 12

Fig. 12 | The Balance of Life

The secret to genius is living in a way that is as much internal as it is external.

e've officially covered what you need to know to employ Spiritual Strategy #1: *Inquiring Inward*. Along the way, you've learned about the 3 S's, Vipassana Crushes, personality tests, Higher Hunches, and what makes the ego tick. You've also had the chance to practice four exercises that you can always return to when you want to inquire inward. Now, what do you do?

If you take away just one thing from these last chapters, let it be this: As Aviva Romm said, *You must commit to spending as much time in the Internal as the External.* The External is easy. You can get your fill of it through the daily mechanics of living. You work. You get food. You see people you love. These events, and most others in our lives, occur on autopilot in the physical, tangible world.

What's much harder is making time for the Internal. But now you know how important it is to prioritize the landscape inside of you. You now see that the quiet space within is where the Inner Genius thrives. You also understand how important it is to preserve the 3 S's of silence, stillness, and solitude, as well as self-awareness, so your Inner Genius can be heard. Finally, you've learned how to tune into and encourage its messages. So, what do you do now that this section is over? How do we go forward and generate the Karma of Success?

We'll start with the Four Affirmations for Inquiring Inward. Affirmations are short statements that allow you to intentionally direct your thoughts. I use them when I'm stuck in a spiral of negative thinking and need to create an alternative path out. You can write them in your notebook multiple times or say them to yourself whenever you're in need of their grounding. They each map to one of the last four chapters:

AFFIRMATION #1: I make time daily for silence, stillness, and solitude.

AFFIRMATION #2: I am insatiably curious about myself and cultivate self-awareness.

AFFIRMATION #3: I listen to my Higher Hunches.

AFFIRMATION #4: I differentiate between my Inner Genius and the ego.

When you begin to master Spiritual Strategy #1, you'll find that you spend more time alone but don't think of this solitude as a punishment or a chore. Reframe it to this: you get to spend time with your favorite person. After all, no one else knows you as deeply.

A productive and joyful way to get into the spirit of Inquiring Inward is to do what my therapist said and take yourself on a Me Date every week. Do something fun by yourself. And while you're on the date or when you're back home, open your journal and record all the insights, feelings, and ideas that came to you while you were cultivating your internal world. Your reflections are treasures and deserve to be preserved. What will you do for your first Me Date this week?

I'll throw in one last affirmation that summarizes what

I hope you feel now after five chapters of celebrating, exploring, and embracing the miraculous inner world within you:

> **AFFIRMATION #5** | *I love myself. I am my own best company.*

In the brief words of the Zen master who called out to the seeking student: *There it is.* Here you are. You have arrived.

MANIFESTING MINDFULLY

✳

CHAPTER 9

ADVICE
FROM SAM

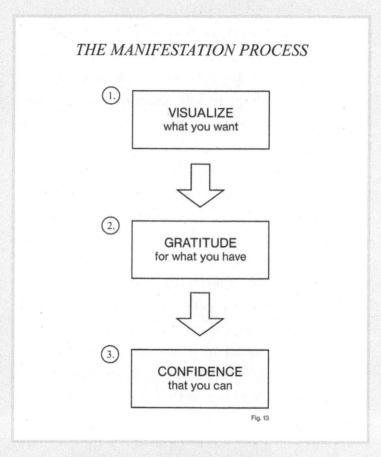

THE MANIFESTATION PROCESS

1. **VISUALIZE**
what you want

2. **GRATITUDE**
for what you have

3. **CONFIDENCE**
that you can

Fig. 13

Fig. 13 | The Manifestation Process

There is no difference between what you believe in your mind and what becomes a reality. You can manifest what you want.

So far, I've said a lot about my interior world. I've shared the questions, fears, and intuitions that rattled in my mind as I pursued my spiritual journey, but I'd be remiss if I gave you the impression that I did it on my own. There were many people who appeared in my life like earthbound guardian angels, ready to offer the exact wisdom, support, or friendship I most needed in tough times. I could go on and on about the magnanimous souls I met on my path toward the Karma of Success, but the person I want to talk about now is someone I haven't spoken to in seven years but I still think about all the time.

I first met Sam after an Ashtanga yoga class. I was almost out the door when he asked me what my birthday was. It turned out we were more than ten years apart in age, but were both in the midst of our Numerology 1 year. We laughed about the coincidence and bonded over the hurdles and stumbles of beginning a new cycle.

Over our first meal together, he told me about his life. His mom was fourteen years old when she gave birth to him. She was a wonderful person and he loved her, but her presence in his life was fleeting. By the time she was twenty-three and Sam was just nine years old, she passed away. Sam went to live with his grandparents. It wasn't a loving upbringing, but at least he had an escape route. Sam was a gifted athlete and had been accepted to university on a full scholarship. There was a new beginning to look forward to. But as fate would have it, right before graduating from high school Sam hurt his leg, and overnight his scholarship and path to college evaporated.

When I met Sam, he was the successful owner of three thriving businesses, including the yoga studio where I met him. He had turned his passions for yoga, surfing, healthy food, and teaching into profitable endeavors, and he was happy. He was the first person I'd ever met who had come from a dysfunctional background like mine and was not only successful but also doing it in a way that he enjoyed. He was truly living the Karma of Success. Back then, I hadn't started Reset yet. I was still going on Me Dates and trying to figure out who I was.

On a daily basis I gave thanks for what seemed like a miracle: I had work and stability, and had narrowly disentangled myself from the chaotic undertow of my childhood. But I wasn't happy or fulfilled. Sam was my first real-world role model for work that was both lucrative and meaningful and was gained without the helping hand of privilege. If he could do it, I thought, maybe I could, too.

I asked Sam how he'd achieved his success. After all, he hadn't gone to business school and lacked previous exposure to entrepreneurship. Sam put his fork down on the table and his face became serious. There are just two things you need to succeed, he said.

1. *Always have a solid, conservative business plan that considers every possible obstacle and weakness.* He explained that he'd read a dozen books on the topic and would dedicate as long as a year to researching and creating his business plan before launching any new endeavor.

Then he told me this:

2. *There's no difference between what you believe in your mind and what becomes a reality. Everything you focus on and imagine happening will eventually occur in real life.*

Sam was talking about manifestation, and it was the first time I'd ever heard a real businessperson talk about it. Before meeting Sam, I believed that my modest success was partially the result of hard work but mostly the random chance of an unpredictable universe. Just as inexplicably as my good luck arrived, the life I'd created for myself could just as easily be taken away. What I learned from Sam that day was that this way of understanding life is wrong. I was the one in charge of my own destiny. All I had to do was change my thoughts and I could guarantee the future I wanted.

Manifestation, at its simplest reduction, is the idea that whatever you focus on becomes a reality. You have the power to create anything with just your mind. If you believe it, they say, it will come.

"I have this weird manifestation gift," pop star Ariana Grande said. She even writes songs about manifesting[*] and tells a great story about her earliest experience with it. A tiny Ariana, age four, called Universal Studios and asked the receptionist if she could audition for a Nickelodeon show. Thirteen years later, she would go on to star in one.

Another music phenomenon, Drake, spent $5,000 a

---

[*] "Just Like Magic" (2020) is the consummate manifestation anthem.

month renting a Rolls-Royce before he made it big. Even though he could barely scrape together the payment each month, it was his way of convincing himself and others that success was on the way. Drake described this gamble as his "extreme way of manifesting." Fifteen years later, his manager tracked down the exact car that Drake had struggled to make payments on and gifted it to him. "Manifestation complete," Drake said of the gift.

Is manifestation as easy and magical as Sam and these stories make it out to be? Should you rent a pricey car or ask a stranger for an audition? Is the world, as some proponents of manifestation say, a mail order catalog of dreams just waiting for you to declare what you want?

The answer is yes, and no. Manifestation isn't magic. It's not a "gift" bestowed on some lucky people, as Ariana Grande says, or a mystical secret for a select few. It's not about transmuting time and space or bending dimensions. There are no spirits waiting to bless you with bounty if you follow the rules.

Manifestation is in fact so real that it's mundane, ordinary, and accessible to anyone who wants it. There's no esoteric code to unlock or special skills to be born with. You don't need to make a vision board or write your goals down thirty-three times a day as some manifestation enthusiasts say. Also, there's no need to go broke renting a car you can't afford because, despite the consumerist messages we all hear, spiritual exploration doesn't require spending money or buying things. Throughout this book, I've mentioned a few times when I've had the privilege to travel or go to retreats as part of my spiritual journey, but I want to be clear that those experiences aren't necessary for the Karma of Success. In fact, for the manifestation process you'll learn here, all you need is a journal, a pen, and your rich inner world.

Yes, all your dreams can come true with something as simple as writing in a notebook. When you do the specific journaling practice that you'll learn over the next few chapters, and when you do it every day, what you're actually doing is rewiring your brain. You're shifting the very nature of how you think about yourself, your capabilities, and the world around you.

You're reprogramming the old, self-defeating patterns that have held you back from getting what you want. Soon you'll be manifesting, and you'll be doing it by building a healthy mind. Now is the time to get everything you want, and all it takes is treating yourself the way you've always deserved to be treated.

CHAPTER 10

WHAT YOU
SEE IS . . .

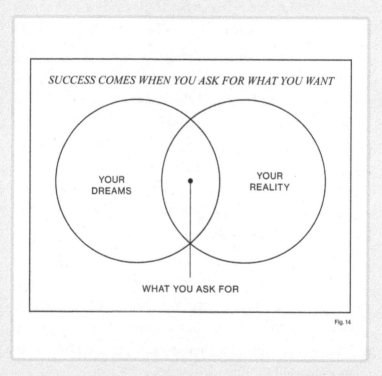

Fig. 14 | **Success Comes When You Ask for What You Want**
You'll never receive what you don't ask for. Declare your dreams loudly to the world.

efore the Buddha became the Buddha, he was a human just like you or me. As legends tell it, he began
his life as Siddhartha Gautama, a wealthy prince so
sheltered that he encountered poverty, old age, and disease
for the first time only at age twenty-nine. Then and there,
Siddhartha cut off his hair, traded his clothes for monk's
robes, renounced his title and wealth, and dedicated his life
to ending the suffering of all beings. He tried fasting, eating
just one grain of rice a day, then nothing at all, until he was
skin and bones and realized that deprivation was not the
path to wisdom. After six years of wandering and meditation, he sat beneath a peepal tree and decided not to
rise until he had reached enlightenment or death. After
seven weeks of challenges, at age thirty-five, Siddhartha
reached nirvana, liberating himself from samsara, the endless cycle of death, rebirth, and suffering in which we all
participate.

Because the Buddha was human, he knew that enlightenment was also possible for everyone. His mission was to
spread the message that any person, no matter their past or
present, possessed Buddha nature and the potential to become awakened.

According to a story told about the Buddha, one day he
traveled to a village where he was met by a skeptic. "You say
that everyone is capable of enlightenment," the man said,
"but if it is true, why aren't we all enlightened?" The Buddha smiled and gave him a simple exercise in response.

"Make a list of everyone in your village and write down what they most wish for next to their names."

"Easy," the man thought, and shortly afterward he returned to the Buddha with his list, pleased with his quick activity. "Tell me," the Buddha asked, "how many of the people on your list seek enlightenment?" The skeptic looked down and saw that his neighbors had asked for oxen, riches, and bigger homes, but not a single person wished for enlightenment. "None," he said, averting his eyes from the Buddha.

"I say that every person is capable of enlightenment, but no one wants to be enlightened," the Buddha said. "How can you get anything which you don't even wish for?" He continued, "The villagers do not ask for enlightenment because they do not see themselves as worthy of it. This must change. If you want it, you must consider it to be possible." Listening to the words of the Buddha, the man understood that in order to achieve anything great, he first had to desire it, and second, he had to believe himself to be deserving.

What about you? Have you wished for what you truly want? If not, take a second to ponder why. Could it be that you, like the villagers, have asked for what you think is possible instead of what you truly desire? When it comes to your career, do you say you want an ox when what you really want is enlightenment? Do you pine for a promotion when what you truly crave is meaning?

It can be a terrifying prospect to admit what we really want. It feels scary to get our hopes up for a dream that we're not sure will happen, so we try to protect ourselves from disappointment by pretending that we never wanted it in the first place. This self-protection mechanism doesn't actually work. Whether we consciously admit it or not, the dreams we have persist. They continue to lurk in the background of our hearts, even when we push them away. So isn't it better to acknowledge them and take action instead of wishing they'd go away? Whether you suppress or act on your dreams, getting hurt is inevitable. But only action holds the possibility for great happiness, too.

Sometimes we turn away from our dreams, convincing ourselves that they're silly, selfish, or greedy. We think to ourselves, *Who am I to want more when what I have is perfectly fine?* A helpful way to work with this guilt of wanting is to remember how accomplishing your dreams will help others. You see, every personal dream also contains the desire to make the world a better place in ways big and small. When it comes to my podcast, to me, success isn't about booking famous guests or having huge numbers. It's purely about supporting as many people as I can to reach their greatest potential. Whenever I sit down to record an episode, I first close my eyes and meditate. I imagine sending loving energy to the wonderful listeners around the world and the Inner Geniuses that reside within them. It's a way of grounding my dream in service.

It's not selfish to have dreams. In fact, they're a natural part of our human existence. Dreams of a better world are what inspired our ancestors to cook with fire, plant crops, and rise up against oppressors. Dreams are as essential to life as breath, and ignoring them erodes your innate energy, confidence, and vitality. As we work through the first step of Manifesting Mindfully, Visualization, you'll learn how to befriend your dreams and thus transform them from a frightening prospect to a deeply comforting part of your life.

Visualization is the simple act of picturing what you want. It's exactly like daydreaming or using your imagination. That's all there is to it. It's both deceptively easy and infinitely powerful because of a unique design feature of our brains; our minds can't actually distinguish between real and imagined activity. So much so, that the mere act of picturing a situation makes your brain believe that it's actually happening to you. That's why watching a video of rock climbing can activate a fear of heights, or why cancer patients who imagine their tumors shrinking experience improved immune function and a higher quality of life. The mind and the body are not so separate after all.

High performance athletes have known this for decades. The East German Olympics team started using visualization practices in the 1960s, and in the seventies, a book of techniques was read by the University of Michigan football team. These days, everyone does it. Michael Phelps, a champion swimmer and the most decorated Olympian of all time, visualizes every race in his mind months in advance. He imagines every detail from the smell of chlorine in the air to the music playing in his headphones. He pictures himself removing his robe and stepping onto the slippery deck. Then, he mentally walks through every stroke of the race, until he sees himself finishing as the winner. When the real race comes along, he is calm and confident because he's already won it a hundred times in his mind.

What we think matters, and our thoughts are precious

resources. On average, we each have over six thousand thoughts a day. That's six thousand chances every twenty-four hours to imagine ourselves reaching our goals. We waste most of these chances because we lack intention. Instead of directing our brains, our brains direct us. Thoughts come in and out at random. We are in the back seat while anxiety and worry drive us around in circular loops. Imagine what would happen if you replaced every anxious thought with a vision of winning. Who would you be if your default mindset was one of success?

The good news is, no matter how little we've done it in the past, we all know how to visualize perfectly right now. Without even realizing it, you've actually had dozens, maybe hundreds of opportunities to practice it. This is because visualization is exactly like ordering food at a restaurant. In one situation, you ask your server for what you want. In the other, you ask the universe to deliver your dreams. It truly is that simple.

Let's practice now. Picture yourself at a restaurant. If you want blueberry pancakes and bacon, what would you say to your server? If your answer is something like, "Can I have the blueberry pancakes and bacon?" then you're right! You did it. You ordered well, and your food is coming. It's just as simple and straightforward when it comes to manifesting your dreams. Unfortunately, most of us present our thoughts as half-formed wishes like, "I want to make more money someday" or "It'd be nice to work for myself." Imagine what would happen if you did this at a restaurant. You'd say, "I might like something sweet with something salty, at some point in the future whenever the timing works out." Not only would your waiter be completely confused, more importantly, they'd have no idea what to bring you. There's almost no chance you'd get the blueberry pancakes and bacon that you want. The same is true for the universe. How can it possibly provide what you want if you don't ask for it specifically?

There's no time like the present, so let's go ahead and visualize together now. First, take a moment to settle into silence and stillness. Take three deep breaths and ask your intuition to join you as you create this visualization. Over the next few moments, you'll be imagining your life five years from now. Think about what year it will be in five years, and how old you'll be then. Now picture having everything you want. Imagine you're living your dream life, and it's happened through a combination of hard work, support from others, and lots of good luck.

Go ahead and picture having the perfect career in five years. What is it? What's your workday like? How much money do you have? What have you accomplished, and what are you most proud of? Next, imagine your surroundings. Where do you live, and what do you love most about your home? Who are the loved ones around you, and what's the general feeling of your life? For example, it could be exhilarating, or peaceful, or both. Finally, what are all the things you love most about being you? Feel free to fill in any details that come to mind, no matter how big or small. Maybe you have the piano you've always wanted, your own charitable foundation, or unconditional love. This is your chance to give your vision depth.

When you're done, take out a piece of paper and get it

all down. If you want, you can start like this: "In five years, it's the year_____, and I am _____ years old," then let it all flow, writing in the present tense. When you're finished, read it again, preferably aloud. If you notice that you were overly general in writing out your dream, go back and state what you want with precision and detail. Say the amount of money in your savings account. Declare the details of your home. Own your vision.

My favorite boss would always say, "You don't get what you don't ask for," and he was right. Throughout my career, I left a lot of opportunities on the table because I hadn't stated my true desires. I was getting promoted and taking on more responsibility, but my path wasn't my greatest wish—it was just happening by default. I didn't have my own plan, so I became a cog in someone else's. After I met Sam, I'd always say, "At some point, I hope I love my work as much as he does. Maybe I could even write a book one day." I was asking for something sweet with something salty, at some point in the future whenever the timing works out. So, if you want the pancakes, ask for the pancakes. If you desire enlightenment, don't ask for an ox. Say the things you want and be clear about it.

Know that the dream you wrote down isn't set in stone. It's okay if what you want today isn't the same in a year. It's natural for our desires to evolve as our life experiences do. I was almost a decade into my career before I started manifesting a future as an executive coach. I didn't even know the job existed until I was thirty-one. The point is, just as we discussed in the first Expansion, your life is meant to change, and it's okay to want blueberry pancakes today and crêpes tomorrow.

Whenever I see a majestic old tree, I like to imagine that it was once a tiny seed. When you really think about it, it seems hard to believe that something so tall and strong emerged from something equally small and fragile. However, the miracle of it happens all the time. It's just what trees do, and it's a normal part of living. Now consider your own life and see how those very same miracles are also possible when it comes to growing your dreams. Just as nature endows the tiny acorn with everything it needs to grow into the mighty oak, you already have everything you require to realize your dreams, no matter how far away or how improbable they seem to you today. You, as you are in this very moment, are worthy of enlightenment.

MANIFESTATION EXERCISE #1

Once you've honed your vision, take out your journal and on a blank page write "My Vision" at the top and get it all down. Dog-ear the page so you can come back and reread it often. Finally, set a recurring calendar invite for every six months to make time to revise your vision, knowing that you're free to add or remove anything you want. Your vision belongs to you and you alone.

CHAPTER 11

$2 COFFEE RICH

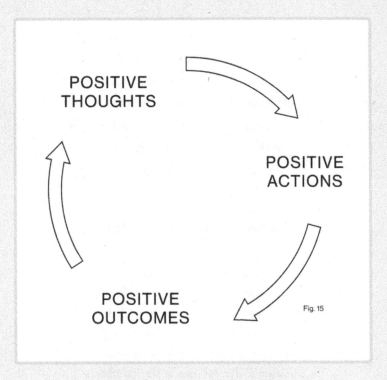

Fig. 15

Fig. 15 | The Law of Attraction

Whatever you focus on multiplies in your life. When you see the world positively, you pave the way for positive outcomes.

For several months in 2019, I did two jobs at once—my venture capital day job that I'd already quit, and the all-consuming process of launching my new company, Reset, a coaching studio for hosting corporate retreats and self-help classes in New York City. I slept very little then. I was scattered and frazzled and didn't do either job particularly well. When the day finally arrived for me to focus only on Reset, I celebrated by sleeping for sixteen hours straight. I thought the worst was behind me, but I hadn't actually done what Sam had suggested about building a very conservative business plan, so the trouble was just starting.

As my new enterprise took flight, so did the costs, with unforeseen bills on a weekly basis. I'd need a new sound system, then summer hit and I had to order commercial air conditioner units. Some clients complained about the discomfort of the seating, so then I bought sixty feet of custom cushions. A few months later, I was in a precarious financial position. I had invested most of my savings, plus a $100,000 loan, into the pricey renovation of the studio, and I was paying rent in one of Manhattan's most expensive neighborhoods. That, combined with all the unforeseen costs that kept coming, meant that I was losing tens of thousands of dollars a month. In order to pay the bills, I liquidated all my stocks, my long-cultivated 401(k) (with huge penalties for withdrawing early), and, against everything I'd learned about sound fiscal decision-making, took out a $40,000 cash advance against my credit card.

In the space of a few short months, I had gone from a

venture capital job with more financial security that I'd ever imagined to shouldering $140,000 in debt that was accruing ungodly amounts of interest. To top off this untenable situation, I got hit with a $30,000 IRS bill because of a recent change in tax law. I owed three times what the average American makes in a year to a bank, a credit company, and the IRS, and I had no real path to paying it back.

Carrying this debt wasn't just emotionally taxing but also psychologically triggering. I had spent decades crawling my way out of poverty, and I couldn't help but think I had ruined my life and returned myself to the same position. I woke up most days with self-loathing for the decisions I had made. Why had I taken such an unknown leap? Why had I been so optimistic in my business plan? Who was I to think I could follow my dreams? During this time, I was working a minimum of fourteen-hour days, hustling for new clients, leading workshops, and coaching, all while trying to appear calm and grounded for everyone who came into the space. In reality, I was falling apart.

I had recurring nightmares of being homeless. I couldn't even bear to look at my bank account. I was so stressed about my finances that I avoided the mail, burying the avalanche of bills under the dusty workout equipment in my closet. Even though I was supposedly "living my dream" and had been featured in prestigious outlets like *The New York Times* and *Marie Claire*, in truth, I was transported to the trauma of my early years. I couldn't sleep. My hair fell out. I chugged caffeine and sugar and gained ten pounds. I withdrew from the people I loved and picked up smoking again.

Amid my anxiety and agitation, there was a sliver of hope—revenue was steadily growing every month. By the six-month mark, I turned a massive corner. Reset was profitable! Just barely, but at least I wasn't losing money. I made a new, more conservative financial model for how I could pay back the debt slowly, and this time it wound up working. Nine months in, I could feel bits of my former, joyful self coming back to life. But just when I thought that I had survived the worst, COVID-19 crashed into the city and destroyed my only revenue stream: in-person gatherings.

Before I can tell you how this story ends, we must first discuss a concept that's critical to understanding what happened to me next. This concept is the Law of Attraction. The fundamental premise is simple enough—it's the idea that *like attracts like*. For instance, the more joyful you are, the more reasons for joy you attract into your life. Conversely, the more you complain, the more life hands you reasons to complain.

Can you spot the Law of Attraction in your own life? Do you know anyone who seems to have everything? Not only are they happy and successful, but they always get what they want? On the other hand, do you know someone who is always mired in chaos? Do they gripe to you about one upsetting event after another?

I do. I've seen the Law of Attraction in action, up close. The first archetype, the person who always gets what they want, is me. I've had more lucky breaks than I can count, some of which you've read about here. The second archetype, the one that bad fortune follows, is also me. For long stretches of my life, I've been a magnet for unfortunate events. My friends even used to joke that I had the reverse Midas Touch because everything in my path turned to chaos. In my career, I've been handed both great fortune and crushing turmoil. And the only factor that differentiates my fate is how grateful I am. Gratitude. That's all it comes down to.

Gratitude is life's greatest magnet for luck. If you remember that the Rule of Attraction indicates that like attracts like, then it stands to reason that the more grateful you feel about the resources in your life, the more resources will come your way. Oprah kept a gratitude list every day without fail for ten years. She attributes her success to the consistency of her practice. By living in a constant state of appreciation, she was handed even more blessings at which to marvel. It was a benevolent flywheel. The more luck she had, the more grateful she felt, and the more grateful she felt, the more luck came her way, and on and on and on, until she became the global superstar we all know today.

Visual artist EJ Hill also attributes his success to gratitude. His specific practice doesn't just live in his journal; it's a public and highly visible form of giving thanks. A few years ago, EJ made the decision to change his professional bio from what you'd normally expect of a working artist to a simple list of all the people for whom he gives thanks. EJ's choice was bold and courageous, especially in the art world, an industry that relies heavily on the currency of accolades and proximity to important people. Galleries, buyers, and institutions assess the worth of an artist based on the awards they've won, the residencies they've attended, and where they've shown their work. EJ chose, in spite of major pushback from others, to leave out all those usual facts and to instead name the teachers, loved ones, and role models who were critical to his success.

His view of gratitude is spacious. He thanks friends from kindergarten that have nothing to do with the art world, and even gives gratitude to people who are no longer in his life. In addition to family and former professors, EJ also thanks the musician Lauryn Hill and the group TLC, women with whom he has no personal relationship but whose songs and music videos influenced him in critical ways when he was growing up. As EJ, a queer, Black artist, explained to me, "I thought about who I am, and how I've come to think in such expanded terms about concepts like feminism, and it doesn't come from dense academic texts. It comes from three young, twentysomething Black women in Atlanta who sang that they weren't too proud to beg for sex in 1992."

Recently, EJ's gratitude list was prominently displayed in North Adams, Massachusetts, when he achieved something most artists only dream of—a solo exhibition at a major museum. There, at MASS MoCA, in a space nearly as large as a football field, EJ debuted his show, *Brake Run Helix*, featuring a 260-foot-long, pale pink, fully functioning roller coaster he created. It was a statement that all people should have access to pleasure and joy, despite the structures that prevent it. There were, of course, immense ups and downs that led EJ to this pinnacle moment. He's often contemplated leaving the art world completely, and at one point he could no longer deny how unhappy he was becoming. His decision to change his bio was so much more than writing words on a page—it was a choice not to contort his innate values or personhood, even if he risked being kicked out of the club for not following the rules. "I've been trying to get back to the core version of me," he said. His biography / gratitude list is the embodiment of his Intuitive Self.

We all have the opportunity to do what EJ did and use the practice of gratitude as a grounding and centering expression of self. However, we've all experienced moments in our lives when it feels impossible to scrounge up any semblance of appreciation. It's a predicament because gratitude works in the same way light does.

When your environment is already sunny, it's easy to generate even more brightness. You can easily walk across the floor, flip on a lamp, and create even more light. But when you're living in pitch black painful darkness, and you can't even see your hand in front of you, how can you possibly make your way to new sources of light? How do you connect with gratitude when there's absolutely nothing to appreciate? That's the question I asked myself after I was forced to shut down the Reset studio just as it had started making money. What could I, at the age of thirty-five, having just lost my life savings, possibly feel grateful for? I took a step back, reconsidered my situation, and found that the answer was *anything*.

The very same day I shut the doors to the studio, I began my gratitude practice. Each evening before bed, I'd list as many things to be grateful for as I could, no matter how insignificant they seemed, and it changed me. Knowing I was responsible for recording good things trained me to notice even the tiniest moments of joy. Through this new lens, there was so much to be grateful for. When I bought myself a $2 cup of coffee, I gave gratitude for being able to afford such a treat. Before every meal, I paused for thirty seconds and gave thanks for the food on my plate, remembering the many people in the world who are hungry. I gave gratitude for the few clients I had left and showered my professional network in thank-you notes and gifts of appreciation. Every month, when I just barely paid my rent, instead of lamenting my deflating account balance, I focused on how lucky I was and the wealth I had to be able to pay my rent on time.

Around this time, I married my partner, Dev, in a pandemic-style wedding of twenty-seven guests in his parents' backyard. Before the pandemic, we'd had a different vision involving a huge gathering of our loved ones in New York City. Now there were more restrictions and fewer options, and I had far less personal resources. Still, with my new mindset of deep gratitude, I thought, "Why wait for perfect when there's so much that we have right now?"

If you had asked me about that year while I was in the midst of it, I would've told you without hesitation that it was the worst year of my life. Now I look back and see that it was also the luckiest. That year was the beginning of everything. It changed me. It transformed me into an optimistic, grateful person, and that paved the way for the Karma of Success. The late Vietnamese Buddhist monk Thích Nhất Hạnh said, "Suffering and happiness, they are both organic, like a flower and garbage." He explained that a flower, through the natural process of decay, ends up in the trash to become garbage. Then, similarly, that garbage decomposes into the soil and eventually creates a flower.

I find great comfort in this idea that suffering and happiness are not so different from each other. They're not opposite ends of the spectrum as we believe them to be, but rather, one transforms into the other. Flowers become garbage, as happiness becomes suffering, and suffering becomes happiness, too. The secret to life isn't running away from suffering, but rather embracing it and learning the miraculous process of turning garbage into flowers.

Without a studio to run, I was underemployed, and after a career of chronic long hours, I finally had leisurely stretches of time. I bought a dozen books on writing, giving gratitude for each one, and inhaled them cover to cover. Then I wrote a hundred pages of emotional little essays that weren't very good; but still, I had this moment to pursue a lifelong dream of writing.

I also had the freedom to listen to my Inner Genius and try out new projects. I created prolifically, launching online courses, a newsletter, and support groups for founders, and I relaunched Reset's Instagram account and podcast, using them both as a way to share my learnings. Some of my efforts were successful and some of them weren't, but I gave gratitude for the failures, building my habit of turning garbage into flowers.

Fast-forward to a year after closing the studio, through a number of lucky breaks and some hard work, I fully paid back every dollar of my debt. I was doing work I loved, coaching a full roster of founders, and six months later I signed a book deal with my dream publisher. Six months after that, Dev and I bought a home in the country, both of us contributing equally. It was beautiful what grew from that garbage, supposedly the worst year of my life.

This is a long, personal story to give color to this rather simple step of how to Manifest Mindfully: Practice gratitude. When you see yourself as having everything you need, you soon receive everything you want. The mistake we often make is to focus only on the first step of manifesting—visualization. We set the vision, fixate on it with our minds, and then go after our goals with rabid fervor. This focus on seeking that which is missing can blind us to what we already have. That's why we need gratitude as its mirror.

As children, we learn that "please" and "thank you" are the most important words, but the truth is that thank you is so much more valuable when it comes to manifesting. Yes, you want your goal. You say, "Dear universe, *please* give me what I want," but the important thing is that the *thank yous* outweigh the *pleases*. Spend twice as much time appreciating what you have as yearning for what you want. Don't worry, this math comes easily. You'll find there is so much to be grateful for now that you know how to look.

MANIFESTATION EXERCISE #2

✳

Begin a daily gratitude practice, ending every day with at least three things you're grateful for. Be sure to look out for garbage transformed into a flower—meaning, think about the worst thing that happened to you that day and reframe it to notice the silver lining. For instance, if your boss gave you constructive feedback, appreciate having a mentor who cares about your growth.

CHAPTER 12

CONFIDENCE BANK

HOW TO BUILD CONFIDENCE

PAST	Make a list of ten moments you're proud of.
PRESENT	Write down three things you did well *every* day.
FUTURE	Visualize yourself realizing your dreams.

Fig. 16

Fig. 16 | How to Build Confidence

We all have the ability to create more confidence. It simply requires opening your mind to your innate greatness.

ow that you've learned how to work with Visualization and Gratitude, the third step of Manifesting Mindfully is Confidence. This chapter will teach you how to cultivate it. Confidence is the great equalizer. It's something we all struggle with across all backgrounds and experiences. So if you've ever wrestled with your self-worth, trust me when I tell you that you're not alone.

It's essential in my coaching work to help my clients develop confidence. Think of the high-stakes hamster wheel they're on. As venture capital–backed founders, they're required to raise millions of dollars every year or two, meaning back-to-back meetings with dozens of investors whose job it is to critique them and their business. The process is a catch-22. Founders go in looking for validation. They want VCs to be interested. They crave confirmation that their business is succeeding. They're hoping that the outcome of the fundraiser will boost their confidence, but what they really need is to have an unshakeable belief in themselves from the beginning.

The definition of confidence is "a feeling or consciousness of one's powers." The key word here is *feeling*; note that confidence is *internal*. Bragging about one's achievements and showing off are not confidence. Those are *external* behaviors that could be linked to confidence but often aren't. It doesn't matter if you are quiet, introverted, or reserved, because confidence is not something we do but rather something we feel within us.

This brings us to the biggest myth when it comes to

confidence. In this material world we live in, we're falsely told that it's something we have to earn. We believe that we have to succeed our way into it. *I'll feel good about myself when I get the job*, we think, but then we get the job and the goal posts move and we think, *I'll feel good about myself after I'm promoted*. After that, it's yet another finish line. Our self-worth is perpetually deferred into the future, ad infinitum, leaving us chasing an unreachable horizon.

Ironically, I only developed *true* self-confidence the year I was in tremendous debt. Before this, my sense of self-worth hinged entirely on what other people thought about me and was dependent on how well I did in school or at work. That year, all my successes had disappeared. I had publicly closed up shop. There was nothing to brag about. No more newspapers and magazines were writing about me, and I was without bosses or colleagues to confirm that I was doing okay. Every channel I had tapped for confidence in the past had dried up.

I had relied on other people to feed me for so long, that when they stopped, I was starving and lacked the means to nourish myself. Eventually I grew exhausted with my self-flagellating thoughts and decided to learn how to love myself, regardless of the external circumstances. I was tired of feeling good only when life was good. I was done with having confidence like a yo-yo fluctuating with the inevitable ups and downs of life. That way of being was unstable, felt terrible, and was preventing me from being bold.

Any trailblazer will tell you that doing something different means that many people won't understand you. There will inevitably be critics who want to reinforce the old way of doing things and disparage your vision. Imagine if you were going after a bold, different dream, but you also needed validation from others. It would be impossible. The two needs of inner authenticity and external approval cannot exist at the same time. If you want to live a life that is uniquely yours, it's essential to build up your confidence from within.

When Alymamah Rashed moved from Kuwait to New York City for school, it was the beginning of many firsts. She was the first in her family to pursue a career in the arts and the first woman to study abroad. In New York City, the firsts continued. She was seventeen, living on her own for the first time, and a complete beginner to the Western conception of art. Sadly, it was also her first experience with racism. As the only Muslim woman in the program, many of Alymamah's professors assumed she wouldn't succeed because of her background. During one studio visit from a teacher, he looked at her hijab and said, "Why are you here? Shouldn't you be back home driving a Ferrari?" In reality, Alymamah could afford her studies only because she had won a selective national scholarship.

After graduating, she applied for dozens of jobs at galleries, and after a few weeks of interviewing, it was clear that the bias she experienced in school was even more prevalent in the working world. Despite many rejections involving her hijab, Alymamah was persistent, and she finally landed a role at a startup gallery. On her first day of work, her coworker took one look at her and asked her if she believed in ISIS. Alymamah later came across more discriminatory messages about her between that coworker and the gallery director.

Over and over, people made constant assumptions about who she was simply because of her appearance. She was assumed to be too conservative, too wealthy, and too Muslim to fit into the art world. Still, she was a trailblazer on a mission, and she never let the opinions of others impact what she thought of herself. Now back in Kuwait, she's built a successful international career as a working artist, represented by dream galleries. Alymamah, just like her work, is confident, bold, and unafraid to take up space, no matter what other people say.

There were two paths she could have taken. If Alymamah had believed what others said, she would have given up on her dreams. Instead, she remained solid in her self-belief despite many tough rejections and discriminatory experiences. We all have the same choice in front of us. Behind door one is a life fraught with ups and downs of self-worth, with your confidence tethered to external events and others' opinions. Behind door two is freedom. You unshackle yourself from the critics, detractors, and the false narratives that say you're unworthy.

There is a second big myth about confidence. It's the idea that either you're born with it or you aren't. We think of it as a fixed and unmovable trait, something bestowed through genetics. The truth is you have power here. The amount of confidence you feel is within your control. Your thoughts and actions shape your self-worth every moment of every day, and it can happen fast. Even if you don't feel confident now, there's nothing stopping you from having an abundance of it soon.

Dr. Nate Zinsser, an expert in the psychology of human performance, compares our confidence levels to a bank account. The balance in the account goes up and down depending on our experiences in life. Say you do well on a project and your boss gives you kudos. That's a deposit into your confidence bank account. Then you're passed over for a promotion and the job goes to your peer. That's a huge withdrawal. The year I closed Reset, my confidence bank account was below zero. I had overdrawn and was left with a negative self-worth.

To fill up your account, you don't have to wait for other people to make deposits through their praise and validation. You can do it for yourself. In fact, you are the only one who gets to decide if you feel good or bad about yourself. You have the sole authority to make deposits and withdrawals, and right now, at your disposal, you have two powerful tools for increasing the balance in your confidence bank account.

The first is called your Top Ten, and we'll do it together now. This is an exercise to mine your memory for evidence that you are a worthy, remarkable person. You simply start from the beginning of your life and write down ten moments of joy or accomplishment that you're proud of. We all accumulate far more than ten over the course of living, but don't feel bad if you have trouble thinking of that many. It's not because you haven't done enough or aren't good enough. It just means that you've gotten out of practice of appreciating yourself, so it's even more critical for you to do this exercise now.

Your Top Ten can be specific achievements or accolades, but they can also be moments that don't involve winning anything. For instance, on my Top Ten, I have my third and fourth years of college. The year before then, I nearly failed out. I was on academic suspension and in a bleak mental state. Instead of giving up, I went to therapy, was gentle with myself, and ended up getting all As and B+s my last two years of school. Top Ten events don't need to be rainbows, butterflies, and awards. You can list times you helped someone you love, moments you've pushed yourself outside of your comfort zone, or instances when you've stood up for yourself. Remember that the Karma of Success is about your internal world, not the external, so think about times when you've felt good about yourself, even if no one praised you for it. The majority of the moments on my Top Ten involve times of failure I found a way to rectify. These aren't obvious wins to anyone else but myself. But these are moments I personally couldn't be more proud of.

The second exercise to build your confidence is part of the journaling practice that you'll do to manifest your greatest goals. Every day, after you've written your gratitude list, you should also make a Self-Gratitude list, writing down all the things you did well that day. It's a moment to do something rare—to appreciate yourself. Journal entry by journal entry, you're rewiring your thoughts to not depend on others for validation. Your Top Ten is a huge check that you deposit into your confidence bank account when funds are low, while your Self-Gratitude list is a daily top off that keeps it at a healthy level.

Just as with the Top Ten, what goes on your Self-Gratitude list doesn't have to be extraordinary. In fact, I'm a big proponent of making deposits from even the smallest situations in life. Back when I was at my lowest in terms of self-worth and energy, I gave myself deposits for small things, like making the bed and doing laundry. I'd feel Self-Gratitude when I cleared out my email inbox, or when I did a good job coaching a client. I'd appreciate myself for doing what I could every day, even if my list wasn't impressive to anyone else besides me.

Pay attention to the circumstances of your life and balance your checkbook accordingly. If there's a day when you feel rejected and you've taken a huge hit to your confidence bank account, counteract it accordingly by rewriting your Top Ten list. If you're learning a new skill and don't feel very good at it yet, be extra diligent about your daily Self-Gratitude list. You can even read your journal entries aloud to really let the deposits sink in.

Self-Gratitude is a powerful tool. By simply noticing what you did well, you're doing the life-altering work of changing your inner dialogue. That little critical voice in your head transforms into your biggest cheerleader. Remember, we think six thousand thoughts a day. That is six thousand chances to appreciate yourself. Over time, you don't just feel confident, you *become* confident, and there are no people or circumstances that can take that from you.

Building your confidence is essential to Manifesting Mindfully. Visualization is a great first step, and Gratitude is also important, of course. But unless you also build the muscle of Confidence, then nothing will happen. Just as the Buddha said to the villagers who shared their greatest desires, you must believe that you're deserving before you can receive what you want in life. By practicing Visualization, you start to believe in your *dreams*. Then with Gratitude, you begin to believe in the *universe*. Finally, when you practice Confidence, you start to believe in *yourself*. Trust in your dreams, the universe, and yourself—that's all manifestation comes down to.

MANIFESTATION EXERCISE #3

Write your Top Ten into your journal. Dog-ear the page so you can return to it anytime you need a big confidence deposit. Today, start your Self-Gratitude list. When you are done, read it aloud, then set a timer for two minutes, close your eyes, say "Thank you" to yourself, and notice how it feels.

Journals
Past and Present

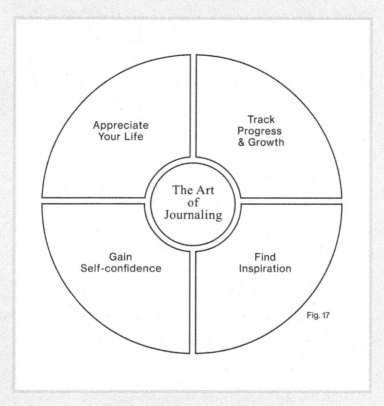

Fig. 17 | The Art of Journaling

Your journal is far more than paper and scribbles. It is your tool for shaping the person you're becoming.

n the tenth century, the ladies of the royal Japanese court began an extraordinary cultural movement. They began keeping pillow books, the first introspective journals in our history. These small notebooks, tucked under bedcovers, held the daily thoughts, feelings, and dreams of these contemplative royal women. We are lucky that some of their writing has been preserved, including that of Sei Shōnagon, who wrote a list in her pillow book entitled "Things That Make One's Heart Beat Faster." Here is what she wrote:

Sparrows feeding their young.

To pass a place where babies are playing.

To sleep in a room where some fine incense has been burnt.

To notice that one's elegant Chinese mirror has become a little cloudy.

To see a gentleman stop his carriage before one's gate and instruct his attendants to announce his arrival.

To wash one's hair, make one's toilet, put on scented robes; even if not a soul sees one, these preparations still produce an inner pleasure . . .

She was, a thousand years before us, writing a gratitude journal of her own. This impulse is ancient. We humans have an innate desire to record and reflect on the particulars of our lives because the practice is so beneficial. Benjamin Franklin attributed his success to adherence to his thirteen virtues. He would dedicate each week to a different virtue and reflect daily about whether he had embodied it. Barack Obama has a long-standing habit of keeping a diary. This practice of writing, he said, "has been an important exercise to clarify what I believe, what I see, what I care about." My favorite, Octavia Butler, epitomizes the art of manifesting through journaling. "I shall be a bestselling writer," she wrote in her notebook. "After *Imago*, each of my books will be on the bestseller lists. . . . I will find the way to do this. So be it! See to it!" As we know, she reached her goals and more.

As you hone your daily practice, you are joining a long lineage of people who have used journaling to improve the quality of their lives. When done consistently over time, not only does this practice help you manifest, it also creates a record of the unique person you are. I've kept journals for fifteen years. That pile of messy Moleskines and spiral-bounds is my prized possession. My journals have been with me as I made mistakes and bad decisions, then grew up and built a career and a family. They and they alone know the complete epiphanies and anxieties of my adult life. Even if I forget the details, the journals always know.

Several years ago, when I was recently divorced, I started daydreaming about a home in the country, somewhere deep in nature where I could grow vegetables and host big groups of people. My Inner Genius yearned for something stable, something permanent, a place to cultivate a grounded way of living. At that point, my desire was the epitome of a pipe dream. I had zero money for a down payment and a bad credit score, and was about to start that job in venture capital that would tie me to the city for many years. I didn't have a car or even a driver's license, so the idea of me on a big plot of land in the country was laughable.

In fact, me in any permanent location seemed ridiculous. I spent most of my childhood moving from one temporary apartment to the next. I changed schools eight times before I was eighteen and felt constant jealousy for my friends with real, green backyards. My heart ached for not just a house but a *home*, with a pantry full of food, a cozy den for watching movies with my brother, and a loving dog by my side. Instead, my only constant was instability. I got used to moving abruptly and without notice, throwing my minimal belongings into trash bags and into the car. Then, when I grew up, I perpetuated that same pattern through my own choices, living in a dozen more places over fifteen years. I could never let myself settle anywhere for very long, even in good situations, and my sudden movements and broken leases hurt many of my friends and roommates in the process. Sean, Bobby, San, Ray, Charlene, Alyssa, and Dolores—thank you for putting up with me.

As I started to let myself dream again of home as an adult, I indulged my desires and wrote a long list of features in my journal. I wrote that I wanted a big piece of land with some small buildings so I could host a dozen people at a time. I wanted a garden, an orchard, and even, unrealistically, a secret passageway. I pictured myself cooking for a busy, bustling house full of people. I saw joy. I saw love. Then, when I filled the pages in that notebook, I stuck it on the shelf and forgot about my dream, busy with my new job and the exciting city life that came with it.

Recently, as Dev and I moved to our new place in the country, my intuition guided me to pull out that old notebook. I was curious what I'd written seven years earlier. When I got to the right page, a distinct chill traveled the length of my body. Everything I'd wanted but forgotten had somehow come true. I manifested my vision, down to the garden, the orchard, and the secret passageway. Then things got even spookier. At the bottom of the page was the name for my dream home—*The Uplands*. I had written those words three years before I'd even met Dev. When I finally did meet him, one of the first things I learned was that he was from Victoria, British Columbia, Canada. It was his favorite place in the world, and he'd grown up in the same house since the age of nine in a picturesque neighborhood called, of all names, The Uplands. As I read my journal, I understood that I hadn't just manifested my list from seven years earlier. I'd also finally realized, at age thirty-seven, that original childhood yearning for a real home.

If you take anything away from this chapter, let it be this: keep a journal. Your life is worth the effort it takes to record it. Your thoughts, feelings, and wishes are meaningful, and they deserve their own perfect lodging. Give them a home where they can settle in. And in that act of recording your life, remember that it's not just about immortalizing *how things were.* Know that you will also be defining *how things will be.* Together, you and your journal will manifest everything you want in life.

In the past few chapters, we've outlined the components to do this.

1. Write down your vision and read it regularly. Close your eyes, and, like Michael Phelps, visualize it happening to you in precise detail.
2. Keep a Gratitude list and a Self-Gratitude list every day. Basking in what you write, consciously fall in love with your life and the person you are.

Remember that none of this works if it's treated like a chore. You must fully engage with these two steps and make them your own. When you open your journal each day, tune into your Inner Genius and ask, what else do I need? Perhaps in addition to Gratitude and Self-Gratitude, you also want to do another exercise from this book, like writing a letter to your Inner Genius, or jotting down a new Top Ten. We humans are not stagnant. What we need vacillates, so use your journaling time as an opportunity to tend to your unique needs that day.

I don't do this all the time, but when I feel off and in need of rerouting, I practice affirmations. For example, I use these affirmations when I'm overwhelmed, writing them down several times in my journal:

I do enough. I have enough. I am enough.

The work will get done at exactly
the right time.

I have a client who is fundraising right now. The business is bigger than ever and growing faster than he can comprehend. "I am deserving. I am worthy" is the affirmation he writes in the morning. Another client uses this one—"I am calm, courageous, and confident"—to remind himself of the CEO he set out to be. When I work with my clients, I don't give them the affirmations to use. They know the right words on their own. That is the beauty of affirmations. Your Inner Genius knows exactly what it needs to help you generate the Karma of Success.

In 400 BCE a sage named Lao Tzu wrote a spiritual text called the *Tao Te Ching*, eighty-one short chapters that read like poetry and describe the Tao, which is the path for all beings to live in harmony with the universe. Despite its age, the *Tao Te Ching* has been translated to Western languages over 250 times and its wisdom still matters for our modern world. This is from chapter twenty-eight, "Turning Back":

Recognize the masculine

But turn back to the feminine

And become the world's riverbed

Always true and unswerving,

Becoming a newborn child again.

Recognize the light

But turn back to the dark

And become a pattern to the world

True and unerring power

Going back again to boundlessness.

These words remind us that life is about movement. We are meant to stay in motion, flowing from yin to yang, dark to light, making progress forward and then reversing. The true nature of your life is dynamic, so why not decide what direction it will take? Now you have all the skills to make your dreams a reality. You've learned how to Manifest Mindfully by expanding your capacity for Vision, Gratitude, and Confidence. You know the journaling process that supports you. What happens to you next need not be up to chance or a stroke of luck; you are the one deciding who you will become.

ENRICHING
YOUR ENERGY

✳

ongratulations. You've arrived at the midpoint of this book having mastered the first two Spiritual Strategies. Through Spiritual Strategy #1, Inquiring Inward, you learned how to make space for your inner world so that you can tune in to the messages from your Inner Genius. Through Spiritual Strategy #2, Manifesting Mindfully, you harnessed the power of your mind to become a visionary, grateful, and confident person who always gets what they want. Now we've arrived at Spiritual Strategy #3, Enriching Your Energy. Over the next few chapters, you'll learn how to provide the fuel your Inner Genius needs to shine, no matter the challenges you face.

CHAPTER 13

THE
THREE
TREASURES

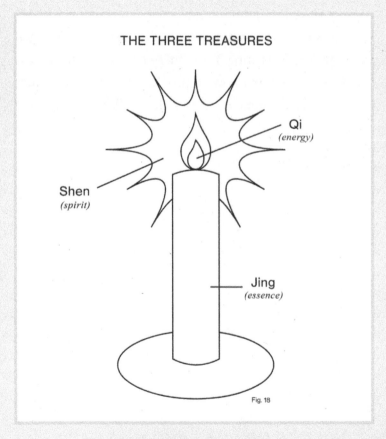

Fig. 18 | The Three Treasures

You are more than just a body and brain. You have three treasures within you that power your brilliance, talent, and capabilities.

've spent my career trying to answer the question of why some founders succeed while others don't. It's not about their background or experience. After all, I've seen founders from Ivy League schools and prestigious companies fail just as often as their less-pedigreed counterparts. I've poured over many years' worth of personality test results and coaching notes, looking for any clue about character or mindset that might signal success.

The first two years of starting a business are the most crucial. This is when founders raise their first institutional capital, their seed round, and then have eighteen to twenty-four months to create a product with enough demand to secure the next round of funding—the Series A. It's a torturous time for most founders. At a minimum, they work twelve-hour days, six days a week, trying to create something out of nothing. They don't sleep well. The product isn't being built fast enough. They have no personal life and hundreds of emails and messages to answer.

Knowing their extreme work schedules, I often ask my clients to check in with themselves and rate their Personal Well-being on a scale from one to five. For these seed stage founders the average is two, meaning that they feel terrible and major changes are needed. No wonder only a small fraction of seed stage companies even makes it to a Series A.

One night a couple years ago, I was coaching a group of Series A and B founders. They were the rare ones, those improbable CEOs who had cleared the seed stage to acquire thousands of clients, bring in significant revenue, and build high-functioning teams in less than two years. As always, I asked each founder to name one suggestion that might be helpful for the rest of the group, assuming that they'd share vendor names, podcast episodes, books, or strategy frameworks they'd found useful. Instead, the founders talked about what they do to support their interior lives. "I give myself a pep talk every morning when I walk to work," one client said. "I read a book that has nothing to do with work at night before bed," another replied. "I do a hundred free throws every day on the basketball court, then come home and play with my kids," one added.

Their faces lit up when they talked about their habits that weren't just healthy but also happy. These activities were sources of joy. When I asked this group to rate their Personal Well-being on a scale from one to five, the average answer was five—peak wellness. I thought about the group of seed stage founders I had seen just the night before with the opposite, rock-bottom scores, and it occurred to me that these two groups of founders had only one year of work separating them, but a world of difference.

The first had figured out how to build a healthy business and then successfully raised an early Series A, while the second group of founders were still waist-deep in muck. Across the two groups, the founders had similar backgrounds and worked in overlapping fields. The only difference between them was what they prioritized. Ironically, the successful founders put their well-being ahead of their jobs. The struggling ones did nothing but work.

We generally think about the concept of self-care as the counterbalance to the pressures of work. We know how important it is to nurture the body and mind after pushing ourselves to the limit. Navigating this interplay, life becomes a seesaw. After a tortuous sprint at work, we may take a long weekend to recuperate, or at the end of a hard day, we'll treat ourselves to yoga and a bath. Then when we feel sufficiently recharged, we jump right back into the fray. While this strategy is certainly better than not taking care of yourself at all, it's missing a critical truth that your Inner Genius knows. To truly unleash the brilliance within you, it's not enough to tend to your body. You must also tend to your *soul*.

As the French philosopher and mystic Pierre Teilhard de Chardin said, "We are not human beings having a spiritual experience. We are spiritual beings having a human experience." Let's consider this for a moment. According to the concept of reincarnation in Buddhism, your primary identity is not with your human body but rather with your soul, which has been reincarnated many times before this life you're in now. There are six realms where you can reincarnate, including good realms like this human one, and evil ones, like the realm of ghosts. Based on the good karma you've accumulated in previous lives, you are here now, in this fortunate experience as a living, breathing human person.

Just think about how special that is. You happen to have made your way onto this giant hunk of spinning rock, endowed with consciousness, passion, and personality. You possess the potential to live out your destiny. You're here to realize your Karma of Success. When you start thinking about yourself primarily as a special soul, instead of just another human worker with obligations, you start to see your life differently. Everyday life isn't just about how you can get by but rather how you can connect with and revitalize your Inner Genius.

There's no way you were given this tremendous gift of human reincarnation just to work like those seed stage founders, clocking endless hours, pushing yourself to the limit, then scrounging up a couple hours of self-care a week just to feel okay. That's definitely not what our souls had in mind when they reincarnated into these precious human lives. Instead, we are here to thrive, flourish, and expand. We're here to free our own Inner Genius and generate the Karma of Success.

That's what Enriching Your Energy is all about. When you learn this Spiritual Strategy, you're not just finding time for self-care in between work commitments. What you're doing is much more profound. You're recognizing that you are a spiritual being experiencing a precious reincarnation, and to honor it, you must put your mind, body, and soul first no matter what.

Energy is a strange and ambiguous word. Most obviously, we think of electricity and fuel. Energy is the power used for providing light and moving machines. The meaning of energy we're talking about here is spiritual energy, also known as Source, Prana, or Universal Life Force. It's the substance that powers all living things—plants, animals, and humans alike. You can't see or touch energy, just as you can't tangibly experience your soul, but they both are real, vital, and exist on the metaphysical plane.

According to traditional Chinese medicine, in the body there are twelve main meridians, energetic passageways that crisscross through the organs and limbs, transporting energy back and forth to give us the ability to thrive. Think of them as twelve powerful extension cords that run head to toe, entwining around your body. When the meridians are open and clear, energy flows freely and powers you and your Inner Genius. When the energy can't flow and gets stuck, this causes mental, spiritual, and physical distress. Enriching Your Energy is about learning how to optimize it so you're functioning at your best—mind, body, and spirit.

We're not accustomed to checking in with our energy the way we know how to pinpoint if we're hungry, tired, or in pain. There's another concept in traditional Chinese medicine called the Three Treasures that offers helpful imagery in understanding how energy serves us (see figure 18). First, bring to mind a candle. That candle is *you*—mind, body and spirt. The first of the three treasures, Jing, which roughly translates to "essence," is the candle wax. Jing is what physically makes the candle a candle, and what makes you physically you. When you have more Jing, you have more wax, and your life will burn longer and stronger than a person with less. To check in with my Jing, I ask myself, *How stable do I feel today?*

The second of the three treasures is Qi, which means "vital life force," and is symbolized by the flame of the candle. When you're low on Qi, you lack vitality, energy, and passion. You have no ability to work. The candle doesn't burn well. No matter what you do, the flame just won't catch. People without enough Qi feel tired and worn out. People with an abundance are lively and active. To check in with my Qi, I ask myself, *How energized do I feel today?*

Finally, the third treasure is Shen. This is your spiritual connection, your true wisdom and consciousness, and is symbolized by the light the candle gives off. When your Shen is strong, your Inner Genius is illuminated and bright. When your Shen is weak, your Inner Genius is dim and obfuscated. You feel anxious, uncertain, and disorganized. When I check in with my Shen, I ask myself, *How clear minded do I feel today?*

When you have enough Energy Resilience, you are like a giant candle, burning strong and giving off beautiful light. You are stable, energized, and clear. Without Energy Resilience. your light and greatest gifts cannot be seen. Let's check in with your Energy Resilience now. Just as I ask my clients, I'll ask you: How is your personal well-being today on a scale from one to five?

5	PERFECT	No changes needed.
4	GOOD	Some things could be better.
3	TOLERABLE	Big adjustments to make.
2	INTOLERABLE	A major overhaul is needed.
1	ROCK-BOTTOM	Completely burned out.

Are you like one of those Series A founders, feeling your best and creating brilliant work despite high pressure and obstacles? Or are you not getting what you want, despite working long and punishing hours? When you start to cultivate your Energy Resilience, you see huge changes in your life, just as those founders did, including:

- **Decisiveness**, so that you think faster with better solutions
- **Creativity** far beyond what you've experienced in the past
- More **confidence, vitality, and enthusiasm** for life
- A consistent feeling of **stability and calm**
- **Better relationships** and communication with your colleagues

What I love most about this third Spiritual Strategy is that it is supportive and nourishing at its core. It all boils down to a simple idea: take care of yourself, and you'll take care of your career. This means going beyond our typical understanding of self-care as a nice to have and something to do when there's extra time. Enriching Your Energy means doing this work consistently for your mind, body, and soul, and especially when it's the hardest to make time for it. This will no doubt require some rewiring if you've been taught that toil equals success.

As you internalize the lessons in this and the next chapter, you will come to understand that prioritizing your personal well-being does not mean you are lazy, unmotivated, or a bad worker. With an open mind, you'll learn habits that, while not directly related to work, will improve your performance more than any office activity can. As you ex-periment with the energetic suggestions in this book, I en-courage you to remember Expansion #1, the Changing Self, and be open to changing your way of thinking. Do not see these suggestions as time drains or diversions from work but rather as the essential soil from which all your greatest successes will grow. That is the Karma of Success.

CHAPTER 14

EASY CLEANSING

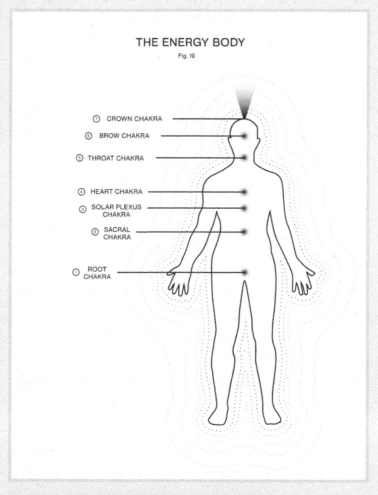

Fig. 19 | The Energy Body

*We intuitively sense one another's energy. Even though it cannot be
seen by the naked eye, the energy body is always making itself known.*

T o remove toxins from our bodies, we sweat, we cry, and we visit the restroom. We rinse our hair, wash our hands, and clean our clothes. We're constantly cleansing the physical form. An important step in Enriching Your Energy is to learn how to cleanse your *energy body*, too. Like a sponge, your energy body absorbs the negativity, chaos, and stress around you, and every once in a while, it needs a big squeeze to release the debris so you can function at your best.

Throughout this book, you've been learning how to sense the unseen. You've practiced tuning in to your Higher Hunches, identifying the ego, and growing your Confidence bank account. These intuitive skills are essential, and also invisible. Unlike the hard skills we apply at work like writing emails, coding, or making spreadsheets, we can't physically see when our intuitive skills need help. We can, however, become fantastic at feeling into them. You can also learn how to assess your own energy body without being able to see it.

This skill comes naturally to us. We all know the feeling of a person with a strong, clear energy. You immediately feel calm, comfortable, and inspired around them. We can also feel when someone seems to have a dark rain cloud over their head. Their energy is taxing to be around. Good or bad, even if it can't be seen with the naked eye, energy always makes itself known.

How is your energy body right now? Start to imagine that you can sense it. See it as a bright sphere of light that surrounds your entire frame. Now begin to give it detail. Turn open the spout of your intuition and answer these questions about the energy surrounding you.

How big is it? Sometimes your energy might fill a room, especially if you're engaging in public speaking or entertaining. Other times, when you don't want attention, like on a crowded plane, your energy retracts, clinging close to your body. Generally, the more expanded your energy, the more noticeable and memorable you are. A big energy field also means more surface area to absorb, so you're more likely to become influenced, for better or worse, by other people.

How bright is it? A strong energy field glows brightly, while a weak field is dim. When I'm hungry, tired, or depleted in any way, my energy field gets dull and dark. When I am coaching, writing, doing yoga, and doing other activities I love, I can sense my energy brightening. How does yours feel right now?

How fast is it moving? Fast energy is active and energizing, but when it's too fast it becomes chaotic. Slow energy is calming and grounded, but when it's too slow it becomes listless. When I'm feeling anxious or frenetic, I intentionally try to slow down and quiet my energy until it gets very still. Other times, when I'm overly lethargic, I'll try to speed it up and get it flowing again. How are you feeling today and how is your energy speed?

When you get into the habit of tuning in to your energy, you'll notice how it naturally shifts throughout the day. Your energy may get bigger and brighter when you hear good news, or it may shrink when you're anxious. Perhaps your energy radiates when you're around someone you love and grows dim when you're with people who drain you. This practice of imagining your energy field may feel like we're playing pretend, but it is essential to learning how to tend to and support your Inner Genius.

In the same way you've learned to recognize hunger, thirst, or annoyance in your physical body, trust yourself here. Know that everything you imagine comes from a place of truth. Your intuitions are valid, and especially so when it comes to your energy field.

In addition to visualizing your energy, you can also troubleshoot by learning how to spot symptoms that your energy needs help. If your energy body is weak, you might feel:

- uninspired, creatively blocked, or disconnected from your passion.
- lethargic or exhausted even though you've been sleeping fine.
- the desire to zone out through behavior like drinking, overeating, or marathoning TV.
- indecisive, uncertain, or overwhelmed by self-doubt.
- frustrated with your output and unable to get work done with ease.

The good news is that it's easy to cleanse your energy when it's not functioning properly. Your three big energy cleansers are as simple as they come: Nature, Movement, and Rest. What you might notice is that these suggestions aren't fancy, complicated, or surprising. There's nothing to buy, no expert to consult, and no esoteric knowledge needed. It's no coincidence that they're meant to occur in our lives on a daily basis without any additional effort. We humans are supposed to exist alongside nature, we're required to sleep every night, and we need to move our bodies in order to get around and live. Energy cleansing was always meant to happen effortlessly.

It is only now that we're living at our desks, attached to computers in tree-scarce neighborhoods, and leading non-stop, busy lives that energy cleansing requires dedication. Think of how disconnected we are. The average kid can identify more than a thousand corporate logos but can't name more than ten plants. Only 22 percent of adults get the daily recommended amount of exercise, and a third of us don't get enough sleep every night. Most of us are running deficits when it comes to these big three energy cleansers, so we must be determined to pursue nature, movement, and sleep for the sake of our Energy Resilience.

Nature

Think of how good it feels to be in the mountains or at the beach. The sights, sounds, and smells calm us. We were born to benefit from the plants and earth around us. The Japanese understand the potency of nature so well that they codified a health practice for it. Shinrin-yoku, or "forest bathing" is a term that was created by the Japanese Ministry of Agriculture, Forestry and Fisheries in 1982. It refers to the simple pleasure of spending time in nature to promote physical and psychological health and has become a vital part of Japanese preventive healthcare.

In Scandinavian countries, babies nap outside in freezing temperatures because the fresh air is good for them. The Indigenous people of the Great Plains were purified by the heat of sweat lodges made of natural materials, and countless bodies of water throughout the world like the Dead Sea are known for their healing properties. When we're sick, we drink tea and eat homemade soup. Nature is always mending us. Trees secrete oils that ward off germs and disease from the bark. When we're near trees and around that same oil, it encourages our human bodies to do the same. Simple proximity to plants boosts our immune systems and filters the air we breathe, removing carbon dioxide and the particulate matter of fossil fuels. Try sitting next to a tree and allowing its energy field to blend into your own. Notice how good that feels.

Even ten minutes outside among plants has an immediate benefit. When I'm stuck in New York City and can't get to nature, I take an Epsom salt bath so I can sit in earth's elements of water and minerals. I go through a lot of salt, several cups every day. Imagine how productive these baths must be to justify lugging a twenty-five-pound sack of salt up the five flights of stairs to my apartment. If you don't have a bathtub, try taking a long shower and imagining the water washing away any unwanted energy from you. Relax and take long slow breaths as you envision the negativity trapped in your energy body washing away and disappearing down the drain.

Movement

According to the chakra system, which comes from ancient Hindu traditions, the body has seven energy centers, starting at the bottom of the pelvis, climbing up the torso, and ending at the top of the head. These spinning wheels of energy are essential in clearing out negative influences. That's why I love yoga. It works the spine, which is the main channel where energy flows up and down, and all the chakras are centered along it. The twisting movements of physical yoga practice wring out the chakras, and I find that just ten minutes of classic sun salutations act like a super-powered washing machine for my energy body. Going from the backbends of upward dog to the forward bends of downward dog moves my energy expertly. Sometimes, when there's a lot of stagnant energy to clear, I'll do a vigorous run or power walk through the park. The pounding of my feet on the pavement helps shake out what's stuck.

Connecting to joy is what matters most, so choose whatever physical movement you love doing. Whether it's pickleball or Pilates, just make sure whatever you do also incorporates the spine work of twisting, forward bending, and back bending that are so helpful in activating the chakras. Sometimes, at my desk, I'll set a three-minute timer and do a few seated cat-cow stretches and then rotate my torso to the left and right. I feel like a new me in a handful of minutes.

Rest

When you're in need of a deep energy cleanse, the best thing you can do is sleep it off. While you rest, your body is hard at work detoxing your whole system. It flushes toxins from the brain so you can function without fogginess, releases hormones to curb inflammation, and at the same time, allows for blood, oxygen, and nutrients to repair any damaged tissues and muscles.

Sleep has the same effect on your energy body. Especially if you sleep in your bed alone, you'll be able to discharge any negative energy you've accumulated. Keep in mind, if you've been running a deficit, cleansing may take a few days of really good sleep.

I used to resent my bedtime. I always believed that there were more emails to do, shows to watch, or friends to catch up with. I worked such long hours that I hardly had any free time, so I resisted wasting even more of those leisure hours on sleep. Now that I know how hard my body and energy field are working to support me while I'm in bed, I look forward to my evening routine, which starts at nine p.m., and those glorious eight hours I spend subconsciously caring for myself mentally, physically, and energetically under the covers.

How are you doing when it comes to nature, movement, and rest? If you're not getting enough for any reason, you must make it your top priority to change that pattern. Given the restrictions of modern life, if we're not intentional about nature, movement, and rest, we quickly slide down to dangerously insufficient levels. Then, our energy fields remain polluted and we can't function at our best.

I've seen so many clients think that they can get more done if they cut "nonproductive" activities like exercise and sleep. They'd rather allocate those hours to their to-do list. Over time, they become foggier, more distractible, exhausted, and uninspired. So, they work even harder but get even less done because their energy is too weak to support them.

Remember that you're playing the long game here. You're learning how to work smart instead of indiscriminately working harder. When you invest your precious time into nature, movement, and rest, your efforts are paid back tenfold as you create and ideate with greater brilliance than you've ever experienced. As you plan out your work week, always make sure that these big three sit at the top of your priority list. They belong above your emails, meetings, and even urgent projects. After all, we're not just talking about feeling good. What is at stake here is survival. These are your natural, human, and incontestable needs. You were meant to get your fill of these three cleansers with ease. So today, choose the life your energy body craves and watch as your genius blossoms.

ENERGY EXERCISE #1: CLEANSE

✳

Choose one of the big three energy cleansers: nature, movement, or rest. Pick the one that is most deficient in your life. Commit to getting your fill of this cleanser for just two days. Notice what happens. Do you feel less lethargic, uncertain, and indecisive? Can you feel your inspiration, creativity and focus expand?

CHAPTER 15

PLAYING DEFENSE

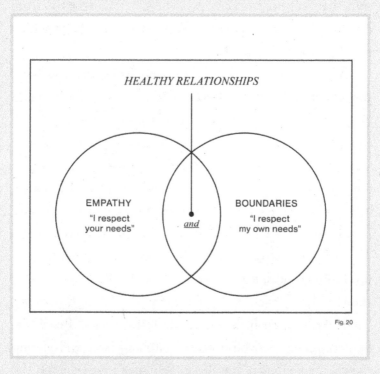

HEALTHY RELATIONSHIPS

EMPATHY
"I respect your needs"

and

BOUNDARIES
"I respect my own needs"

Fig. 20

Fig. 20 | Healthy Relationships

It is not often discussed, but upholding your boundaries is the key to healthy, supportive relationships that do not drain you.

rinity Mouzon Wofford, cofounder of the super-
foods brand Golde, grew up seeing her mother suffer from rheumatoid arthritis, a chronic condition of
inflammation that often left her bedridden. With a front-
row seat to the challenges her mom faced, Trinity was inspired to support others' well-being, and shortly after
college she launched Golde, collaborating with her partner
in love and work, Issey Kobori.

While their friends went to parties, Trinity and Issey
stayed in at night to work on Golde, the two of them playing all the roles in the company. Trinity listened to her
Inner Genius as it guided her in developing new products.
One of Golde's bestsellers, the Clean Greens Face Mask,
emerged from a spontaneous discovery process. The city air
had caused Trinity's face to erupt in breakouts and clogged
pores. She hadn't found anything that helped, so one day
she raided the Golde product development cabinet, mixed
up chlorella and spirulina powder, and put it on her face. As
soon as she washed it off, she knew she had a hit on her
hands. From their little apartment in Bushwick, Brooklyn,
bootstrapping their business, Trinity and Issey were living
the third expansion, the Joyful Self, and experiencing the
Karma of Success in the process.

Within a year of starting Golde, Trinity and Issey began
to attract attention from investors who were interested in
scaling the nascent business. Back then, they could have
used the cash. Neither was taking a salary, and they put all
the money they made back into the company, pulling out

just enough to cover their rent each month. Every week, they took forty dollars and went to the farmers market to get groceries. They would then pickle the vegetables and eat them over rice every day.

Despite the draw of financial stability that external investment could offer, Trinity said no to that first investor and continued to say no for years as new investors reached out to her. Most founders consider outside funding the holy grail, but Trinity's intuition knew with profound clarity that she needed to continue bootstrapping Golde to focus on her unique vision, the quality of the products, and her connection with the customer. Through saying no she protected the energy of her company.

When the time intuitively felt right, Trinity did eventually accept investment, but she has stayed strong to her practice of saying no and creating boundaries. To protect their energy, Trinity and Issey said goodbye to Brooklyn and moved to the Hudson Valley, where the access to nature energizes them. Then they had a baby, Ruby, and even with a busy company to run they continue to put family ahead of all else. Trinity makes time throughout the day to feed and play with Ruby. She and Issey cook delicious, healthy meals together and continue to find joy in experimenting with Golde's products.

Over six years, Trinity has come a long way from her original goal of just making enough money to pay rent. Golde has blossomed into a cult-favorite brand of products on the shelves at Target and Ulta. Much of her power has come from her ability to say no over and over again in pivotal career moments. She said no to early investors, no to the busyness of the city, and no to the toxic expectation that she, as a young founder, must defer family life to put her company first. Trinity knows what drains her energy, and she's learned how to protect herself from it. That's her secret to the Karma of Success.

Learning how to say no is essential to Enriching Your Energy. After all, your energy body is a boundary like any other, and not only do you decide what comes in (like nature, movement, and rest), you, like Trinity, also get to choose what you keep out. In this chapter, we'll explore what's draining your energy, when you need to say no, and how you can build better boundaries.

For my clients who feel constantly exhausted, I have them do an Energy Audit exercise so we can understand what people, situations, and responsibilities are depleting them. Using their online calendar, they mark every energetically positive interaction with one color. These are meetings, work events, and tasks that leave them feeling energized. Next, they mark all the depleting activities with another color. These are the day-to-day responsibilities that leave them feeling drained and exhausted. At the end of the week, the calendar tells a clear story. We know with a simple glance what needs to change.

For this next week, I want you to keep your own Energy Audit. As you go, notice the balance between energizing and draining activities throughout your day. What fills you up and what tires you out? Pay special attention to the people, situations, and moments that cause you to feel the most exhausted. What is it about them specifically that drains you?

Consider that you might be an empath. Empaths are people who are highly attuned to the emotions and inclinations of the people around them. It's like they have an extra antenna on the top of their heads that is especially sensitive to the thoughts and feelings of others. When an empath is in a meeting, they not only understand what is verbally said, but they can also intuit the deeper emotions in the dialogue. What seems obvious to them is often unseen by others.

If this description resonates with you, you need to be even more determined to protect your energetic boundaries. You need to be clear about what is allowed in your world and what isn't, because empaths feel drained by people and situations much more than others. Non-empaths certainly absorb negativity and toxicity, but empaths take on those negative influences as if they are their own, leaving them feeling discombobulated for hours or days and making it much harder to return to a positive energy state. For empaths, it is better to ensure that those influences aren't allowed in to begin with.

For empaths and non-empaths alike, the first step to protecting your energy is to examine the people in your life, considering who might be an Energy Vampire. Energy Vampires are described as such because they intentionally or subconsciously drain your energy. They are attracted to people who are kind, compassionate, and empathetic because those are the easiest sources to feed off of. They want your attention. They need validation from you. They constantly crave emotional connection.

The biggest clue that someone in your life might be an

Energy Vampire is to notice how you feel when you are around them. Do you feel exhausted after spending time with them? Do you find yourself thinking more pessimistically, or feeling frustrated, confused, or down? Do you find it hard to disconnect from their energy even after you've physically separated? Start paying attention to the tactics Energy Vampires use. Here are a few.

- **Undervaluing you:** They don't see you as a full person. They think of you only in relation to themselves and what role you play for them.
- **Not listening to you and talking nonstop:** Energy Vampires dominate the conversation, unload their stress onto you, and often repeat the same stories over and over. They're talking at you, not with you.
- **Arguing, bickering, and yelling:** Interpersonal tension makes them feel comfortable and energized, while it exhausts everyone else.
- **Playing the victim:** They don't know how to be accountable. It's never their fault, and there's always someone or something else to blame.
- **Being passive-aggressive:** Energy Vampires can get upset but refuse to communicate directly about it. This unwillingness to express their negative feelings creates a dark cloud around them that everyone feels, too.

The Energy Vampires in your life might do all of those behaviors or it might be just one. At the root of all those actions is the (often subconscious) desire to be unhappy, upset, or at odds. Energy Vampires don't see the glass as half full. In fact, they don't really see the glass at all, because they're obsessing over and fixating on their own issues.

The wonderful news is that you have the agency to open or shut your energy to whomever you want. You can choose to spend less time with the Energy Vampires in your life. You can say no to their ploys for your attention. If you've been taught that being agreeable and cooperative is the key to success at work, it's time to revise this narrative. There are three techniques you need to defend your energy: protect your peace, build boundaries, and assert yourself.

Protect Your Peace

Forget what's "polite" or "considerate." You're allowed to walk away from draining conversations. My friend Jackson lives by a simple motto: Protect your peace. You can end any commitment that isn't in line with your integrity. You can and should say no to the people who exhaust you. This work isn't physically hard to do but requires intention if you default to placing other people's needs ahead of your own.

If you are an empath or a recovering people-pleaser, this step is essential for you to master. Realize that you're not being selfish for protecting yourself. There is no reason for you to accommodate other people at the expense of your own well-being. You are the only person who has the responsibility for protecting yourself, so you must take that job seriously. Every time you find yourself in a situation where you have to choose between what you need and what someone else wants, ask yourself, "How do I protect my peace?" The resulting answer is always the right path to walk. Whenever you stand up for your right to inner peace, your energy field grows brighter and stronger, emboldened by your resolve.

Build Boundaries

You can create effective energy boundaries by simply using your mind. Whenever I'm in a situation with a high likelihood of draining my energy, I simply visualize a boundary around me. I call to mind the image of my energy body, the ball of light surrounding me, and envision it as a golden bubble protecting me from any negative influences. I always feel immediate relief.

If you find that, despite your best efforts, a negative interaction with someone else still lingers, you can take a couple minutes to do a "cord cutting" visualization. It's a simple technique that unhooks you from unhealthy relationship dynamics. You simply close your eyes and imagine the person who has drained your energy sitting across from you with a thick golden rope connecting both your hearts. Then, you visualize that connection being sliced by a sword or a large pair of scissors. Freed from the other person, you and they both float away from each other happily. The whole process takes under three minutes.

If you find that visualization isn't enough, you can build a physical boundary, too. If you work at an office, you can line your desk with pictures of loved ones, mementos, or sacred objects that reverberate positive energy. As soon as you sit down for the workday, put on your noise-cancelling headphones, draw that golden bubble around you, and imagine yourself safe and protected within your own energy field.

Assert Yourself

The emotional body and the energy body are interconnected. One affects the other. If your emotional boundaries are intact, your energy boundaries will be, too. That's why the act of standing up for yourself is essential in protecting your energy. Challenge yourself to be more assertive: ask for what you want at least once a day. Every time you stand up for yourself, it builds up your energy field's ability to withstand negative influences. I love this practice because it pushes me past my comfort zone and forces me to articulate my needs, no matter how small I write them off to be.

At the end of every day, I ask myself, *Have I been assertive today?* If I haven't stood up for my needs enough, I'll then go through my email, see what I may be avoiding, and write a clear, candid email that champions my needs and preferences. It's the most empowering feeling to end my workday on. So often, we find reasons not to do this work. We minimize our own needs with thoughts like:

That person is not so bad—I should feel okay with spending time with them.

I shouldn't rock the boat—the situation isn't that terrible.

I have to do it because they need me to.

Start to be wary of your brain saying things like "I should," "I shouldn't," or "I have to." Those words are red flags that you are actively prioritizing someone or something else over your own needs. Make the commitment to stop this behavior now because you must, at all costs, protect yourself.

Remember that this work is driven by your Inner Genius, not your logical mind. You don't ever need to justify your boundaries to anyone, even yourself. You don't need to offer reasons why. Somehow, we have all gotten into the habit of needing to explain why it is we're taking care of ourselves, when a simple "it doesn't feel right" is reason enough.

That's it. Today, decide that you come first. When you practice protecting your peace, building boundaries, and asserting yourself, you'll soon feel such complete calm in your life that you'll wonder how you ever lived without it before.

ENERGY EXERCISE #2: PROTECT

Think about a relationship, whether personally or professionally, where you haven't been prioritizing yourself. Recall past situations when you've fulfilled the other person's asks at the expense of your own needs. Make a commitment to behavior that will end this pattern. Write this commitment in your notebook three times.

CHAPTER 16

BIGGER, BRIGHTER, AMPLIFIED

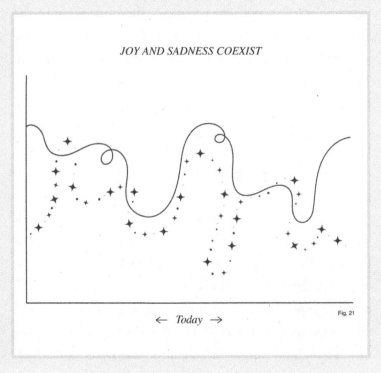

Fig. 21 | Joy And Sadness Coexist

There is a Buddhist saying that life is ten thousand joys and ten thousand sorrows. The secret is to accept that they are both fundamental to life.

When I was a child, I never met a single adult who enjoyed their work. In every example I could see, work was something to be endured, not enjoyed. Back in Vietnam before they immigrated and started from zero, my mom's family had been so wealthy that up until the day Saigon fell, she had never planned to work. My mom was adept at arranging flowers and playing instruments, but nothing practical. She took pride in the fact that she didn't learn how to boil water until she was seventeen, and even after her life circumstances changed, she was never particularly interested in working.

I remember her in a part-time job behind the makeup counter at Macy's and a brief stint as a social worker, where I'd sit in her break room on days when I was sick from school. For many years she worked as a paralegal for a couple different personal injury attorneys, but she always struggled to get out of bed and in the car by eleven a.m. It wasn't that my mom didn't care about money. In fact, it was the opposite. She constantly plotted new ways to have more of it, but these plans usually involved a romantic partner, or some superstitions, but not actual work. In the world I was raised in, jobs meant status. It was best to be a doctor or a lawyer, and money, which there was never enough of, should be prioritized over all else.

It's funny how things work out. I tried my hardest to become the opposite of my mom, but in some ways I grew up to be exactly like her. Unlike my mom, I didn't have an aversion to work. Far from it—I became a workaholic.

What I did inherit was her belief that work is a hardship. There was never a point in my life when I asked myself what job I might like, let alone love. In fact, I never thought of myself as particularly passionate about any vocation. I knew there were people in the world for whom work was fun, but I was certainly not one of them.

Well into my job in the finance world, I had an unusual experience at a stranger's home that cracked open these beliefs I held about work. I'd been seeing an executive coach of my own for a couple of years, and she invited me, along with some other clients and friends, to a healing workshop of a therapeutic method called Family Constellations she'd organized. My coach had recently taken the workshop herself and was so moved that she invited the facilitator, a French woman, to work with us, too. There, with a dozen other people, the goal was to heal the generational trauma we'd all inherited from our ancestors.

We each took turns, one by one going through the process, which would begin with the facilitator identifying the most toxic family pattern that needed to be broken. Then, the other participants would serve as stand-ins for the family members involved, both living and dead. Finally, the facilitator directed the group to act out the breaking of those patterns in order to reverse the trauma and commit to a new path.

The French woman had never met any of us before, and she wasn't social or particularly interested in getting to know us. Between sessions, she stood alone outside chain-smoking cigarettes. But somehow, even with her limited interaction, she knew everything about every person in the group. It blew my mind. When a new session would start, the person whose turn it was wouldn't say a single word, not even their name. We'd all just sit there quietly, and the French woman would stare at them for a few seconds, and then as if reading the weather forecast, she'd tell them the most destructive pattern they'd inherited from their family.

She knew that one man's grandparents had emigrated from Russia because of war, and all of the family members they'd left behind had died. This man had grown up in the US, gone to Stanford, and worked at Google, but deep in his heart he'd inherited his grandparents' sadness of losing their family, and it now prevented him from connecting with his own children. She told another participant that he was having trouble finding a romantic partner because his mom thought of him as her own romantic partner and she had treated him like that since he was a kid. When it was my turn, the French woman said this to me: "You come from a long line of people who have suffered because of circumstances. Your grandmother suffered so much she tried to kill herself. Your grandfather had to do a job that was painful for him. Now you believe that it is your destiny to suffer, too." She knew.

My grandmother had indeed tried to hang herself as a young woman. Both her parents had passed away, leaving her an orphan in the care of an uncle who beat her up so badly that her cousin begged her to run away before the uncle could take her life. My grandfather, her husband, had always wanted to be a poet, but his family didn't have enough money to make this path a reality for him, so instead he spent his entire adult life in battlefields. First he was a common soldier; eventually, he became a two-star general in the South Vietnamese army. Neither of my grandparents, the two people who I had loved most in the world, had the chance to fulfill their dreams, and the same was true for every other person in my lineage. By the end of my turn with the French woman, I understood that it was my duty to break this pattern. This was my purpose in life. I would be the first person in my family history to be happy.

At the end of the day, I walked outside to seek out the facilitator. I needed to know how she had done it. *How do you know all this?* I asked. With a wave of her hand and a puff of smoke she said, *I hear it.* She was in touch with a source of wisdom unavailable to most of us, and of course she had no interest in explaining this to me, a clueless tech worker. Even so, I walked away satisfied.

After that session, I started working with my executive coach on how to change this inherited belief that I should suffer in life, especially when it came to work. In the past, when deciding anything related to my job, I'd always used one of two filters. The first: "What will be the best thing for my career?" And the second, "What will make me look good?" Two variants of the same superficial yearning.

With my coach's help, I discarded them for a new filter, something that at first seemed preposterous. I began to ask myself, "What will be most fun for me?" I started off with low-hanging fruit like avoiding annoying colleagues, and I constantly audited my energy to make sure I had more energizing meetings on my calendar than draining ones. I remember taking my first big step. I removed myself from a high-visibility project that my boss loved but I hated, and instead handed it to someone else on my team to take the glory.

It wasn't perfect. I still had many unfulfilling responsibilities, but as time went by and I got more comfortable prioritizing myself, they became fewer and fewer, and magically in the process I got better at my job. I never expected that to happen. I was certain that prioritizing fun would make me less productive, but within a few months of making the shift to joy, I was promoted and given a huge raise, and my opinion was valued more than ever.

I didn't realize it at the time, but I was actually doing the third step of Enriching Your Energy—I had amplified it. Because I was happy and having fun, my energy body was vibrant and strong, allowing me to be seen and respected. People saw me as an authority. They wanted to be around me and to help me succeed. Just as the Law of Attraction states, I had always considered work a grind, so that's how it was. As soon as I reframed it as easy and fun, it became that way, too.

How much joy do you feel in your life? Do you wake up and go to bed happy? What is the predominant look on your face throughout the day? One of my favorite Buddhist phrases describes life as ten thousand joys and ten thousand sorrows. While there are always things to be upset about, there is also an abundance of happiness. To master this third step of Enriching Your Energy and amplify it, your job is to search for as many of those ten thousand moments of joy as you can every day. Here are some dependable places to look.

Your Morning Routine

Our energy levels naturally decline throughout the day. We can start off feeling great, but then the train is late, a meeting runs long, or someone at work is rude. You know this and feel this. By the time you're halfway through, you're *tired*. You have only a fraction of the juice you started with. This is why it's so important to squirrel away all the positive energy you can before your workday even begins. If you start your day feeling like a five, you'll be a zero by lunch time. But if start your day at a ten, you'll still have energy in the afternoon.

You must have a morning routine you love, so what is that you love? For some of my clients, it's an iced coffee, reading fiction, cycling, or a walk. Every morning I get dressed and eat breakfast at warp speed so I can still have forty-five minutes to do Pilates, do pranayama, talk to my husband, or do something else I love. Yes, it's a lot of time, but it's worth the effort and more. When you start with a full tank, you can go anywhere.

Micro-fun

It is appalling how many of my busy clients neglect to eat lunch. Some are so back-to-back that they don't have time to even use the restroom. Imagine, taking a risk to pursue your big dream and successfully raising millions of funding, only to be in the position where you don't have time for normal human functions. What kind of life is that? Just as your computer needs to be shut down every so often, you need breaks, too. Especially if the browser that is your brain is overloaded with open tabs.

Studies have shown that the ideal productivity ratio is forty-five minutes on, then fifteen minutes off on break. An easy way to amplify your energy is to fill your day with micro moments of fun. Take fifteen minutes to call a friend, stretch, pet your cat, or slowly sip your tea. It doesn't matter what you do, as long as you enjoy yourself. While it may be challenging to take a break every forty-five minutes, it is essential that you never go any longer than three hours without a period of micro-fun.

Zone of Genius

In *The Big Leap* by Gay Hendricks, he explains that there are four buckets of activity, Genius, Excellence, Competence, and Incompetence, and every action we take at work falls into one of them. Your Zone of Incompetence are the tasks that you're terrible at. Your Zone of Competence are the things you're okay at, but other people do much better. Your Zone of Excellence is the trickiest category. It's the work that you're great at and for which you're likely well-paid but leaves you feeling depleted. You get it done, but you don't like it.

Where you want to be is in your Zone of Genius. It's work that you find endlessly fascinating. Time stands still and speeds by simultaneously. Not only are you good at it—it's the work that you were placed on this planet to do. What's in your Zone of Genius? The most effective way to amplify your energy at work is to live as much as you can in your Zone of Genius. It's impossible to be there all the time, but this doesn't mean that we shouldn't try. For the sake of our mental health, we must try. Start with spending 10 percent of your day in your Zone of Genius and expand that amount over time. As the ratio grows, you'll notice how much more alive, refreshed, and effective you become.

I had a yoga teacher who would pretzel the class into uncomfortable, awkward postures—the type that make your muscles tremble—and just when we couldn't take any more, he'd add on yet another instruction: "Now, gently turn up the corners of your mouth." He called his pose Smile-Asana. "If you can't smile during the hardest moments," he'd say, "you're doing it wrong."

I've heard the same advice when it comes to running, and it is equally relevant for our careers. The more uncomfortable, frustrating, or challenging the work at hand, the more important it is to look for ways to find joy to balance it. If you have a dozen sorrows on your plate, you cannot survive unless you can access a dozen complementary joys.

I will say something now that it took me three decades on this Earth to understand: You deserve to be happy. Joy is your birthright, and now you have the permission to do whatever you can to get yourself more of it.

Everything shifted when I made this realization. I am sure that my grandfather, who passed away almost twenty years ago, can see me now, having the most fun of my life writing a book and getting paid for it. Because I changed my relationship to work and started experiencing the Karma of Success, I now get to live his literary dreams for him, and I cannot imagine a sweeter reward.

ENERGY EXERCISE #3:
AMPLIFY

❊

Set a timer for two minutes and make an exhaustive list of every activity that brings you joy—big or small, work related or not. Your list can include actions as simple as texting your mom or making a sandwich, or as complex as perfecting a new skill.

When you're finished, find ways to slot these energy boosters into your day, whether it's in your morning routine, during micro-fun breaks, or by making more time for your Zone of Genius. Then, as a last step, remind yourself to smile.

Forty-Eight-Hour Energy Reset

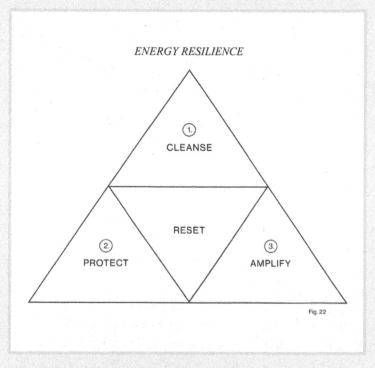

ENERGY RESILIENCE

1.
CLEANSE

RESET

2.
PROTECT

3.
AMPLIFY

Fig. 22

Fig. 22 | Energy Resilience

To show up as your optimal self, make sure you prioritize the time it takes to complete the three steps of enriching your energy on a regular basis.

here you have it, the three steps for Enriching Your Energy: cleanse, protect, and amplify. In the past few chapters, you've learned a number of ways to work with these steps, and now you'll put it all together to create a game plan for your specific life. How do we do that? Well, it's really up to you. Remember that our work here is always inwardly focused. This is your chance to explore the contours of your own preferences, passions, and process. I'm merely here to share information and provide the questions. You are the one with the answers.

As you consider now what is best for you, tune into your Inner Genius, and ask yourself this:

How can I take better care of myself? (Cleanse)

What boundaries do I need in my life? (Protect)

How can I fill my days with joy? (Amplify)

Now you get to choose. Perhaps you'll begin with low-hanging fruit, or an area of your life that's utterly broken. Whatever your Inner Genius intuits is exactly what you need. Here are my three. I cleanse my energy by improving my sleep, my lifelong Achilles' heel. I take melatonin, turn off my devices, and start my wind-down process when my friends are just meeting up for dinner.

To protect my energy, I have a blunt boundary: I simply do not interact with people who drain me. Not potential clients. Not old pals. No one. Renegotiating long-held toxic relationships is often painful, but I've learned the hard way that putting others' needs before mine zaps me every time. Finally, to amplify my energy, I make my morning routine sacred. I schedule my meetings to give me plenty of buffer so I can enjoy the activities that bring me joy.

If you are thinking that you don't have the time or energy to make big-habit changes right now, you may be in a need of a Forty-Eight-Hour Energy Reset. Ironically, it takes some energy to change one's habits to create more energy, so if you've been in a slump for a while, then you need something fast and potent to break your low-energy pattern.

The Forty-Eight-Hour Energy Reset is a simple break away from your normal day-to-day where you allow yourself to focus on the big three energy cleansers: nature, movement, and rest. Ideally, you're alone or with someone calming and in proximity to Mother Nature, even if it's just a few trees (nature). Once a day, practice your favorite physical activity, whether walking or yoga (movement), and avoid having any meetings or responsibilities on your plate so you can sleep, nap, and relax as much as you want (rest). It's helpful to kick off your Reset with an energy treatment, such as Reiki or acupuncture, or even a massage if that's more relaxing for you.

Reiki is a form of Japanese energy work that promotes both emotional and physical healing, stress reduction, and relaxation. The treatment is performed fully clothed laying on a massage table with your eyes closed. Your practitioner is what's called a Reiki master. They are someone who's gone through the training and been "attuned" by another Reiki master. Attunement is the powerful spiritual experience of having your energetic pathways opened. Even though I am a Reiki master myself and have experienced many Reiki treatments, I'm still blown away by the feeling.

Reiki is the only time I've ever *physically* felt energy in an obvious way. As the practitioner floats their hands a few inches above your body, you feel an undeniable heat on you that is deeply comforting. The first time I got Reiki, I couldn't believe that I could experience such a strong sensation from someone who wasn't even touching me, so I opened my eyes, sat up, and demanded to know what was happening. Whenever I get Reiki, it feels like my nervous system is completely reset, and I feel calmer and more spirituality aligned than I'm usually able to experience through my day-to-day practices.

Acupuncture holds a special place in my heart because my mom would take me to an acupuncturist when I was sick instead of a Western medical doctor. At the time, I wanted to fit in and be "American," so I hated it, but now I'm grateful she did because it's been a huge source of support for me as an adult in dealing with extreme fatigue, high stress, throwing out my back, and poor sleep. Consistent acupuncture over time can do incredible things. When my grandfather was in his seventies, he had a heart attack and stroke in quick succession, and his doctors said he'd never walk again. After six months of acupuncture and herbal medicine, he recovered movement in his lower body and walked without a cane, and he lived for another fifteen years.

Some people are scared off by the fact that acupuncture

involves many little needles going into your body, but allow me to reassure you. The needles are tiny—as small in diameter as an eyebrow hair—so you don't even feel them as they are very gently tapped into your skin, just a fraction of an inch. Acupuncturists study for three years, learning the hundreds of points along the body, so they know exactly what they're doing. Once they've put in all the needles, you rest on the table for about thirty minutes. I usually fall into a deep sleep right away and feel magnitudes better—mind, body, and soul—by the time I leave.

While I am a huge proponent of both of these treatments, I want to be clear that neither of them are necessary for a Forty-Eight-Hour Reset. You can fully accomplish the mission by nourishing your energy through activities that don't cost anything. I also highly recommend trying pranayama as a free and effective way to work with your energy. It's an ancient set of breathing techniques from the yogic tradition that cleanse, protect, or amplify your energy, depending which ones you do. There are many free online resources that teach the very simple techniques to beginners.* I personally do a ten-minute energizing pranayama routine every single day before I write or work on something that requires deep work. I don't drink caffeine anymore because I'm able to keep my energy high holistically.

Whether you stick to the activities you know or want to explore new energy-improving modalities, the most

---

*Ira Trivedi offers a simple but powerful fifteen-minute pranayama practice for beginners here: "Daily Pranayama Practice with Ira Trivedi," *YOG LOVE*, YouTube, March 30, 2020, www.youtube.com /watch?v=ZLxPCT-mw2g.

important thing is to listen to your intuition to choose a schedule you love. One of my clients does his Resets only on sunny weekends because the sun is so rejuvenating for him. Another stays off of social media and email during the first twenty-four hours and focuses his Reset on exercising his physical body. Your Resets may vary each time based on what you intuitively need in that exact moment. Don't overthink it too much. Just do what makes you happy, and make sure to hit the three categories of cleanse, protect, and amplify.

The important thing is to get on a regular cadence with your Resets. Some of my clients even have their Resets pre-scheduled in their calendars for intervals that vary between eight and twelve weeks. When work has me tethered to New York City for long stretches, I schedule a Reset for the day after my work commitments end. I'm especially sensitive to energy pollution and city life makes cleansing and protecting my energy a challenge.

The big thing I want to stress is there is no right answer here, no pressure, no bar to meet. There is no best way to Reset, and there are no silver-bullet habits that enrich your energy. What works for you is what works for you. Your only mission is to have fun while you figure out, through trial and error, how to set up a life that just feels good. That's all you need for your energy to flow.

BECOMING
BRILLIANT

CHAPTER 17

THE
GENTLE WAY

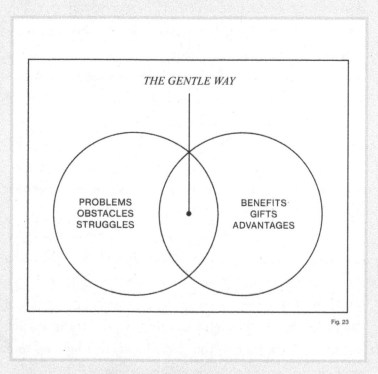

Fig. 23 | The Gentle Way

You can learn how to transform the most challenging parts of your life into benefits, gifts, and advantages.

A martial arts student approached his teacher and said, "I am very dedicated to my studies. How long will it take me to become a master?" The teacher said, "Ten years."

"But what if I am diligent, work hard, and practice more than the other students?" the eager youngster asked. The teacher examined the student again, considering his words. "Twenty years," he said.

The student made three wrong assumptions about success that his teacher knew would impede his mastery of martial arts. Many of us hold the same assumptions, and we are equally prevented from realizing our full potential. Over the next chapters, we will go deeper into these wrong assumptions, and in doing so, uncover the fourth and final of the Spiritual Strategies, Becoming Brilliant.

You've now learned the first three Spiritual Strategies. By Inquiring Inward, you spent time in your internal world so you can hear your Inner Genius. By Manifesting Mindfully, you learned how to become a visionary, grateful, and confident person through journaling. In the third section, Enriching Your Energy, you chose habits that light up your soul, no matter the challenges on your plate.

Those three strategies were to prepare you for this moment. You have honed your intuition, vision, and lifestyle, and are ready to become brilliant and achieve success in any endeavor. This description of "becoming brilliant" isn't wholly accurate. After all, you are already brilliant. The work here isn't to change who you are but rather to realize the genius within you.

Nowadays, *genius* is a loaded word, used sparingly with connotations of bravado and bluster, but it was never meant that way. The origin of the word first came from the ancient Romans who believed that every person has a guiding spirit who looks after them for their entire life. This spirit was the one responsible for inspiration, ideas, and breakthroughs. They named it *genius*, and they believed that every person was literally born with it. The original conception of genius is a birthright—an innate component of the human experience. You have it. I have it. We all have it.

The first step in Becoming Brilliant is for you to acknowledge this. Can you appreciate that you have genius within you, or does it feel challenging? Do you worry about being boastful, full of yourself, or untethered to reality? What you must remember is that in admitting your genius, you are not putting yourself at a level above anyone else. You are simply owning what is true for you. Each person in the world possesses the seed of genius. The only difference between those who express it versus others has nothing to do with talent and everything to do with state of mind.

To free the genius within you and experience the Karma of Success, you must unlearn limiting beliefs you have been taught throughout your life. Just like the martial arts student in the parable, we've been fed three wrong assumptions about work and success. Our job now is to dismantle the assumptions and replace them with Genius Truths— new ways of viewing your work that allow you to tap into your brilliance. These are the wrong assumptions that we and the eager martial arts students falsely believe:

WRONG ASSUMPTION #1: The harder you push yourself, the more successful you'll be.

WRONG ASSUMPTION #2: Success should follow a specific process and timeline.

WRONG ASSUMPTION #3: Success comes from the mastery of skill.

These assumptions are so common in our culture. We must think differently now to get in touch with the Inner Genius.

I have a dear friend who I met when I was eighteen. By now we've been friends for half our lives, witness to each other's many ups and downs. She always did well in school, better than me, and after university she continued to strive for perfection, going to the best graduate school and onward to great jobs. As you now know, that wasn't the case for me.

The other day she remarked on the success of my company and my podcast, and how much I enjoy my work, while she's lacked fulfillment in hers for years, despite making the perfect choices. "Everything happens so easily for you," she said. It took me a moment to respond, because her words seemed both true and untrue at the same time.

In the 1880s in Japan, Kanō Jigorō founded judo, a martial art that was not just a sport but also a way of life. In

English, judo means "the Gentle Way," and the foundational premise is to use the strength of your opponent for your own benefit. Instead of striking *against* your opponent, trying to meet their force with even greater force, you leverage their own effort and then direct it skillfully to get what you want. When they pull, you push in the same direction. When they push, you pull. Kanō described this as seiryoku zen'yō—"maximum efficiency, minimum effort." You go with the flow of what's happening.

If you've ever watched a judo match, you might at first believe that the practice is anything but gentle, as the name implies. The judokas are lifted, slammed, and pinned down to the ground. Yes, there is much exertion, effort, and force, but look closely and you see the Gentle Way beneath. You notice that one judoka's attack is transformed into the other one's strategy. It is maximum efficiency and minimum effort.

When I first learned about this philosophy, it helped me make sense of the fortuitous unfolding of my own career. It wasn't as simple as my friend had said, that everything comes so easily to me. Just like every person in this world, I've had my share of obstacles, disappointments, and failures, but the difference has been the Gentle Way. Instead of protecting myself from their attack, I move with them in the same direction. When they pushed, I pulled and tried to transform the strikes against me into strategy.

This is the work of Becoming Brilliant. Instead of letting your flaws embarrass you, you lean into what they teach you. When you feel the sting of failure, you find a way to move in the same direction. When the struggle feels endless, you dig and dig until it becomes a gift. The Gentle Way means releasing control and perfectionism. You understand that it is a fool's wish to try to avoid disappointment, mistakes, and hardship. Instead, like a master of judo, you embrace them. Over the next few chapters, I will teach you how to fail and fight with ease, and in the process you will experience the Karma of Success. This is the Gentle Way, and we begin with gentleness toward yourself.

CHAPTER 18

REVERSE GOLDEN RULE

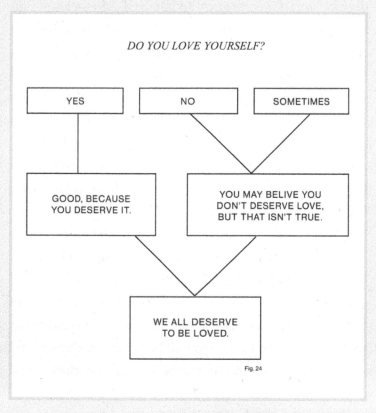

DO YOU LOVE YOURSELF?

YES — NO — SOMETIMES

GOOD, BECAUSE YOU DESERVE IT.

YOU MAY BELIVE YOU DON'T DESERVE LOVE, BUT THAT ISN'T TRUE.

WE ALL DESERVE TO BE LOVED.

Fig. 24

Fig. 24 | Do You Love Yourself?

We are often our own worst critics. We beat ourselves up in ways we'd never treat others. When you can let this go, and unlock self-love, you deepen your connection to genius.

When Piera Gelardi was twenty-four years old, she started a company called Refinery29. At the time, she wasn't sure where the experience would lead her, but she was excited to create a platform with more complex stories and portrayals of women. A decade later, her company had hundreds of employees, an audience count in the millions, and a passionate communications team that wanted Piera out in the world giving talks to further the company's mission.

With care and diligence, the team outlined the topics they wanted her to present and hired a media trainer to coach her. Piera and the media trainer spent long hours together. She'd rehearse the speeches as he corrected her on her posture, movements, and delivery. He videotaped her live talks and played back the footage, making note of every "um" and "like" she said, and every line she failed to hit. The work was frustrating and dejecting, but Piera worked overtime, determined not to let her team down.

When the moment came to deliver, Piera's brain overflowed with the trainer's reminders of how to stand, what to say, and who to be. Despite all her practice, Piera would immediately black out as she began her speeches. She'd grope her way through the memorized words with no awareness of what she was doing or the audience response. The moment she stepped offstage the performance would come flooding back to her, every mistake highlighted in bold. Piera would berate herself for her failure to excel, despite the many long hours put into practicing.

After a string of demoralizing speeches, Piera's assistant suggested she submit herself for a slot at the popular South by Southwest Conference and Festivals (abbreviated SXSW). It wasn't yet a sure thing. First, they'd have to propose a topic for the attendees to vote on, and only the top vote-getters would secure a speaking spot. This time, Piera chose a topic she was inherently passionate about—courageous creativity—and she won. She would be the headline speaker.

Piera's Inner Genius knew this was not only a great opportunity, but also the moment for change. Instead of building her speech from talking points, she took a new approach and focused on the stories she wanted to tell. In lieu of the punishing media trainer, she hired a pair of speaking coaches with a background in theater. With her new trainers, Piera focused on feeling comfortable. She sang songs from *The Little Mermaid*, learned to stand with confidence, and practiced visualization.

Piera chose the Gentle Way. Instead of attacking her imperfections with relentless critique, she leaned into creating from a place of joy. She worked just as diligently to prepare this talk as she'd done with all the others, but this time, the work was enlivening and not punishing.

The morning of Piera's speech, she ate a delicious breakfast and she danced and laughed and practiced her visualization. She even wrote herself a supportive love note, setting a simple goal for the speech: as long as she was generous, present, and had fun, she'd consider it a success. She wasn't fixated on the mistakes to avoid or the points to hit. Instead she just had to be her. Not only did Piera enjoy herself, but she gave such a rousing performance that the audience erupted in a standing ovation. Just a few hours later, the festival organizers called her and asked her for an encore. That's how much her words mattered. In the audience that day was an organizer for a conference called Inbound, who loved Piera's speech so much that she wanted her on the Inbound mainstage alongside other headliners like Michelle Obama and Brené Brown. Piera was thrilled at how many people she could support and inspire with her message. And while she'd pushed herself to grow and perform at her best, hard work was not the primary reason for her success. What mattered was *self-love*.

Unfortunately, most of us do what Piera did in the beginning without ever learning to amend our strategy. We are just like the martial arts student in the parable. We ask, "But what if I am diligent, work hard, and practice more than the other students?" We think that if we put in the long hours, do the unseen work, and push ourselves to the point of breaking, we'll get to the goal faster. We internalize Wrong Assumption #1, believing the harder you push yourself, the more successful you'll be.

Just as the teacher in the parable understood that diligence, hard work, and endless practice do not translate to success, Piera learned this lesson for herself. When she worked relentlessly with the media trainer, it didn't make her a good speaker; in fact, it made her worse. Her success came only when she replaced the voice of self-critique with that of self-love. This brings us to the rebuttal of this wrong assumption, Genius Truth #1: The more you love yourself, the more successful you'll be.

Let's look for proof of the Genius Truth in your own life. Can you bring to mind a teacher, coach, or role model who helped you, no matter how far back in the past? This person could be a relative, a coach, or an educator of some sort, just as long as they helped you in some meaningful way. Now, think back to your relationship with them. What did they see in you? How did they treat you? What actions did they take to support your learning and growth?

My person is Mrs. Albright. She was the head of the International Baccalaureate program at the high school I attended after I moved in with my cousins, and she acted as a guidance counselor to me and the other students in the program. Mrs. Albright was the first person in my life who told me I was smart enough to go to any college I wanted. Then, she helped me follow through. She talked to me about my applications and showed me how to apply for low-income fee waivers. Outside of school, she even hired me to babysit for her kids, knowing that I needed the money, and paying me more than the market rate. Mrs. Albright believed in me before I knew how to believe in myself. Even though she didn't have to, she treated me with love. I was just a fleeting person in the program, one of dozens of students she helped every year, but to me, she was everything. I have no doubt that all that is good in my life now started there in eleventh grade at Annandale High School, with her.

I imagine the person you're thinking of bears some resemblance to Mrs. Albright, too. Did your person believe in you and treat you with respect? Did they recognize the gifts and talents you had, even if you couldn't see them yourself? Was your person fond of you and kind to you, and did they cheer you on? I know that if Mrs. Albright had been too hard on me or pushed me with endless critiques, then it wouldn't have worked. Of course, she challenged me to work hard on my grades and dedicate time to my college applications, but what made all the difference was the foundation of love she showed me. When you think of your person, can you see how love is an infinitely more powerful motivator than critique?

The same applies for the voice inside of you. You can push yourself as hard as you want, but success won't follow until you can show yourself love and support, as well. In the 1960s, psychologists Robert Rosenthal and Lenore Jacobson studied students at an elementary school in California. At the beginning of the year, they gave the kids an IQ test, then told the teachers that some of them scored high enough to be considered gifted "Intellectual Bloomers." In reality, these "gifted" students were chosen at random. At the end of the year, the same IQ test was given again, and amazingly, the randomly selected Bloomers had much higher scores than the other students.

This study shows us the Pygmalion effect in action, which is when high expectations lead to high performance. The students in the study who were believed to be smarter became smarter. The way they were treated became a self-fulfilling prophecy. This matters for all of us. When you're expected to be brilliant, you rise to the occasion. But if you're told that you will fail, so it will be. With the kids in the study, with Piera Gelardi, with Mrs. Albright and me, the simple act of expecting the best from yourself makes anything possible.

We've all heard of the Golden Rule, which says you must treat others as you would like to be treated. It's a helpful reminder to practice empathy, compassion, and kindness for others. But something just as important but never talked about is the Reverse Golden Rule—it's about treating yourself the way you'd treat someone you love.

Imagine that your best friend had just given a speech they'd spent countless hours preparing. Would you berate them with criticisms as soon as they got offstage? Would you replay every detail of what they did wrong? Never. You'd never treat your best friend the way Piera treated herself at first. Not only would that be unloving, but following the Pygmalion effect, it'd also be ineffective.

How often do you practice the Reverse Golden Rule? Do you treat yourself the way you'd treat someone you love? Is your internal voice critical or loving? What percentage of your thoughts are self-effacing? I asked a client of mine these questions the other day. He is a successful, well-respected CEO with an Ivy League degree and a string of successes under his belt. Without skipping a beat, he answered 95 percent. Meaning, nineteen out of every twenty thoughts he has about himself involve what he's done wrong. Somewhere along the way, despite information to the contrary, he forgot how to treat himself like someone he loves.

The Dalai Lama said, "Give the ones you love wings to fly." Never forget that you are someone you love, too. Our human lives are short and fleeting. Why not be your own biggest supporter? What else is there to do besides believe in yourself before anyone else does? You have a choice, so why be Piera's media trainer when you can be your own Mrs. Albright?

Now we are here at the first step of Becoming Brilliant. It is Genius Truth #1: The more you love yourself, the more successful you'll be. My favorite part of this first step is how much freedom it gives you. You can start this moment. You can stop waiting for approval and support from other people. Right here and right now, you can give yourself all the love you've yearned for. From today forward, you'll treat yourself like someone you love and watch as your performance rises to the occasion. This is about you, not anyone else. It's the Karma of Success in action.

GENIUS EXERCISE #1

Practice the Reverse Golden Rule by writing yourself a love note with all the things, big and small, that you love about yourself. Write down all the words you've been waiting to hear from someone else. Then, choose one way you can support yourself, some act in which you give yourself wings to fly, then do it this week.

CHAPTER 19

NO TIMELINES ALLOWED

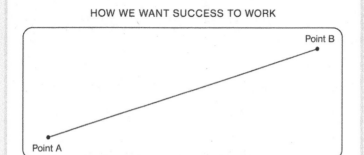

HOW WE WANT SUCCESS TO WORK

Point B

Point A

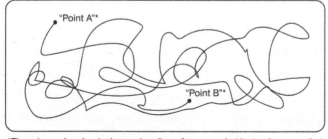

HOW SUCCESS ACTUALLY WORKS

"Point A"*

"Point B"*

*There is no clear beginning and ending of success, but instead a somewhat cyclical yet unpredictable journey that surpasses linear time and space and encompasses the experience of life itself.

Fig. 25

Fig. 25 | How Success Works

We are not robots. Life is not linear. As much as we like to think we can determine the future, we can't. Embrace this, and let it be a joy.

W hat does it mean to be a Buddhist? Is it an identity or a state of mind? What type of life does it mean signing up for?

These were the questions I asked myself as I deepened my learning of Buddhism. At the time, I understood the rules of meditation retreats well. Of course, there was Noble Silence, the practice of finding quiet both outside and within, and then there were also the Five Precepts, which required that we:

1. Refrain from harming any living, sentient beings.
2. Refrain from stealing or coveting what is not freely given.
3. Refrain from the misuse of sexual energy.
4. Refrain from lying, gossip, and other harmful speech.
5. Refrain from alcohol, drugs, and other intoxicants.

The precepts were easy to follow while on retreat. After all, the setup makes numbers 1, 3, 4, and 5 nearly impossible, and there's not much temptation for the second precept, because everyone is equally restricted in what they're allowed to bring. I felt strong, moral, and clear while I was on retreats. However, my real life was a different story. Following these precepts day-to-day, as the monastics do, was proving to be much harder.

I tried my best to follow them around the time I was getting divorced and starting my life again, but alongside my new spiritual practices, I also had a slew of unhealthy coping mechanisms. I was committed to my daily meditation and yoga practice, but I was also just as interested in going out and partying. The former helped me tune in, while the latter was for escape. I needed both those things, presence and distraction, in equal measure during that heart-wrenching period. But my choices weighed on me. I felt guilty about regularly breaking the Five Precepts, and I wanted to become the best Buddhist possible, as quickly as possible.

That summer I went to the Insight Meditation Society for their annual People of Color Retreat. The experience was supportive in every way, but I still worried about my progress. Halfway into the retreat, we broke into small groups to ask questions of our teachers. I was placed with Sharon Salzberg, a cofounder of IMS and one of my greatest heroes. She too had come from a fractured childhood and had struggled for years with developing self-love. I'd read every book she'd written, and it was a dream to be guided by her in person.

We each got to ask one question, and after mulling over mine for many days, this is what I asked: "I love practicing Buddhism and meditation, but I also still drink and go out and often have unkind words and thoughts. I want to stop all those things now so I can be the best Buddhist possible. Do you have any recommendations for me?" I was embarrassed to ask this question, to admit my shortcomings to my hero, but I wanted tough love and guidance. I needed her to tell me the exact steps of what to do. Instead, this is what I got:

"Don't worry so much," she said. "Just keep practicing

meditation, and at some point, the drinking and the going out will naturally drop out of your life until they eventually disappear." That was it. Her advice was essentially, *Chill, and let life run its course*. I nodded and thanked her, but I didn't quite understand. I had a goal in mind. I wanted to become the best Buddhist, and I didn't see how relaxing was going to help me do that.

Back then, I was just like the martial arts student in the parable who demands to know the exact program to follow for achieving success. The both of us, eager and focused students, were fixated on our goal, and thus held onto a major misconception that would hold us back. We were both believers in Wrong Assumption #2 that says success should follow a specific process and timeline. I didn't just think this way about Buddhism, I also wanted a blueprint for how the rest of my life would unfold. What I wish I had known then was Genius Truth #2: Timelines are an illusion, and your journey is unique.

When I got engaged at twenty-six, I was thrilled to be ahead of my peers. I had found my life partner while everyone else was still dating around, and I was smug about the apartment we shared, so grown up with real furniture and art in comparison to my friends' places. My husband and I were playing house—planning dinner parties, redecorating, and hosting Thanksgiving dinner for our families. I was satisfied to have checked off so many boxes on my adult to-do list at such a young age, especially for New York City.

Of course, I loved my partner, but I was perpetually in a rush back then, racing toward a finish line of achievement, and that was the major reason why I pushed for us to be married. Unfortunately, it backfired, and five years later I was no longer ahead of the pack, but trailing so far behind we weren't even in the same race. By thirty, all my friends were in stable relationships and committing to marriage, while I was alone in a cheap sublet, further from my desired outcome than I'd been at twenty-five. The year that I got divorced, I went to seven weddings, all of them alone, and instead of realizing the wisdom of Genius Truth #2 and throwing my timeline out the window, I made a destructive mistake, becoming even more determined to catch up.

This was when I put myself on a strict timeline for getting remarried. I thought, "If I meet someone in the next twelve months, then we can be married in two years, and I can still have two kids by the time I'm thirty-five." With this timeline in mind, I was frenzied and chaotic. I went on too many dates during a time when I should have been healing. I wasn't discerning enough about my partners and pushed them for commitment too soon. Of course, none of this worked, and I kept missing the deadlines I set for myself. Instead of giving up this pressure to catch up, I'd recalculate the timelines in my mind and set new, equally unrealistic goals.

One day, I finally grew tired of putting this pressure on myself. Three years had passed, and after countless first dates, two dramatic breakups, and one matchmaker, I was still single. I had reached my limit of feeling bad about myself just because my path looked different than the paths of those around me. By this time, Sharon Salzberg's prediction had actually come true. While I was frenetically pursuing love, I had relaxed into my practice of Buddhism, expecting nothing from myself except presence, and shortly after that retreat at IMS, I felt organically drawn to take a six-month break from drinking and partying, and after that, I never went back. Instead of nights slamming shots, I learned how to enjoy the 3 S's quietly at home, and it was in one of those moments when I chose freedom from this self-imposed timeline for love.

I decided then that I'd happily wait for the right partner even if it took me until my forties or fifties. I could adopt the kids I'd always wanted, I thought. Making this decision released me from an oppressive weight. With my timeline in the trash, I made peace with not having a plan. Ironically, the very next month, despite pausing my romantic efforts, I went on my first date with Dev, who I'd marry two years later. None of the process of getting married and building a family was remotely close to the timeline I set for myself at age thirty, but it was right for me. It's the wisdom of Sharon Salzberg and Genius Truth #2: Timelines are an illusion, and your journey is unique.

This wasn't just the case for me in love. I've always been off the path of what's considered "normal." I was a late bloomer through much of life. I was the best friend that no one wanted to date in high school. I had braces as an adult (twice!), and it took me until I was thirty-four to choose my true career. But in many other ways, important life milestones, both internal and external, arrived more quickly for me than I ever imagined. When I look back on my life, I can see that the predictions never paid off, and there was never a time when putting myself on a timeline worked, even when I desperately wanted it to.

Maya Angelou was forty-one when she published her first book, *I Know Why the Caged Bird Sings*. She went on to write dozens more, win three Grammys, and receive the Presidential Medal of Freedom. Actor and comedian Ken Jeong was a doctor until he was forty. Julia Child wrote her first cookbook when she was fifty, and Momofuku Ando invented Cup Noodles when he was sixty-one. The world's most generative artists, activists, and entrepreneurs have no timeline for their own blossoming, so why should you?

Why do we make ourselves feel like winners or losers based on the artificial deadlines we pluck from the sky? Why do we believe that life events are better because they happened before age thirty, or occurred in tandem with our peers? Who's to say that the plans we create for ourselves are even the ones that will lead to success?

There was once a farmer whose fence became damaged, allowing his horse to run away. "What bad luck!" his neighbors said. Now he'd have no horse to plow his fields. His response was, "We'll see." A week later his horse returned home with two other wild horses who the farmer then successfully tamed. "What good luck!" his neighbors exclaimed, and again, the farmer simply said, "We'll see."

Later that month, the farmer's son was riding one of the wild horses when it became frightened and tossed him off. The son broke his leg. "What bad luck!" the neighbors said, knowing the farmer would miss his son's help in the fields. And all he said again was, "We'll see." The next day, military officers visited the village to conscript all the young men into the army. With a broken leg, the son was passed by. "What good luck!" the neighbors exclaimed, knowing the son would be safe from the dangers of battle, and as always, the farmer smiled and said, "We'll see."

We humans are the only animals that think about our futures, but just as the neighbors in the story, we are remarkably bad at predicting what is best for our lives. We pick a process and timeline we think will make us happy and successful, creating it based on the limitations of past experiences and what we know in the moment. Then, we work hard to reach our goals, and by the time the future arrives, it winds up being very different from what we imagined.

I consider myself so lucky that my life didn't unfold according to plan. When I was nineteen, I wanted to marry my college boyfriend. That would've been the worst idea. When I was twenty-two, I planned to become a lawyer. Now I see how little that made sense for my passions and talents. Just as the farmer reacted to every event with "We'll see," the same can be done with the perceived wins and losses of our lives. Sometimes getting exactly what we want turns into disappointment, while it's often the setbacks that place us on the right path. When it comes to our timelines and plans, the best we can say is "We'll see."

So, what does this mean about the goals we have for life? If events never unfold according to plan anyway, then what is the point of even trying? To understand the balance between planning and relaxing, imagine your life as one long road trip across the country. Let's say you live in New York, and you want to drive to California. Of course, you would create a plan to organize your trip, but under no circumstances would you stick to that plan precisely, never deviating. If the weather was bad, you'd stop and rest. On a day when you had plenty of energy, you might drive for longer. You'd never try to drive in one nonstop, straight line from east to west. If you did, you'd miss so many cities, adventures, and experiences along the way. Instead, you would let yourself get a little lost.

As with a road trip and with life, you must create room for the unknowable and the unplannable. You should stay in Nashville for three nights instead of one if you love it. You can give yourself permission to reroute through New Mexico when you hear of a town that piques your interest. When your car breaks down, you make the best of it, stopping to enjoy the city you've found yourself in. Of course you should still make plans. Don't let anyone stop you from wanting to drive to California. But the secret to success is to hold onto plans lightly.

You use the Gentle Way. When life pushes, you pull. You don't resist the forces that attack you. Instead, you take the surprises you never wanted and run with them as if you had. Rumi said, "Try not to resist the changes that come your way. Instead, let life live through you. And do not worry that your life is turning upside down. How do you know the one side you are used to is better than the one to come?" When you get thrown off the path in your life, instead of lamenting your failure, you simply smile and say, "We'll see."

When we fixate too much on the right timeline or the perfect process, it's because we're not happy with who we are in the moment. We do not feel enough for whatever reason and reach out for comfort that we are at least on the

correct path. I wish I had known then what I know now—
the more unique your timeline is to you, the better it will
be. The surest way to make yourself unhappy is to try and
live someone else's life.

The truly impressive feat is to wear your life well—to
do it your way. The Karma of Success can happen only
when you have the courage to break society's structures and
timeframes just as Maya Angelou and Julia Child did. The
only thing that matters is that the choices are yours and
only yours. Genius can emerge only when you chart your
own path and travel at your own speed. This is your precious life. Why copy and paste someone else's?

When you feel the urge to compare your progress to
others or beat yourself up for "where you should be by
now," resist and remind yourself of Genius Truth #2:
Timelines are an illusion, and your journey is unique.
Loosen your grip on the wheel, roll down the window, and
put on your favorite music. However long it takes, it is all
unfolding perfectly for you.

GENIUS EXERCISE #2

✳

*Choose the area of your life where you
feel most pressure to follow a specific
timeline or process, no matter if this pressure is coming from society, from others,
or from yourself. Choose an affirmation
to rebut this pressure, write it in your
notebook ten times, and repeat it to*

yourself whenever anxiety strikes. Here
are some ideas:

- *My timing is always perfect. My timing
  is always right.*
- *My future will be better and different
  than what I imagine now.*
- *Life only gets better when I follow my
  own timing.*
- *There is no need to rush. What I desire
  will arrive at the perfect time.*

CHAPTER 20

LET YOUR
STRUGGLE BE
YOUR MAKING

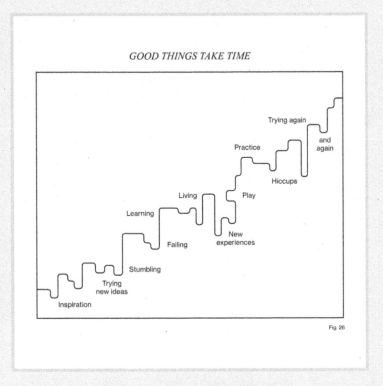

GOOD THINGS TAKE TIME

Trying again

and
again

Practice

Hiccups

Living   Play

Learning

New
experiences

Failing

Stumbling

Trying
new ideas

Inspiration

Fig. 26

Fig. 26 | Good Things Take Time

Our tendency is to want everything right now, and when it doesn't come, we take that as a sign it will never happen. Let this go and remember that all good things take time.

ow that we've arrived at the last step of this fourth and final Spiritual Strategy, I'll say something unpopular. Hard things will happen to you on your path to success; it's an inescapable certainty. The road toward achievement is lined with obstacles, rejection, and struggle, and to expect any different is foolish. I say this not to dishearten you but to give you strength. Using the Gentle Way, you can transform challenges to your advantage and in the process, free your Inner Genius.

All the world's geniuses are deeply familiar with the rocky path. After graduating top of her class from Harvard Law School, Ruth Bader Ginsburg struggled to find a job while her less-accomplished male peers got offers from top firms. "No law firm in the entire city of New York would employ me," she said. "I struck out on three grounds: I was Jewish, a woman, and a mother." Vera Wang missed out on her two largest career goals, professional ice skating and becoming an editor in chief, before she started her own fashion line at age forty. Harrison Ford was a full-time carpenter until he was thirty-five. Melanie Perkins was rejected more than a hundred times over three years before she raised Canva's first round of funding. Today, she's a billionaire.

Even Michelle Obama had setbacks. She dedicated six years to law school and working at a big firm before she realized that the path that she'd chosen would never bring her fulfillment. The majority of my clients, who have all built successful businesses, have also suffered massive disappointments and defeats, and have logged countless rejections over the years.

In school, we learn about the breakthroughs of brilliant people, but we are rarely told about the losses it took them to get there. We grow up believing the same thing the martial arts student in the parable did, which is Wrong Assumption #3: Success comes from the mastery of skill. So we double down on our strengths, stick to what we're good at, and retreat at the first sign of struggle. We make it our goal to be good and in the process, miss out on what it takes to be exceptional. The true secret to success is not about the mastery of skill, but rather, from Genius Truth #3: Success comes from the mastery of failure.

In 1997, Octavia Spencer drove from Alabama to Los Angeles in a ten-year-old car with duct tape holding the taillights on. She brought with her everything she had—$3,000, a suitcase, a 46-inch TV, and, as she put it, "a heart full of dreams." Despite her undeniable talent and charisma, she didn't fit the traditional movie star stereotype and was considered only for minor roles like bus driver and nurse, again and again. For more than a decade, she faced constant rejection in Hollywood and struggled to make a living, often borrowing money from her sisters for rent. Finally, in 2011, Octavia got her big break when she was cast as Minny in *The Help*, the role for which she won a Golden Globe, a BAFTA, a SAG, a Critics' Choice, and an Academy Award for Best Supporting Actress. The world now unanimously agreed that Octavia Spencer was a star.

Fourteen years of constant rejection and disappointment could have easily caused her heart to harden. After all, many people in similar positions begin to doubt their talents, they become cynical and jaded, and eventually, they give up on their dreams. Instead, she's taken the opposite perspective. Not only has she learned how to thrive in the face of adversity, but she is also determined to lift up others at the same time.

Octavia quietly funds a nonprofit learning center to help domestic abuse survivors get back on their feet. Despite her dyslexia, she wrote not just one but two inspirational books for middle school girls. Recently, when Octavia was inducted into the Hollywood Walk of Fame, Allison Janney paid this tribute to Octavia and her heart: "She is the actor and producer who not only opens the doors but pulls her friends through. . . . Every time someone has helped her succeed, she has paid it forward three times."

Octavia Spencer never let the nonstop rejections diminish her "heart full of dreams." Instead, she used them as an opportunity to become even more empathetic, more generous, and more giving. That is the Gentle Way.

There is a Japanese proverb, "Nana korobi ya oki," which means "Fall seven times, get up eight." These simple words speak to what it takes to become brilliant. The geniuses among us don't have special skills or abilities, but rather, they use failure as their stepping stones.

I want to be clear that the struggles I speak of do not include oppressive obstacles like racism, prejudice, gender inequality, abuse, or harassment of any kind. We should not condone them nor believe it is our responsibility to accept them and find the silver lining. What I'm talking about here are the natural and inevitable disappointments we all face as people. Just as we talked about in chapter 16, life is made up of ten thousand joys and ten thousand sorrows. There will be ups and downs no matter how much we resist. The waves keep coming, and this natural unfolding of life's disappointments is what we're talking about now.

The Arrival Fallacy

Most of my life, I believed that happiness meant the absence of hardship or struggle. I would think to myself, "I'll finally be happy when I get promoted" or "Everything will change in my new apartment." I had bought into the Arrival Fallacy, which is a psychological tendency to believe that lasting happiness will come as soon as a major goal is reached. It is a huge factor in why we chase after wins, believing them to be a panacea, and do all we can to avoid losses.

Have you felt this for yourself? Have you yearned for some development in the future, believing it will bring you the happiness and satisfaction you've waited for? Perhaps it was graduating, getting a certain job, or becoming engaged. Maybe you feel it now with a big work project, a competition, or a fitness milestone. The big problem with the Arrival Fallacy, however, is that it's an illusion. We arrive at our long-awaited destination only to find that nothing has changed or even worse, that we're disappointed.

Its why lottery winners aren't statistically happier than non-lottery winners, and why nearly 50 percent of new brides in a 2016 study reported feeling let down or depressed after their wedding. The things we believe will make us happy often don't, and when they do, the effects are more fleeting than we imagine. The achievement we worked so hard for is quickly forgotten and we're left chasing another goal, then another, and yet another. The horizon line is always moving. We spend our lives yearning for an emotional payday that never comes, perpetually caught in the Arrival Fallacy.

If we are always waiting for life to be perfect in order to be happy, then happiness will always elude us. The truth is, happiness isn't the result of the absence of hardship but rather it is from owning and activating your own power, no matter how challenging the situation.

Expression

When we struggle with obstacles and challenges, we must first make room for our feelings to be heard. As my current therapist says, every feeling has its own need that we must respect and do our best to fulfill. It took me two full years with my old therapist to completely work through the anger I had toward my mom. "Should we talk about your dad?" she asked when we were about a year in. "I can't even go there," I said, because there was so much to unspool about my mom. It was a long but ultimately productive process, and only when I was done could I rally any graciousness or compassion toward my childhood years.

We want to turn our obstacles into advantages, but going straight into the silver linings of our suffering doesn't work. That's called spiritual bypassing, and it serves only to bury your feelings deeper down where they fester below. If you are not in a place right now to consider your hardships as advantages, then that is fair and understandable. Sometimes we need to go through all the stages of anger and sadness that our deepest traumas require.

Something that helps is to write a complaint letter. In it, I express every single reason, big or small, why I am upset. I don't push myself to be calm or reasonable. No, I give myself full permission to be aggressively mad or sad and let myself blame whomever I want. The primary goal of this process is catharsis, so don't hold anything back. Then when you feel done with complaining, write yourself a response to the complaint letter. It's called the compassion letter, and I start with something like, "Dear Liz, I hear you, I see you, that must be so hard . . ." I don't suggest solutions or silver linings, I simply give myself bottomless empathy and understanding.

Acceptance

For much of my life, my natural coping mechanism was to play the victim. I believed that life wasn't fair, and I had been left holding the short end of the stick. I'd think about my unknown father and disconnected mother and lament, "Why me?" I felt jealously toward many people, and I blamed everyone I could—including my mom, my friends, and the Universe. It was the opposite of the Gentle Way. Instead of working with reality, I exhausted myself protesting it. I was too busy hurting to get on with living.

There are two affirmations I use when I'm having a hard time spinning in victimhood, blame, or projection. The first is this: *There's no one to blame. Especially myself.*

This affirmation is essential because we can be as harsh on ourselves as we are on others. We look at the challenges we're facing and eviscerate ourselves for the role we believed we played. This affirmation is critical because any blame, whether toward yourself or others, is not only false but unproductive. This affirmation can help you move past it.

The second affirmation I use is this: *I hate this situation, but I accept that I am here.* This one works for me because it doesn't expect the impossible. Affirmations are effective only when some part of you believes them, so to say of your greatest hardship "I love this situation" probably won't work. Let your affirmations be reasonable and truthful— just a little bit of a stretch. That creates the right balance for your brain to feel safe while it challenges an old belief. I can get behind *I hate this situation, but I accept that I am here.* It's what's real.

Acceptance is the key to unearthing your genius, because without acceptance there isn't enough energy left to become brilliant. Imagine you are calmly sitting in a boat and then suddenly someone tosses you into the river. You are thrashing and panicking, frantically trying to swim against the current to get back to the boat. If you struggle like this, you will quickly tire and sink. But if you accept your new circumstance and accept where you are, then you can simply float and wait for the current to carry you to shore. That is the Gentle Way. You are where you are, and the only thing left to do is to make the most of it.

The First Five Hours

The next step to turning your obstacles into an advantage is to practice Nana korobi ya oki: fall seven times, get up eight. In an unhelpful pop culture moment, Malcolm Gladwell told us we need ten thousand hours of practice to become a master at any skill. This idea is irrelevant for most of us. That's five years of practicing something full-time, forty hours a week. Or, if you spend as much time as most people do on hobbies, about five hours a week, then mastery would take you forty years. Whether this idea is true is beside the point. It is largely unhelpful, because the most important part of doing anything hard is not the end, but rather the *first five hours.*

They are the toughest, because that's when you are the worst at whatever it is you are trying to learn. If you decide to get up every time you fall down during those first five hours, you suddenly become capable of doing anything, learning everything, and accomplishing your dreams. I stayed mostly inside when I was a kid and never did any extracurricular sports until high school, so I was terrible at anything athletic until later in my life. I got deep into yoga when I was twenty-eight, sat on my first road bike when I was thirty-five, and I'm still learning how to swim now.

The first time I taught a yoga class, I was so nervous I cried at the end. By the fifth time, my anxiety was entirely gone, and by the twentieth, I was a pro. My first foray on a road bike, I gripped the bars so hard from fear I got callouses. By the fifth ride, I was flying down hills, and ten weeks later I was biking with the best down the West Side Highway doing my first duathlon.

On the road to realizing your genius, you will have to do many hard things for the first time. Unless you learn how to get comfortable with discomfort you'll never go anywhere. So, when you're trying something hard, something new, something unknown, bring to mind the concept of the first five hours, and remind yourself that ease is right on the other side of the extreme novice stage.

As an adult, I tried every sport I never did as a kid— kickball, basketball, spin, and Pilates. Even though I was generally terrible at first, over the years I've become athletic. There was no talent involved. It was all mindset. I forced myself to become an expert at *beginning*.

Can you be an expert at beginning, too? Can you feel okay with being bad at something? Will you consistently try new things, no matter how uncomfortable? The next time you are struggling or failing, use the Gentle Way. Instead of berating yourself for how badly you're doing, congratulate yourself for your courage to begin. Reframe your thoughts. You are not failing; you are brave for trying. You are not inept; you are getting better. It might take ten thousand hours to become a master, but it takes only five hours to stop being a novice, and through that tough stretch, the beginning is what matters most.

Look for the Lesson

Sometimes hardship continues for so long that we wonder how much more we can endure. We fall down, then get up, and do it again and again until we are too bruised and demoralized to keep going. In these moments, we lament, *Why is this happening to me?*

As of the moment I'm writing this, I have been trying to get pregnant for three years, working very hard and actively. I've changed my diet, taken vitamins, gone to acupuncture, seen a dozen doctors, and spent hundreds of hours and a big chunk of money on fertility treatments that my insurance doesn't cover. I have been poked and prodded and had every type of test under the sun, but no doctor can tell me why it's not working. Because I never had a conventional family, I've always had a deep, hungry yearning to create one of my own, so every month, when my period comes, I am devastated. It's been thirty-six failures and counting.

That is one way to look at it, but there is also another way, and after some time, I was finally able to see it. The change I made was to understand that this experience was not *happening to me*, but rather, it was *happening for me*. Of course there have been countless hard moments, and I still haven't gotten what I want, but with these disappointments have come a bountiful gift—major life lessons and personal growth that would've alluded me otherwise.

There are too many to list here, but one example of a lesson learned is empathy. From this long struggle, I got the gift of understanding people with chronic and time-consuming health issues of any sort. I never had any patience for this in the past. Ironically, I remember a friend many years ago telling me about her fertility struggles over dinner, and I, young and single, dismissed her feelings as inane, uninteresting overreactions. This hardship, the chance to be in another's shoes, has made me more kind.

Second, it has been my lifelong fear that if I emotionally unravel in front of my partner, they won't love me. This belief was created back when I was a kid and I wasn't allowed to cry or be upset. My mom was superstitious, and she believed that sadness invites bad luck upon the house. So, when my tears flowed, she would become upset and yell that I had cursed our family. I learned how to hide when I was upset and never ask for help. I prided myself on being independent and self-sufficient, and created a long-held story that it was best not to need anyone.

So, even when Reset was going through its darkest period, I never asked my husband for help, emotionally or otherwise. Then, my fertility challenges gave me the sweetest gift. They forced me to change. I was depressed and despondent, drowning in a trough of sadness, and I had no choice but to break my pattern. Not only did I ask, but I demanded support from my husband. I pushed him to show up for me in a way that he was not accustomed to. To my surprise, he met me. Only from hitting rock bottom could I see that I too deserve unconditional love. It's hard to imagine a richer treasure.

In the second year, during the worst of it, I woke up at two a.m. inconsolable. It started with a nightmare in which a group of doctors told me that I would never have children, then they listed everything I'd done in my life to deserve it. I woke up shaking and crying so violently that all I could do was roll myself off the bed and curl up on the floor hyperventilating until my husband helped me back into bed. Eventually my emotions settled, but I had disrupted our night for hours. *I hate that I ruined our sleep,* I said. But he didn't mind at all——*It's okay,* he said back. *At least we get to be awake together in the middle of the night.*

At least we get to be awake together in the middle of the night. It is a metaphor for how I think of these three years of struggle and counting. I am deep into the night and there is much hardship, but at least I am awake and learning—— uncovering treasures I would not have known otherwise. There is joy in the sorrow, lessons in the letdowns. I used to think of every monthly disappointment as a hardship. Now I know it is the opportunity to love myself more.

Pema Chödrön said, "Nothing goes away until it teaches us what we need to know." I believe this. It was true in my financial woes with Reset. There were many changes I had to make on the inside before I saw results on the outside. And now the same is true in this moment. I am still waiting for the resolution to this story, for my so-called happy ending, for when I get to look back and say something like, "It all worked eventually, and I can't imagine it any other way!" It's not there yet. I'm not there yet. But that's okay. I can accept where I am. I am fine to be here with all these lessons that I've been blessed to learn the hard way.

What obstacles and struggles are most potent for you right now? What part of your life feels uncomfortable, unsettled, or just plain hard? The most important question we ask now during this sensitive time is this: *What is it you most need right now?*

Do you need to **express** your feelings, **accept** your situation, get through **the first five hours**, or **look for**

lessons? Whatever it is you need, commit to giving it to yourself with an abundance of love and gentleness. These trying times are gifts, because it is only through them that you get to decide the kind of person you want to be. When life is peachy and all is right in the world, we are never forced to transform. After all, why change a good thing that's working? These low points are the only moments we have to carve ourselves out of marble. So, who will you be today?

- Will you value yourself for not failing, or will you love yourself for never giving up?
- Will you lament the struggles that come your way, or will you embrace them as a sign that you're learning and growing?
- When hard things come your way, will you ask why is this *happening to me*, or will you understand that it is all *happening for you*?

GENIUS EXERCISE #3

✳

Think about the most challenging and frustrating situation in your life right now. If you have strong feelings you need to express, write yourself a complaint letter and then write your compassion letter with empathy and understanding. Once you've done that, ask yourself the follow-

ing questions about your situation and record your answers in a notebook:

- *What lesson does this teach me?*
- *What gift does this give me?*
- *How can this struggle become my making?*

The Genius Truths

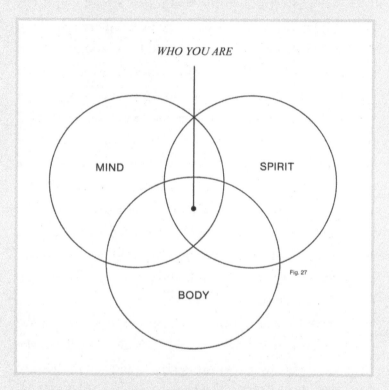

Fig. 27 | Who You Are

You are more than where you went to school, where you work, or the number in your bank account. Your genius comes from a far richer place your body, mind, and spirit.

f you take one thing from this fourth and final Spiritual Strategy, let it be this: don't give anyone else the power to define your path in life.

As we move through the world, we are all inundated with opinions as to whether we are talented enough to get what we want. We take standardized tests from which we are placed in percentiles of performance, then we're herded into buckets as overachievers or underachievers. We go on to schools that are considered tier 1, tier 2, or tier 3, as if this defines our individual worth. Or we don't go to school at all, and people make inferences about what this means about us. All of these external assumptions are rubbish. You are not your grades, the schools you went to, the family you come from, or the companies you worked for. That's the Mechanical Work way of seeing the world, and it reduces every person to a series of bullet points, none of which can tell you whether you will succeed.

Every achievement test that Amy Tan took told her she was more suited for the sciences than writing. Then she went on to pen award-winning novels and sell millions of books. The legendary Michael Jordan was cut from his high school varsity team. Einstein was told by his teacher that he wouldn't amount to anything, and Oprah was demoted from her job as a news anchor because she wasn't "fit for television." I myself barely graduated from college, and I am more fulfilled by my work than most people I know. This is the moral of the story. No one else has the right to define the limits of your capabilities.

This is also true for the readers out there who shine in conventional ways. If you are a great test taker and went to the best schools, of course you should be proud of your achievements, but always remember that you are more than that. What you've accomplished does not make you. It is not why you have worth. The achievements are something wonderful you *did*, but they are not who you *are*. Just because you are a whiz at finance does not mean you should forget about your passion for music. It is fantastic if you have made your teachers and bosses happy, but that's not all you have to offer.

In the simple parable to which we returned again and again, the martial arts student did exactly what I'm encouraging you *not* to do here—he looked to someone else, an authority figure, to dictate his life path. He believed that someone else could gauge his capacity for success better than he could. If I were to speak to him, I'd tell him this: No teacher, test, or boss knows what will happen to your life. You are the only one with that power.

Becoming Brilliant means shifting away from needing external validation and instead becoming that source of validation for yourself. You don't need to ask others if you're good enough. No one else can confirm that you're okay. Empower yourself now and always by holding the Genius Truths close to your mind and heart:

GENIUS TRUTH #1: The more you love yourself, the more successful you'll be.

GENIUS TRUTH #2: Timelines are an illusion, and your journey is unique.

GENIUS TRUTH #3: Success comes from the mastery of failure.

Now that we understand the Genius Truths, how should the story have unfolded? If the martial arts student were firmly living by the Genius Truths, what would he have done? What questions would he have asked the teacher? In what way would he have responded to the wisdom?

The answer is this: *There is no answer.* We cannot claim to know what the student would have asked the teacher, because his path is uniquely his own. There is no cookie-cutter way of being that exists for me, you, him, or anyone else.

Even though all my coaching clients have the same type of job, I never give the same advice twice. I share the same stories and data and ask the same questions, but every one of my clients is a unique person who responds to those prompts in their own unique way. The thought that *there is not one "right way"* can be terrifying or it can be liberating. It's terrifying if you are afraid to steer your own course but empowering if you are tired of others driving for you.

Are you working hard enough or taking it too easy? *Only you know.*

Are you following the correct timeline and process for your life? *Depends.*

Have you mastered the skills you need to get what you want? *I don't know. What do you think?*

I have a friend who got offered a job that seemed so much better than the one he currently had. He asked all his friends and family what he should do and 100 percent of them, including me, very enthusiastically told him to take the new job. I was sure that the opportunity was exactly what he needed to shake out of an old rut, express his genius, and finally be happy after many years of ambivalence about work. He took the new job, but then I spoke to him a few months after and found out he had already quit and was back at his old job. I was shocked. I couldn't understand how any person could prefer the original role to the one he was offered. *What happened?* I asked him of his sudden about-face. *I listened to what everyone else told me*, he said. That was his mistake. He chose the voice of the crowd over his Inner Genius.

Perhaps now you are feeling that this is a lot of pressure to put on yourself, to be the only one who decides your fate in this world. Maybe now you are thinking you cannot ask your friends and advisors for guidance. This is not what I am saying. Of course you can ask for others' opinions. I am just saying to take them with a grain of salt. No one knows what you know. Not even your parents, partner, or best friend know the full range of your emotions, preferences, and needs at this exact moment. By nature, outside advice will always be limited in the truth it holds.

Don't be afraid of this power. You were born for it. This is why you came into this world with the spirit of genius as the ancient Romans said, and why your Inner Genius exists. You may not always know what to do in the moment, but I promise you have all the tools it takes to get there. Love yourself, listen to yourself, trust the Genius Truths, ask yourself the tough questions, and give honest answers. You are now in full possession of Spiritual Strategy #4. You have everything you need to become brilliant and generate the Karma of Success.

IN
TWO
WORDS

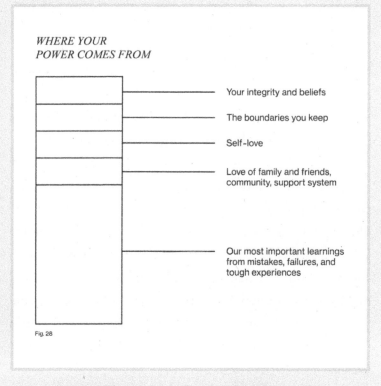

WHERE YOUR
POWER COMES FROM

Your integrity and beliefs

The boundaries you keep

Self-love

Love of family and friends, community, support system

Our most important learnings from mistakes, failures, and tough experiences

Fig. 28

Fig. 28 | Where Your Power Comes From

Your power comes from the unseen, internal world. Your mindset, beliefs, boundaries, and wisdom are what free the Inner Genius.

n the first chapter of this book, we heard of the time when a student asked Suzuki Roshi to explain Buddhism in one sentence. He replied quickly and easily with just two words: *Everything changes.* Throughout this book, you've learned the four spiritual strategies, explored the concepts at the root of them, and heard stories of many people who applied them to find success. Now, inspired by Suzuki Roshi, I'll boil down this book to a single sentence myself. Just two simple words: *Trust yourself.*

When it comes to your life, there are many decisions that are binary—yes or no—and oftentimes the answer is clear. We ask if it will rain today or if there is a cheaper flight we should book. We look at the mountains of online information at our disposal and then clearly comprehend the nature of our reality. When it comes to careers, however, the data is more uncertain. Not only is the "right choice" often ambiguous in the moment, but it is usually only later when we see how those decisions truly unfold. Like the farmer in the story in chapter 19, we have to wait and see. While this may seem like a frightening prospect to most, now you know the process of Intuitive Work, and you have everything you need to move swiftly and confidently toward your future. You've connected to your Inner Genius.

Kim Pham, Cheri Maples, EJ Hill, and Octavia Spencer. Your name belongs there alongside every example of genius we explored together in this book. You have the same spirit of genius that they, and every other person in this world, was born with, and now you've freed yours. The only thing left to do is trust yourself and pleasantly await what will unfold in the unique, precious adventure that is your life. Welcome to the Karma of Success.

ACKNOWLEDGMENTS

This book would not exist if not for Lynn Johnston, my agent, who plucked my proposal from a pile of cold queries and told me, "There's something missing here. This book needs more *you*." Lynn, your encouragement to be fully me, idiosyncrasies and all, is the reason we're here.

I owe just as much gratitude to my editors, Merry Sun and Veronica Velasco, at Portfolio. It's no short of magic how you pushed and supported me in the exact ways the book needed. Truly, this book is as much a product of your Inner Geniuses as it is mine. I'm also grateful to Adrian Zackheim for coming up with the title, and Alison Rich, Kate Berner, Zehra Kayi, Esin Coskun, Heather Faulls, and the rest of the phenomenal team at Penguin Random House.

Thank you to Tessa Forrest, who is responsible for the Reset aesthetic and designed every chart in these pages. Tessa, I am eternally grateful for your talents and collaboration over the past four years.

Dev Aujla, my husband and first reader—thank you for building a shelter for my imagination. It's not lost on me how you dropped everything, no matter what was going on, to hear a chapter, assuage my insecurities, or offer advice and a hug. Thank you to the rest of my family: Andrew Tran, Pam Pham-Le, Riley Ferrell, Nick Pham, Alex Pham,

Sheila Aujla, David Aujla, Aaron Aujla, Emily Bode Aujla, and Grover.

When I was first learning how to write, my intuition guided me to take a class with John Evans, and what good luck that was. John, thank you for seeing a spark in my clunky, early essays and for giving me the toolkit to express my inner world. I also owe a debt to my friends who supported me in the writing process by cheering me on, making introductions, and pretending that my writing was great even when it wasn't. Vanessa Hardy, Carla Fernandez, Alua Arthur, Scott Shigeoka, Madison Morales, Amir Sharif, Victoria Rogers, Owen Laub, Julia Pontecorvo, Charlene Caronan Mercier, Dolores Stevens, Lauren Shirley, Mỹ Tâm Nguyễn, and Liya Shuster-Bier—thank you.

This book was inspired by the work I do with my remarkable, brilliant coaching clients, many of whom I've worked with for years but continue to learn from every day. How lucky am I to know your Inner Geniuses? To every podcast listener, you are my muse, and this book is for you. One of my favorite parts of writing this book was getting to tell stories of people I admire. Alua, Alymamah, Aviva, EJ, Kim, Piera, and Trinity—thank you for trusting me.

Beyond time and space, I'm grateful to the ancestors of my maternal line—my mother; my grandparents, Ông Ngoại and Bà Ngoại; their mothers; and all the other mothers who came before them. I am also grateful for the future. For my future, older, wiser self, and my children who have yet to come.

NOTES

INTRODUCTION: INTUITIVE WORK

x **"I always had to be willing to stand alone"**: Robinson, Roxana. *Georgia O'Keeffe: A Life*. Waltham, Mass.: Brandeis University Press, 2020.

x **"often made with high confidence"**: Seligman, Martin, and Michael Kahana "Unpacking Intuition: A Conjecture," *Perspectives on Psychological Science* 4(4): 399–402. doi: 10.1111 /j.1745-6924.2009.01145.x. PMID: 20300491; PMCID: PMC2839455.

CHAPTER 1: THE CHANGING SELF

6 **he replied, "Everything changes"**: Chadwick, David. *To Shine One Corner of the World: Moments with Shunryu Suzuki: Stories of a Zen Teacher Told by His Students*. New York: Broadway Books, 2001.

CHAPTER 3: THE JOYFUL SELF

21 **"We cannot solve"**: Isaacson, Walter. *Einstein: His Life and Universe*. New York: Simon & Schuster, 2008.

22 **"joy is possible"**: Gay, Ross. "Ross Gay—Tending Joy and Practicing Delight." The On Being Project, updated March 26, 2020, onbeing.org/programs/ross-gay-tending-joy-and -practicing-delight.

23 **"I am a professional laugher"**: Lama, Dalai, and Sofia Stril-Rever. *My Spiritual Journey: Personal Reflections, Teachings, and Talks*. New York: HarperOne, 2011.

24 **"I just don't trust myself"**: Olmstead, Molly. "Simone Biles Explains Withdrawl: 'I Just Don't Trust Myself as

Much as I Used to.'" *Slate*, July 27, 2021, slate.com/culture
/2021/07/simone-biles-olympics-gymnastics-statement
.html.

24 **"hurts my heart":** Miranda, Gabriela. "Here's What Simone
Biles Told Reporters after Withdrawing from Tokyo Olympics
Team Final." *USA Today*, Gannett Satellite Information
Network, July 27, 2021, usatoday.com/story
/sports/olympics/2021/07/27/simone-biles-quotes-mental
-health-after-2021-tokyo-olympics-final/5385472001.

24 **children laugh about one hundred fifty times a day:**
Holden, Robert. *Living Wonderfully: A Joyful Guide to Conscious-
Creative Living*. New York: Thorsons, 1994.

24 **average adult laughs less than twenty:** Martin, Rod A.,
and Nicholas A. Kuiper. "Daily Occurrence of Laughter:
Relationships with Age, Gender, and Type A Personality."
Humor: International Journal of Humor Research 12(4) (1999):
355–84. https://doi.org/10.1515/humr.1999.12.4.355.

CHAPTER 5: THE 3 S'S

45 **blood flows to your brain:** Bernardi, L., C. Porta, and
P. Sleight. "Cardiovascular, Cerebrovascular, and Respiratory
Changes Induced by Different Types of Music in Musicians
and Non-musicians: The Importance of Silence." *Heart* 92(4)
(April 2006): 445–52. doi: 10.1136/hrt.2005.064600. Epub
September 30, 2005. PMID: 16199412; PMCID:
PMC1860846.

45 **Focus and creativity also increase with silence:** Dent,
Maggie. *Saving Our Children from Our Chaotic World: Teaching
Children the Magic of Silence and Stillness*. Gerringong, New
South Wales: Pennington Pub., 2009.

45 **grow new brain cells:** Kirste, Imke, Zeina Nicola,
Golo Kronenberg, Tara Walker, Robert Liu, and Gerd
Kempermann. "Is Silence Golden? Effects of Auditory Stimuli
and Their Absence on Adult Hippocampal Neurogenesis."
Brain Structure & Function 220(2) (March 2015): 1221–28.
10.1007/s00429-013-0679-3.

48 **"Meditation is just gently coming back:"** Chödrön, Pema. *How to Meditate: A Practical Guide to Making Friends with Your Mind.* Boulder, Colo.: Sounds True, 2022.

CHAPTER 6: WHAT'S YOUR TYPE?

62 **Cheri had listened to her intuition:** "Thich Nhat Hanh, Cheri Maples, and Larry Ward—Being Peace in a World of Trauma." SoundCloud, soundcloud.com/onbeing/thich-nhat -hanh-cheri-maples-and-larry-ward-being-peace-in-a-world-of -trauma.

CHAPTER 9: ADVICE FROM SAM

89 **"Manifestation complete," Drake said:** Plante, Chandler. "Drake Gifted Rolls-Royce He Used to Rent to 'Keep Up Appearances': 'Manifestation Complete'." *People*, October 25, 2021, people.com/music/drake-gifted-rolls-royce-he-used-to -rent-to-keep-up-appearances-manifestation-complete.

CHAPTER 10: WHAT YOU SEE IS . . .

95 **our minds can't actually distinguish:** Reddan, Marianne Cumella, Tor Dessart Wager, and Daniela Schiller. "Attenuating Neural Threat Expression with Imagination." *Neuron.* November 21, 2018;100(4) (November 2018): 994–1005.e4. doi: 10.1016/j.neuron.2018.10.047. PMID: 30465766; PMCID: PMC6314478.

95 **cancer patients who imagine:** Lengacher, Cecile A., Mary P. Bennett, Lois Gonzalez, et al. "Immune Responses to Guided Imagery During Breast Cancer Treatment." *Biological Research for Nursing* 9(3) (January 2008): 205–14. doi:10.1177/1099800407309374.

95 **The East German Olympics team:** Raiport, Grigori, and Monique Raphael High. *Red Gold: Peak Performance Techniques of the Russian and East German Olympic Victors.* New York: J.P. Tarcher, Inc, 1988.

95 **University of Michigan football team:** Goldenbach, Alan. *University of Michigan: Where Have You Gone?: Gene Derricotte,*

Garvie Craw, Jake Sweeney, and Other Wolverine Greats. New York: Sports Publishing, 2012.

96 **six thousand thoughts a day:** Tseng, J., and J. Poppenk. "Brain Meta-state Transitions Demarcate Thoughts Across Task Contexts Exposing the Mental Noise of Trait Neuroticism." *Nature Communications* 11 (2020): 3480. doi.org /10.1038/s41467-020-17255-9.

CHAPTER 11: $2 COFFEE RICH

104 **Oprah kept a gratitude list:** Skidmore College. "Skidmore College 2017 Commencement Ceremony." YouTube, May 24, 2017, youtube.com/watch?v=kN6nvXfuzUk.

107 **"Suffering and happiness":** "Remembering Thich Nhat Hanh, Brother Thay." The On Being Project, January 27, 2022, onbeing.org/programs/remembering-thich-nhat-hanh -brother-thay.

CHAPTER 12: CONFIDENCE BANK

112 **The definition of confidence:** "Confidence Definition & Meaning." *Merriam-Webster*, merriam-webster.com/dictionary /confidence.

116 **compares our confidence levels:** Zinsser, Nathaniel. *The Confident Mind: A Battle-Tested Guide to Unshakable Performance.* New York: Custom House, 2022.

SYNTHESIS: JOURNALS PAST AND PRESENT

122 **"Things That Make One's Heart Beat Faster":** Shōnagon Sei. *The Pillow Book.* Bletchley, Buckinghamshire, England: Jiahu Books, 2017.

123 **Benjamin Franklin attributed his success:** Franklin, Benjamin. *Autobiography.* Garden City, NY: Dover Publications Inc., 1996.

123 **Barack Obama has a long-standing habit:** Scherer, Michael. "2012 Person of the Year: Barack Obama, the President." *Time,* December 19, 2012, poy.time.com/2012 /12/19/person-of-the-year-barack-obama/5.

123 **Octavia Butler, epitomizes the art:** Russell, Natalie. "The Octavia E. Butler Collection." Art Papers, June 22, 2018, artpapers.org/the-octavia-e-butler-collection.

127 **"Turning Back":** Le Guin, Ursula K. *Lao Tzu: Tao Te Ching.* New York: Random House, 2019.

CHAPTER 13: THE THREE TREASURES

135 **"We are spiritual beings":** Covey, Stephen R. *Living the 7 Habits: The Courage to Change.* New York: Fireside Book, 2000.

CHAPTER 14: EASY CLEANSING

146 **like the Dead Sea:** Uriel, Katz, Yehuda Shoenfeld, Varda Zakin, Yaniv Sherer, and Shaul Sukenik. "Scientific Evidence of the Therapeutic Effects of Dead Sea Treatments: A Systematic Review." *Seminars in Arthritis and Rheumatism* 42(2) (October 2012): 186–200. doi: 10.1016/j.semarthrit.2012.02.006. Epub April 12, 2012. PMID: 22503590.

146 **Trees secrete oils:** Andersen, L., S.S.S. Corazon, U.K.K. Stigsdotter. "Nature Exposure and Its Effects on Immune System Functioning: A Systematic Review." *International Journal of Environmental Research and Public Health.* 18(4): (February 2021): 1416. doi: 10.3390/ijerph18041416. PMID: 33546397; PMCID: PMC7913501.

148 **It flushes toxins:** Lulu, Xie, Hongyi Kang, and Qiwu Xu, et al. "Sleep Drives Metabolite Clearance from the Adult Brain." *Science* 342(6156) (October 2013): 373–77. doi: 10.11 26/science.1241224. PMID: 24136970; PMCID: PMC3880190.

148 **releases hormones to curb inflammation:** Mullington, J.M., N.S. Simpson, H.K. Meier-Ewert, and M. Haack. "Sleep Loss and Inflammation." *Best Practice & Research. Clinical Endocrinology & Metabolism* 24(5) (October 2010): 775–84. doi: 10.1016/j.beem.2010.08.014. PMID: 21112025; PMCID: PMC3548567.

148 **repair any damaged tissues:** Vyazovskiy, Vladyslav V. "Sleep, Recovery, and Metaregulation: Explaining the Benefits of Sleep." *Nature and Science of Sleep* 7 (December 2015):

171–84. doi: 10.2147/NSS.S54036. PMID: 26719733; PMCID: PMC4689288.

CHAPTER 16: BIGGER, BRIGHTER, AMPLIFIED

168 **Genius, Excellence, Competence, and Incompetance:** Hendricks, Gay. *The Big Leap*. New York: HarperCollins, 2009.

CHAPTER 18: REVERSE GOLDEN RULE

190 **"gifted" students were chosen at random:** Rosenthal, Robert, and Lenore Jacobson. *Pygmalion in the Classroom: Teacher Expectation and Pupils' Intellectual Development*. New York, Holt, Rinehart and Winston, 1968.

CHAPTER 19: NO TIMELINES ALLOWED

201 **"Try not to resist the changes":** "A Quote by Rumi." Rumi, *Drops of Enlightenment (Quotes & Poems)*, edited by Murat Durmus (independently published, 2022).

CHAPTER 20: LET YOUR STRUGGLE BE YOUR MAKING

205 **"I struck out on three grounds":** "Ruth Bader Ginsburg: Who Was She and Why Was She So Important? "BBC Newsround." BBC News, bbc.co.uk/newsround /54235799.

206 **Octavia Spencer drove:** "Octavia Spencer Receives Star on Hollywood Walk of Fame." Performance by Octavia Spencer, *Variety*, YouTube, December 8, 2022, https://www.youtube .com/watch?v=-3V4CFbc29k.

206 **considered only for minor roles:** "Octavia Spencer Receives Star on Hollywood Walk of Fame." Performance by Allison Janney, *Variety*, YouTube, December 8, 2022, https://www.youtube.com/watch?v=-3V4CFbc29k.

207 **"she has paid it forward":** "Octavia Spencer Receives Star on Hollywood Walk of Fame."

216 **Nothing goes away until:** Chödrön, Pema. *When Things Fall Apart: Heart Advice for Difficult Times* (anniversary edition). Boulder, Colo.: Shambhala, 2016.

SYNTHESIS: THE GENIUS TRUTHS

220 **Every achievement test:** Tan, Amy. *The Opposite of Fate: Memories of a Writing Life.* New York: Penguin Books, 2004.

220 **Michael Jordan was cut:** "Michael Jordan Didn't Make Varsity—at First." *Newsweek*, April 25, 2016, www.newsweek .com/missing-cut-382954.

220 **Einstein was told:** "What Teacher Said about . . ." *The Guardian*, January 11, 2005, theguardian.com/education /2005/jan/11/schools.uk1.

220 **Oprah was demoted:** Winfrey, Oprah. *The Path Made Clear.* New York: Flatiron Books, 2019.

ABOUT THE AUTHOR

Liz Tran is the founder of Reset, an executive coaching company for CEOs and founders. Before founding Reset, Liz spent over a decade working in the tech industry, most recently as the only female executive at a leading venture capital firm. She is a trained meditation teacher and Reiki master and studied yoga at the Samyak Ashram. She lives in New York City and Norfolk, Connecticut, with her husband, Dev, and their dog, Grover.